The
International
Student's
Guide

The International Student's Guide

Studying in English at University

Ricky Lowes,
Helen Peters and
Marie Turner

⑤ SAGE Publications
London • Thousand Oaks • New Delhi

First published 2004

SAGE Publications Ltd
1 Oliver's Yard
55 City Road
London EC1Y 1SP

SAGE Publications Inc.
2455 Teller Road
Thousand Oaks, California 91320

SAGE Publications India Pvt Ltd
B-42. Panchsheel Enclave
Post Box 4109
New Delhi 110 017

British Library Cataloguing in Publication data
A catalogue record for this book is available from the British
Library

ISBN 0-7619-4252-1
ISBN 0-7619-4253-X (pbk)

Library of Congress Control Number: 2003115341

Typeset by GCS, Leighton Buzzard, Beds.
Printed and bound in Great Britain by Athenaenum Press

Contents

Acknowledgements   vi
How to use this book   vii

 1 Introduction   1
 2 Being an effective learner   14
 3 Understanding spoken English   40
 4 Building vocabulary   66
 5 Speaking English at university   88
 6 Giving oral presentations   120
 7 Reading   160
 8 Making notes   191
 9 Writing   222
10 Studying at postgraduate level   258
11 Preparing for exams   278
12 Coping with life as an international student   297

Index   309

Acknowledgements

The authors would like to thank the following:

Marion Bull for the photographs on pages 58, 60, 96, 97, 102, 107, 158, 159, 167 and 176.

Our students at London Metropolitan University whose words we have quoted and those who read and commented on chapters of this book.

Cambridge University Press for the extracts from the *Cambridge Advanced Learner's Dictionary* (2003), pages 18 and 19.

Peter Collin Publishing (a division of Bloomsbury Reference) for the extract from Green, J. (1999) *English Thesaurus for Students*, page 31.

Collins Publishers for the extract from the *Collins Cobuild English Language Dictionary for Advanced Learners* (2004), pages 109 and 110.

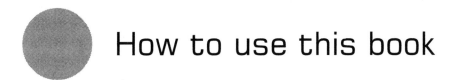

How to use this book

Chapter aims

These tell you what the chapter will cover and what you should learn if you study the chapter and do the activities.

Glossary

The words listed in the glossary appear in the chapter used with the particular meanings given. Remember, a word can have more than one meaning, but the particular meaning given in the glossary is the sense in which the word is used in the chapter. If you feel you need to know more about any particular word, look it up in your dictionary.

Definitions in the glossary are taken from or based on the *Cambridge Advanced Learner's Dictionary* (2003), Cambridge: Cambridge University Press, available online at http://dictionary.cambridge.org/

Tasks

You should take time to do the tasks. They are designed to make you study actively. Take a piece of paper and a pen to do the tasks. If you do the tasks properly, you will learn much more from the book.

Useful resources

These are books and other resources for you to find out more about the things you have been studying in the chapter and to do further practice.

1 Introduction

This book is organized into twelve chapters, each of which deals with a major aspect of studying at university. Each chapter contains information, examples, quotations from students and tasks for readers to do. Answers to the tasks, where necessary, are included at the end of each chapter. We have also included a glossary at the beginning of each chapter to explain any words which may be unfamiliar, and a list of useful resources at the end of each chapter, which we hope will stimulate readers to go further in developing their studies.

AIMS

By studying and doing the activities in this chapter you should:

- understand the purpose of this book;
- discover how it could be useful for you;
- get some ideas about what other students think about studying in the UK;
- start thinking about the advantages and disadvantages you will have; and
- find out some information about each of the chapters in the book.

GLOSSARY

These key words will be useful to you while reading this chapter:

Asset: A useful quality or skill.
Coping: Dealing successfully with a difficult situation.
Motivated: Wanting to do something well.
Relationships: The way in which people behave towards each other.
Specialist: Someone who has a lot of experience, knowledge or skill in a particular subject.
Strategies: Plans for achieving success.
Summarize: Express the most important facts or ideas in a short and clear form.

The purpose of this book

WHO ARE WE?

We are lecturers who teach students from other countries at university in the UK. Our work is to help students coming to study in the UK to be successful in their studies. Over the years we have learnt a lot about our students, what strengths they have and what help they need. The purpose of this book is to share our experience and that of our students with you to help you succeed at university.

WHO ARE YOU?

You are from a country where English is not the main language, or where the variety of English used is different from the one used in the UK. You want to study or are already studying in a university where English is the medium of instruction. Your English may be very good already, or you may be working on it in preparation for your studies, or studying a specialist subject and improving your English at the same time. You may speak one or more languages besides English and therefore already be a skilled linguist. You also come from a culture which may be different from the culture of the UK.

We are all formed by the culture in which we live and when we move around the world we have to adapt to other cultures. It is important to remember that although in an English medium university everything may be very different from where you have studied before, the knowledge and skills that you have gained from previous study will be your most valuable asset. The subject knowledge you have will be useful even if things are done differently in your new university. You will need to learn to adapt that knowledge to the new environment. Your knowledge of your own language and other languages will help you to develop and refine your knowledge of English. Because everything is new and different you must not forget that you already know a lot and have the ability to study successfully.

How this book could be useful to you

LANGUAGE

First, there is the language. Even if you know the language of the country well, you will probably find that it is spoken in many different ways from those you are used to. There are regional differences: people speak differently in different parts of the country and there may be people from many different countries teaching and studying in your university, all with different accents. There are also social differences: people speak in one way when they are with friends and in other ways at work, to lecturers or to people they don't know very well. You may not be familiar with all the different ways of speaking English in the country where you will be studying, and it may take time to get used to them. We will give you some advice on coping with these differences.

Here are some comments that students made about English in the UK:

Everybody has different pronunciations, even if they're British.
(Japanese student)

People don't understand my accent.
(Bangladeshi student)

I didn't understand the way they say numbers like 'nought' for 'zero'.
(Filipino student)

What we've learnt from university and what we've heard from local people are quite different.
(Chinese student)

People seemed to speak too quickly and I had to ask them to repeat what they say all the time.
(Kenyan student)

BEHAVIOUR

People also behave differently in different countries. People may not be as friendly in the country where you are studying as they are in your home country. This is often especially true if you are studying in a big city but have come from a small town or island. There are also different customs, so the behaviour of people in your host country may surprise you and your behaviour may surprise them. You may sometimes need to explain your actions or behaviour if people misunderstand you and, likewise, you may need to ask others for explanations of their behaviour. We will describe some of the expectations your lecturers and fellow students may have in the university where you will be studying.

Students say some positive things and some more negative things about different ways of behaving:

> *They are more easygoing and sometimes very bold.*
> **(Chinese student)**

> *People here won't even give you directions if you're lost.*
> **(Ghanaian student)**

> *More chips, more potatoes, we must have rice every day but English maybe not.*
> **(Chinese student)**

> *Everyone I meet is very friendly and polite, but I was surprised to see almost everyone smoking.*
> **(Ethiopian student)**

> *They like our foreign accent.*
> **(French student)**

> *People are courteous and always say 'please' and 'excuse me' though at times I find it not necessary.*
> **(Kenyan student)**

> *English people do like quiet, but do make noise when they are drunk.*
> **(Chinese student)**

APPROACHES TO STUDYING

Approaches to studying are also different in different countries. In the UK and other countries where most education is in English, students at university are expected to be very independent. You do not have many classes but are given work to do and expected to go to find out information and do the work by yourself. We will give you some advice and strategies for becoming an independent learner, for helping yourself and for getting the help you need from others when you need it. Relationships between students and teachers are also different from country to country.

Students we spoke to made the following comments:

Teachers are more distant from students in my country.
(Bangladeshi student)

The relationship between teachers and students but also between students themselves is quite impersonal.
(Polish student)

Tutorials after class are very, very helpful. I really like that kind of atmosphere.
(Pakistani student)

It encourages students to do more self-education. In my country the teachers try to tell you everything according to the book no matter whether you like it or not.
(Chinese student)

Self-study takes more time than study in my country.
(Vietnamese student)

Few hours in the class, I am used to more time at school and less at home.
(Chinese student)

YOU, THE LEARNER

You will also need to understand yourself as a learner. What approach to studying suits you best and how can you make the most of your skills and improve where you need to? We will describe ways of finding out how you learn best and building on your strengths to learn as much as possible.

YOUR SITUATION

You will learn best if you are happy in what you are doing. Make sure you have chosen the right course. If you think you have made a mistake in choosing your course, speak to your tutor as soon as possible about it. Make sure you will be able to study in your accommodation or, if that is not possible, that you will be able to use the library or another appropriate space at the university. Make sure you will have enough money and that you will be able to find a suitable part-time job near the university if you need to work. If you have any health problems, find out where you can get medical treatment. If you are disabled, find out what provision there is in the university to help you. All universities will have staff to help you with all these issues but you will need to find them and ask for help if you need it.

Signpost

See Chapter 12 for more information on coping with life at university as an international student.

I found accommodation through the university website.
(Filipino student)

I can find almost all the information I need in the Student Services Centre.
(Chinese student)

The student handbook will help students to know where they can go for help if they need any.
(Ethiopian student)

Task 1.1

Think about any differences you would expect to find between student life in your country and in the UK, and make a list of them.

SUCCESS

One thing you can be sure of – if you want to succeed, you will. If you are motivated in your studies, nothing will stop you. There may be difficult lessons to be learnt but nothing is impossible. We hope that this book will help you.

Before continuing, take a few minutes to think about what your aims are and what you need to do to achieve them. Think also about what advantages you have already. Then think about any areas where you think you might need to improve or get help.

Task 1.2

Write down your aims, starting your sentence: 'My aims at university are ...'

(For example: to get a qualification: BA, postgraduate diploma, masters, PhD, to study abroad for a year and get x credits for my degree in my country, to improve my English, to gain further knowledge of ..., to carry out research in ...,to meet people and enjoy myself.)

Task 1.3

Now think of the advantages you are starting out with and write them down, beginning with: 'The advantages I have already are ...'

(For example: I speak English fluently/to a high standard/quite well, I read quickly, I make friends with people easily, I am very hard working, I already have a lot of knowledge in my subject area, I am good at writing/maths/ languages, I am an experienced/quite experienced user of IT.)

Task 1.4

Now think of any areas where you think you may need to improve or get help, starting with: 'I need to improve or may need help in ...'

(For example: I need to read more in depth and get more understanding from my reading, I need practice in discussions and speaking in class, I need to be more accurate in my writing, I need to learn more about the uses of IT in studying, I need to be more organized, I need to find out more about research techniques, I need special equipment to help me study because ...)

Now that you have some idea of what you are looking for, we suggest you read through the summaries of the chapters below and decide which ones will be useful for you. Each chapter will include explanations and theory, examples and activities for you to carry out as well as references to other books, websites and sources of information in case you want to go further in your studies.

Summaries of chapters

CHAPTER 2

This chapter aims to help you understand yourself as a learner and to take responsibility for your own learning. It encourages you to look at your past learning and think about where you were successful and where you were less successful and why. The aim is to help you understand cultural differences in learning methods and the advantages and disadvantages of different methods. Here we look at some theories of how we learn and at how these can be applied in particular situations to help you learn more productively. The chapter will also explain how you can observe yourself as a learner and plan for effective learning, and suggest some strategies to help you improve your English.

Which parts of this chapter will be most useful for you?

Understanding yourself as a learner	☐
Taking responsibility for learning	☐
Looking at past learning	☐
Understanding cultural differences	☐
Theories of learning	☐
Observing yourself and planning	☐
Improving your English	☐

CHAPTER 3

In this chapter the focus will be on listening and understanding. It will help you to assess your level of listening ability in the different contexts in which you will be listening and tell you about strategies for understanding lectures, seminars and fellow students. All these require different skills and involve you in understanding different types of language. Lectures will require an understanding of the specialist language of your subjects and particular strategies for listening. In seminars and groups you will also be listening to specialist language but it will be used in a more informal way. The chapter will give you hints for preparing for these activities and ideas for how to improve your listening skills.

Which parts of this chapter will be most useful for you?

Factors that affect understanding	☐
Understanding in lectures and seminars	☐
Working in small groups	☐
Strategies for listening	☐
Ways of improving listening	☐

CHAPTER 4

An important aspect of studying at university is building a good vocabulary. This chapter explains how to do this. You should learn a little about how English vocabulary is different from many other languages. The chapter will give you strategies for understanding and remembering new words, and will also explain how words are used to create different ways of speaking English, formal and informal, specialized for a particular subject or general for communicating socially. It will help you to recognize which is appropriate in which situation and explain ways of increasing your vocabulary and using dictionaries.

Which parts of this chapter will be most useful for you?

What it means to 'know' a word	☐
Understanding and remembering new words	☐
Knowing the difference between formal and informal English	☐
Ways of learning vocabulary	☐
Choosing and using dictionaries	☐

CHAPTER 5

Here strategies for improving your spoken language will be outlined. As a new student from another country you will probably have plenty of questions to ask and will need to be prepared sometimes to make mistakes. You may need to build up your courage and practise before speaking out in a seminar or asking a question in a lecture. The chapter will give you some idea of the kind of language to use in these situations and helpful ways of preparing to communicate with your lecturers and your fellow students. It will give you ways of improving your confidence and practising your pronunciation.

Which parts of this chapter will be most useful for you?

Communicating in another language	☐
Learning how to ask questions in seminars	☐
Developing strategies for participating in seminars	☐
Developing skills for group work	☐
Improving confidence in speaking	☐
Practising pronunciation	☐

CHAPTER 6

In English medium universities it is common practice to ask students to give oral presentations. This means that the students, either individually or in a small group, prepare a topic and then present it formally to the lecturer and the other students in a seminar. For all students, but sometimes especially for those whose first language is not English, presentations may be frightening. This chapter will explain what is usually expected in an oral presentation and give advice on how to prepare for them, including how to build up your confidence and hold the interest of your audience, body language and the use of audio-visual aids.

Which parts of this chapter will be most useful for you?

Planning and preparing a presentation	☐
Building confidence in speaking to an audience	☐
Using your voice and body language effectively	☐
Preparing and using audio-visual aids	☐
Preparing group presentations	☐

CHAPTER 7

One of the most important activities at university will be reading. All students need to be able to read and understand a wide range of texts from books, journals and electronic sources. Strategies for effective use of the library will be explained. Here you will find details of how to improve your reading skills and get the most out of your reading. You will learn how to choose your reading and to approach texts from a critical standpoint and recognize bias. The chapter will also cover strategies for remembering what you have read, including different ways of making notes such as pattern notes and linear notes, and using index cards.

Which parts of this chapter will be most useful for you?

Using the library	☐
Choosing what to read	☐
Improving your reading skills	☐
Learning to recognize bias	☐
Remembering what you have read	☐

CHAPTER 8

Following on from reading, this chapter deals with ways of making notes. This will be very important to you as you collect information from a range of different sources during your studies. The way you make notes relates to your understanding of the information you read or hear, and is dependent on you being able to select what is important. The chapter covers how to choose what to write down in your notes, and different ways of writing notes that will help you to understand and remember later.

Which parts of this chapter will be most useful for you?

Selecting important information from a text or lecture	☐
Making notes from reading	☐
Making notes from lectures	☐
Writing notes in different ways	☐
Using notes to understand and remember information	☐

CHAPTER 9

This chapter covers perhaps the other most important activity at university – writing. Throughout your time at university you will be required to write a great deal in a variety of forms. These may include essays, reports, case studies, summaries, book reviews and dissertations, even at undergraduate level. This chapter will explain the different forms and also examine cultural differences in writing. It will explain plagiarism and how to avoid it by referring to your reading in your written work through referencing and bibliography. It will explain how to construct an argument and to make sure that your writing follows a logical structure, and will also deal with the important and difficult skills of editing and proofreading.

Which parts of this chapter will be most useful for you?

Learning about different forms of writing	☐
Understanding plagiarism and how to avoid it	☐
Constructing an argument	☐
Referencing and bibliography	☐
Editing and proofreading	☐

CHAPTER 10

All the information in the preceding chapters is relevant to postgraduate as well as undergraduate students. However postgraduate study is a different stage involving further skills which will be described in this chapter. At this stage students are carrying out more research and dealing with knowledge in a more sophisticated way. The chapter will explain the difference between undergraduate and postgraduate study and give advice on approaching the higher research skills and the demands of the Master's dissertation and the PhD thesis. Types of research methodology and ways of collecting information will be explained as well as ways of analysing and storing data and working with a supervisor.

Which parts of this chapter will be most useful for you?

Understanding the difference between undergraduate and postgraduate study	☐
Research methods	☐
Analysing data	☐
Writing at postgraduate level	☐
Working with a supervisor	☐

CHAPTER 11

All students need to take exams, but in most English medium universities these can take a variety of forms. There are also various conventions and attitudes to exams which may be different from other countries. It is important for students to understand these in order to be able to prepare properly for exams and to have the best possible chance of doing well. In the exam situation the student whose first language is not English is under pressure because of the requirement to write within a time limit. Ways of preparing for and coping with this will be explained.

Which parts of this chapter will be most useful for you?

Understanding attitudes to exams in the UK	☐
Learning about different types of exams	☐
Strategies for preparing for exams	☐
How to do your best in an exam	☐

CHAPTER 12

This chapter covers aspects of university life which do not relate directly to your studies, although they will be a part of your life and will make a difference to your well-being and happiness. Information is given about social and sporting activities at university, as well as clubs and societies in which you can meet people and learn about a range of topics. Practical issues such as finance, accommodation, finding a job and getting medical care are also covered.

Which parts of this chapter will be most useful for you?

Information about social and sporting activities	☐
Details of clubs and societies	☐
Where to go for practical help	☐

You should now have a good idea of which parts of the book will be especially relevant to you. We hope you will find this book useful and would welcome any comments you wish to make, or any suggestions for additions or improvements.

Good luck with your studies!

Being an effective learner

AIMS

By studying and doing the activities in this chapter you should:

- know how to take responsibility for your own learning;
- consider what it means to study in English;
- consider the effect of your past education on your attitude to learning;
- explore cultural differences to learning;
- read what the experts say about how we learn;
- think about your own individual way of learning and observe your own learning;
- be able to plan learning effectively; and
- discover strategies to improve your English.

GLOSSARY

These key words will be useful to you while reading this chapter:

Assignments: A piece of work you do as part of your studies.
Consolidate: To become, or cause something to become, stronger and more certain.
Current: A movement of water, air or electricity in a certain direction.
Initiate: To cause something to begin.
Night owl: A person who prefers to be awake and active at night.
Proactive: Taking action and not just reacting to the things that happen.
Resources: The information (in the form of books, magazines, Web-pages or other computer based information) equipment and people who can help you in your studies.

Strategy: A detailed plan for achieving success.
Terminology: Special words or expressions used in relation to a particular subject.
Transmit: To pass on information, to communicate.

Being an independent learner

A successful learner is motivated, knows how to study and is independent!

+ I like my course.
+ I know what my aim in studying is.
+ I know how to study.
+ I understand the way I learn best.
+ I am prepared to work hard.
+ I can work effectively with others.
+ I take care of myself.
+ I know how to make best use of my time.
+ I know how to get help from my tutors.
+ I know how to find and use resources.
+ I know the requirements of my institution.

Task 2.1

Look carefully at the list again. Which of these statements are true of you?

If you can honestly say all these things are true for you, you probably do not need to read this chapter. If you cannot, study this chapter thoroughly and, when you reach the end, turn back to this page. If you really learn what is in this chapter, these statements should then also be true for you.

Taking responsibility

Being prepared to take responsibility for yourself and your learning is the key to being an independent learner. When you decide to study at a university or college in the UK, you have to take responsibility for your own learning. No one will tell what to do and how to do it. In education at this level in the UK students are expected to make decisions themselves and to make sure they do everything they need to. You have to be *pro-active*; that is, you must:

- find out what you need to know;
- ask for help if you need it;
- organize your studying yourself;
- make sure you do all the work you need to; and
- complete your work on time.

Some students may find this hard at first if they are used to their teachers or their parents organizing things for them. Taking responsibility for yourself is, of course, an essential part of becoming a mature adult and many people take this step when they begin to study at college or university. Below is a checklist of things you should do as an independent, responsible student. Our advice to you is to do these things! Tick the things you already do (be honest). If there are some things you don't, highlight them and make sure you begin to do them!

Checklist: THINGS YOU SHOULD DO AS AN INDEPENDENT LEARNER

Attend classes regularly and arrive punctually	☐
Do all the set work	☐
Read background and any other recommended texts	☐
Find out when your assignments are due in	☐
Make sure you hand them in on time	☐
Find out when and where your exams are held	☐
Make sure you arrive for exams in plenty of time and are well prepared	☐
Ask about anything you do not understand	☐
Take care of your health and well-being	☐

No one will force you to do these things but if you do not, there will be negative consequences for you. Here are some of the things that can happen (*all* of which have happened to our students at one time or another):

- You miss the deadline.
- You get ill and tired and cannot work well.
- You may miss important information.

- You are not well prepared and have difficulty understanding classes.
- You arrive at the exam stressed and nervous (and probably don't do your best).
- You do not consolidate your learning or get feedback from the tutor.
- You miss important information and fall behind in your learning.
- You are penalized (and may fail the course).
- You miss the exam (and may fail the course).

Task 2.2

See if you can make the link between each thing you should do and the negative consequence for not doing it.

Key

For suggested links see 'Key to tasks' at the end of this chapter.

Ask yourself honestly if you want any of these things to happen to you. If the answer is no, you must be prepared to do everything in the first list, to prevent the things in the second list from happening. This sounds simple and it is. However, it is also *hard work*! You have to be prepared to be organized and to work hard if you want to succeed.

Motivation is the key

Something that greatly affects your learning and your ability to work hard is your motivation. Motivation is sometimes called 'drive' and it is like the fuel you put into a car; it is the power that keeps you going. Even the best car cannot run without fuel. In the same way we cannot succeed without motivation.

Motivation can be divided into two types:

1 *Extrinsic motivation*:   this is related to external rewards, such as a good mark, praise from the teacher, the approval of parents or the promise of a good job if you are successful in your studies.

2 *Intrinsic motivation:* this comes from the sense of achievement and pleasure you get from studying.

Task 2.3

Read what students have said about their motivation and decide what kind it is:

1 My mother has promised me that if I do well in my exams, she will pay for an extra flight so that I can spend the holidays with my family and friends. So, I am working very hard now!
2 Our statistics lesson drives me crazy but I know I have to understand the subject in order to be able to do my research project. Anyway, I hate to be defeated, so I am determined to learn this subject and to be one of the best in the class.
3 I love food science. I find nutrition absolutely absorbing and I am happy if I spend the whole day studying.

Key

For suggested answers, see 'Key to tasks' at the end of this chapter.

At some points in your studying you will feel discouraged and it is then that reminding yourself of your motivation can help you. What motivates you?

Task 2.4

Take a piece of paper and write down your reasons for studying your subject. Is your motivation mainly extrinsic or intrinsic?

If you find that all your reasons for studying are linked to extrinsic motivation, perhaps you should consider carefully if you have made the right choice of course.

Illustration: Choosing the right course

I noticed one of the students on our International Foundation Programme looking much happier and more confident. When I asked him how he was getting on, he told me with a big smile that he had changed courses from Computer Science to Architecture and Design and that he was suddenly enjoying his studies much more. He had originally chosen Computer Science because it had seemed a promising area for future work, but in the end he found it was better to study a subject closer to his heart.

Of the two types of motivation, intrinsic motivation is much more powerful. That is why it is important to study a subject you are interested in and to make the process of studying interesting and enjoyable where possible. The way to make studying easier is to plan ahead and find strategies for dealing with difficult or boring subjects. (However much you love your subject, parts of it will inevitably be difficult or boring.) Ways to do this are:

- ◆ study in short periods, with a rewarding activity at the end;
- ◆ study with a friend. This is more active and enjoyable; and
- ◆ use different methods – don't get stuck in a routine.

If the material is difficult, studying using your preferred learning style may make a difference.

Signpost

For more information, see the section, Individual styles of learning, below.

Also, remember that it is important to study at the right level of challenge for you:

- ◆ If the material is too easy, you are likely to become bored. Try to push yourself a bit harder.
- ◆ If the material is too difficult, it is also easy to lose motivation and to want to give

up. Look for help, from your teachers, from other students or from easier textbooks.

Studying through English

Having chosen to study through the medium of English, you are one of a growing number of international students who decide to study in another language. This is for most an enormously positive and rewarding experience. However, it can present challenges and it is worth considering what studying in another language means.

Studying in another language is very different from studying in your own language, particularly if you feel you are still learning that language at the time you start to study. Many people, all over the world, study in languages which are not their mother tongue. While some people study in a second language they are completely fluent in, others may be less than fluent or even have to learn the language in a very short time in order to study in it.

One of the challenges of learning in another language is that the subject-matter is new and unfamiliar and the language it is being transmitted in may be, too. So, at first, while you are getting used to the terminology of your subject and the way your teachers speak, you may find your classes quite hard work. One thing to remember is, though, that you would probably experience some of the same difficulties even in your mother tongue. When we start to study a new subject, there is always a certain amount of new language and new ideas that take time to understand.

This is the way one student dealt with difficulties she had:

> *At first I tried to read the recommended textbooks. However, the systems are different from Japan and the words that explain them are difficult to understand. So, I changed my method. I now go to the library and borrow books for secondary-school students, because they explain the concepts in simple language. In other words, I think I need basic knowledge about my course. It is an effective way both of preparation and to review the class. I also have a specialist dictionary for my subject. This helps me to understand the vocabulary and the concepts behind the words. It is hard work but it is good for both my English and my studies.*
> **(Japanese student)**

This student obviously feels positive about the challenges while acknowledging the difficulties. However, some students find it quite hard at first and feel the fact that they are studying in English is making their studies more difficult:

> *If I understood all that the teacher said I think I would have more ideas about my subject.*
> **(Japanese student)**

Despite the difficulties, international students generally feel that the effort is worth while because of the advantages. Once they finish their course, they not only have a qualification but also a very good command of the language they have been studying in. Many appreciate the value of being fluent in English:

> *English is very important for me because I will communicate about business and trade with people from all over the world.*
> **(Chinese student)**

Some students also find that the challenge of studying in another language is a pleasure in itself:

> *In the humanities class I read and write poems. It is quite difficult for me to understand poems which are written in English. I always try to express my feelings when I write poems in class. However, I find it difficult to express all of my feelings perfectly for writing poems. I do enjoy the humanities course because that is what I want to learn. Writing and reading poems are difficult but I find joy in the difficulty.*
> **(Japanese student)**

One thing it is important to remember is that you can use what you already know to help you. Your mother tongue may prove a great help in developing your English. Greek students are often surprised and pleased at how much vocabulary is the same in English as in Greek. Chinese Mandarin-speaking students find they can pronounce English sounds that many other learners of English have problems with, such as the 'ur' /3:/ sound in 'bird', 'world' and 'turn'. You can also draw on the knowledge you have from your previous studies, both in terms of subject knowledge and knowledge about how to study:

> *I thought before that it would be very difficult but from the first lecture I understood everything. I was studying computing in Cyprus for about three years. I didn't have any*

problems here because the terminology is exactly the same. It doesn't change in English or in Greek.

(Student from Cyprus)

Your past learning

We are all affected by our past. It shapes what we are today. How you have learnt in the past, your previous experience of education, has not only given you the knowledge and skills you have now but it has also given you your beliefs about learning itself.

Stop reading now and take some minutes to do the following task before continuing to read.

Task 2.5

Think of something (e.g. a poem, algebra, how to use a computer, etc.) that you learnt at school or college:

- What helped you to learn it?
- What made it difficult?
- Did you enjoy learning it? Why?/Why not?
- Was this experience of learning typical for you?

Perhaps you have been very successful and learning has been a positive experience for you. You have enjoyed learning and see it as a stimulating and interesting experience, which brings rewards and pleasure. The methods you have followed in the past have worked, and you might believe that the way you have learnt in the past is the best, and perhaps the only way to learn.

However, perhaps it was not like that for you. Maybe your experience of learning was not so positive. You may have experienced education as boring or painful. You may have felt it was often a waste of time, or a humiliation when you were not successful and were made to feel a failure. The methods of learning you experienced may have seemed completely ineffective. Perhaps, for you, education itself was a meaningless process.

Our beliefs about how things are, or how something should be done, are often unconscious but they affect us very powerfully. When we experience a very different way of doing things, we may find it stimulating or confusing. As you have come to study in another culture, you will find methods that are different. It is a fresh start. Therefore it is important for you to examine your own attitudes, your habits and beliefs and to try to understand them. You need to notice the differences between the ways you have done things in the past and the new ways open to you now. You will probably be able to continue to use strategies that have helped you in the past. However, you will certainly need to consider trying new methods and ideas, and adapting these to suit you.

Stop reading now and take some minutes to do the following task before continuing to read.

Task 2.6

Think of something you have learnt recently at the university or college where you are studying now. What helped you to learn it? What made it difficult? Did you enjoy learning it? Why?/Why not? How was this experience of learning different from the ways in which you have learnt in the past?

Finally, let's think about the strategies you have used in your learning up until now. Some of them will continue to serve you but others may no longer be useful. You may need to adapt them or abandon them. This may be because the type of learning you are doing now is different, because you have changed as a person or because your situation is different.

Read what these students have to say about one strategy that they all used in their previous studies – memorization:

I used to learn information by heart for my exams. I would spend hours reciting passages from the textbook, over and over again but at this university assessment is mainly by coursework, so I really don't need to do this anymore. I just memorize facts or short quotes for my presentations. Besides, I find it difficult to memorize passages in English, which is not my mother tongue. So now I just make sure I understand the main ideas and can explain them in my own words, when I need to.
(Iraqi student)

In our society, students learn their lessons by heart, otherwise they are considered lazy. To be honest, they do a lot of work but they don't necessarily do a lot of thinking! I prefer to read more and to think about what I am reading and to discuss it with other students. For me this is a new method. I enjoy it and I believe it helps my understanding. But I do memorize some words and sentences because it helps my English.
(Chinese student)

Task 2.7

Think about the methods you have used to learn up until now. Then consider how effective they are. Can you continue to use them? Read the examples below written by a student and then take a piece of paper and do the same for the methods you use:

Method	*Comments*	*Still useful now?*
Reciting a text	Helped me learn facts, (but boring)	Not really – we use different texts, not just one
Highlighting passages in the book, writing in the margin	An active way to read. Helped me when revising	We don't use just one textbook for my present course, but this is still useful when using photocopies
Listening silently while the teacher speaks	OK when teacher is interesting, but I used to fall asleep!	Sometimes, in lectures, but we mainly have to work actively in groups or pairs

Look back at your list. Which of the methods did you most enjoy or most dislike? Did you have a choice about which methods you used in the past? Do you have a choice now? Which methods do you think you will use from now on? Why?

Cultural differences in learning

You will probably have noticed some differences between your previous learning and the type of learning you are expected to do at the college or university where you are studying now. Partly this is because higher education is very different from secondary education but partly it will be because other cultures have different views of what learning actually is. Some societies value detailed knowledge; others value developing individual skills. Some appreciate students who follow the traditions of established scholars and reproduce their opinions; others encourage and reward original thought.

Task 2.8

What is learning for you? When do you feel you are really learning? What is the aim of learning? Try to answer these questions in writing.

Key

Turn to the suggested answers at the end of this chapter to see what other people have thought about learning and education.

METHODS OF LEARNING

In addition, different societies may have very different ideas of the most effective and appropriate ways of learning. Each country has its own traditions and will favour certain learning methods.

Is there a big difference between the methods you have used previously and those you are using now? Are you happy with the methods you are using? Some students find they have to make an effort to adapt:

> *Finally, I learnt how to put myself in this different education system. It is very different from the education system in China. You cannot hand in the coursework after the deadline, you do not need to read much textbook, but you have to borrow some relevant books to do self-study and you have to spend a lot of time on your coursework. All of this is different from what I used to do in China. So I have to adjust myself to the system.*
> **(Chinese student)**

Task 2.9

Below is a list of methods. Mark the ones you have experienced, either in your previous education or at your current institution. Put a ✓ if you like the method or a ✗ if you do not like the method:

	Previous	Current
Students sit and listen to the teacher talk at length		
Students work actively in groups to discuss ideas		
Students ask the teacher questions		
Students discuss ideas with the teacher and sometimes disagree		
The teacher asks the students questions		
Students follow the ideas of the teacher or another established scholar		
Students follow their own opinions or ideas		
Students speak out if they don't understand or if they don't agree		
Students keep quiet if they don't understand or if they don't agree		
Students research a topic and give a presentation		
Students are told the correct ideas/answers by the teacher		
Students discover the correct ideas/answers for themselves		
When students write an essay they use their own ideas and words		
When students write an essay they use the ideas and words of established scholars		

For most students, settling down to study in a different country, in a new language, at a higher level is a challenge. The majority, however, find that the experience is very rewarding:

> *This course has been a great opportunity for me. Meeting many students from different countries is a marvellous opportunity to learn their respective culture, history, geography and heritage. The teaching system is markedly different from my culture. Here, to cope with daily learning, I am to study a lot, think about the subject and be prepared accordingly, which was not the system I followed in Bangladesh. To say honestly, the English system compels you to study a lot, not by force but by intelligence. So my learning habit is developing and at the same time, progress in study is being attained.*
> **(Bangladeshi student)**

You can make the process of adjusting to a different system of education easier for yourself. Try to notice the differences and consider how you can help yourself to adapt to them. If you are consciously aware of the differences, you are probably halfway to dealing with any problems you have. One shy student devised a strategy for overcoming her difficulties in participating in class:

> *In my country it is not customary to speak out in class. I would be ashamed to make a mistake or reveal my ignorance. Here we are expected to participate in class discussion. At the beginning this frightened me, but I found if I discuss the points first with my partner or group, it was easier for me to speak. Often, I simply ask a question or contribute to the discussion with one or two sentences. I have explained to the teachers that I am shy and they don't put any pressure on me. Perhaps in the future I will be able to speak at length.*
> **(Korean student)**

Task 2.10

Can you say what you find difficult about the methods of learning at your present institution? Can you think of strategies you can use to cope with your difficulties?

How We Learn

There has been a lot of research into learning and, although no one can say exactly how we learn, experts believe there are certain stages in the learning process which are common to most people. They have also identified strategies which successful learners use.

THE LEARNING CYCLE

David Kolb (1984) produced a model which describes four stages in learning. These are:

1 having an experience;
2 looking at the experience and reflecting on it;
3 drawing conclusions from the experience; and
4 using these conclusions to plan future learning.

If we take the example of doing an exam, we can see how these stages can work together to improve learning:

* First, you sit the exam – this is having the experience.
* When you leave the exam, you reflect on how you felt and what you did. This is looking at the experience and reflecting on it. Let's say you felt nervous because you hadn't prepared enough and were tired because you had stayed up half the night before, studying. You couldn't finish the exam because you ran out of time.
* Then you draw conclusions: you might decide that it is important to be better prepared and that you need more time before to revise. You realize that during the exam you must divide your time equally between questions.
* The fourth stage is to apply what you have thought about to future learning: for the next exam you make sure you have a timetable which guarantees you enough study time in the weeks before, and that in the exam itself you will make a plan and follow it.

In this way you can refine and improve your learning. It is something that most people naturally do to some extent, but if you are aware of the process you can make it more effective. Taking time to reflect on your learning and then translating your conclusions into action can make you a much better learner.

OBSERVING YOUR LEARNING

Task 2.11

Think about one learning experience you have had recently. Try to remember the experience in detail. What happened? How did you feel? What did you learn? Were you satisfied with it? What would you do if you could have that experience again? Would you change anything?

If you take the time to reflect on your learning and to identify small improvements that you can make, you can make a big difference in your learning over time. One way of doing this is by keeping a learning diary where you write down your reflections systematically. Many courses now have such a task as one of their assignments.

Example: learning diary

This is an example of an entry in a student's learning diary

Learning diary week 2

Today we studied the difference between fact and opinion. It is important to recognize them in reading and when we write an essay. Most of the time we spent on reading an article and understanding what was fact and what was opinion. It was a recent article, so I felt it was interesting to know. In fact it was difficult for me to recognize the difference between fact and opinion. Sometimes one sentence included both, which really confused me. However, by the end of the lesson, I felt a little clearer.

I can see that my English is really at an elementary level. Recently, I have felt that my vocabulary is not good enough, so I cannot read easily. I need to read more in order to develop my grammar and vocabulary. The way I can think of improving is to read books and newspapers. I have started to use my dictionary more when I hear unknown words on TV. I am going to make a special notebook of these words and try to use them in my conversation.
(Ethiopian student)

If you do not already keep a diary, try to do it for a few weeks. Reflect on what you do and how you learn. At the end of a month or so, re-read what you have written and you may find it interesting to see how you have progressed.

PERSONAL LINK

Other theorists give useful advice about various aspects of learning, and one piece of advice is that it is important to try to find a personal interest or link with material you are studying. If you can do this you will be able to understand it and remember it more easily:

> *Accounting is not going to be my major subject in the future, but I know for sure that I am going to run my own business and I want to be able to understand all the entries: where the money goes to and where it comes from, how much I owe and how much credit I give and so on.*
> **(Russian business student)**

> *After reading the article on town planning and development, I went for a walk along the Thames. I could see similar things. However, in London, unlike Delhi, the modern buildings do not take over. The journal was difficult to read but it was good practice and it really made me think about what I see around me.*
> **(Japanese architecture student)**

ACTIVE LEARNING

It is important above all to be *active* in learning; learning is not like filling a jug with water. You are not a passive receiver of knowledge. It is more like building a house: you need to be very active in finding and arranging your materials and you need to work hard!

PRACTICE

Obviously, the more you practise something, the better you will learn it. There is a theory called 'over-learning' which reminds us that for real excellence we must continue to practise and repeat after the knowledge has been learnt, in the way that an accomplished musician continues to practise even after they can play the piece perfectly well.

BEING COMFORTABLE

Another principle of learning is that the brain can only work effectively under certain conditions. It is important for you to be physically comfortable and that the room should be at the right temperature. You should not be hungry or tired. It is also necessary to think about the time you spend studying. You cannot concentrate effectively for long periods without a break. You may feel you need to continue working but, in fact, you will learn less if you work without breaks.

Experiments have shown that we remember information better when we have a break or a change of activity. Most of us need a break of about 10 minutes after 40–50 minutes. This is because of the fact that you learn best at the beginning and the end of a period of study. So, if you have a number of beginnings and endings within your study period, with time for consolidation in between, you should have the ideal conditions for learning.

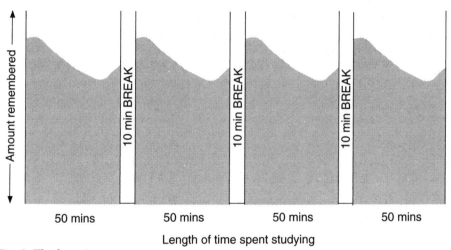

Fig. 2 The learning curve

It is also recommended to pace your study. It is much better to study for 3–4 hours a day than to leave it all to the last minute and then study for long hours. You may feel that this suits you personally but tests have shown that this is not an effective way to study.

One student confirms these theories:

I cannot read sitting down for hours on end. So, after contemplating or reading for about thirty to forty minutes, I have a break for fifteen minutes and let my brain mull over what I have learnt.

(Bangladeshi student)

Task 2.12

Think back over the studying you have done this past week. How many hours did you study for? When did you take breaks? How long were they? How could you have arranged your studying to be more efficient?

Individual styles of learning

While there are principles of learning that apply generally and strategies that can be useful to everyone, it is also important to realize that you will have you own individual style of learning. What this means is that because you are a unique human being, with your own individual characteristics, you will also have your own particular way of learning.

ENERGY

Different people experience variations in energy levels at different times of day. Some people are lively in the morning, others feel at their best later in the day. These fluctuations in energy can be used to your advantage if you notice how you feel and plan your studying accordingly. Obviously, it is best to tackle difficult subjects when your energy is highest and to do routine tasks when you are feeling slow or dull.

Task 2.13

Are you an early bird or a night owl? When do you have most energy and feel freshest? Over the next day or two, observe how you feel at different points in the day. Notice when your energy levels are high and when you feel most able to concentrate. These will be good times for you to study. Also notice when you feel sleepy or restless and plan other activities for these periods.

USING YOUR SENSES

I really couldn't understand the lecture at all. Then I went to the library and found a book which explained the topic with the help of diagrams. Suddenly, it all made sense!
(Mauritian student)

It has been shown that people also favour different senses. Some people are more visual; they like to see information. They may enjoy reading or using pictures and charts. Others prefer to hear information and understand most easily when they are listening or discussing. They will enjoy lectures and listening to tapes. These are auditory learners. Some people, a minority, like to be physically involved with what they are learning and they benefit from being able to move about and handle objects. They may enjoy role play or doing experiments. These are physical learners. If you use the sense you prefer, you may find it easier to learn, especially when you are learning something difficult for you. Academic institutions tend to favour the visual learner, as a lot of higher study involves reading. If you are an auditory or physical learner, you may need to adapt your style but you should still look for opportunities to learn in the way that suits you.

Ideas for those who prefer listening:

+ Get information from audio tapes, radio programmes or sound files on the Internet.
+ Get information from lectures as far as possible.
+ Form a study group where you all report back on a piece of reading you have done. This means you only have to read one text but you get to hear about many more.
+ Discuss ideas with friends.

Or physical activity:

+ Move around as you study (this isn't as crazy as it sounds).
+ Put information on cards that you can handle and move around (you may find it helpful to stick them up around your home).
+ If you can, choose options that allow you to do practical work or primary research (such as interviews, experiments or other forms of data collection that take you out of libraries and into the real world).

It is very important that you take account of your personal style of learning and devise ways of studying that suit you. Trying to study in ways that don't suit you is like trying to sail against the current. The secret of successful studying is to find a way of going with the current – but making sure it takes you where you want to go.

Planning your study

To study effectively you need a plan. You should consider carefully all the factors we have discussed so far that affect learning and then plan so that you can study in the best way possible.

Think of something you need to learn. It might be some information you need to prepare (for a lecture or a seminar) or a skill you need to develop (writing a clear paragraph).

Make an action plan. Consider:

- What you need to do – set yourself a realistic, achievable goal.
- When you will do it – give yourself a clear time period that you will dedicate to this work, at a time when you have energy.
- Where you will do it – choose the best place to work, where you will be comfortable and have few distractions.
- What resources you need – think carefully about what information or equipment you will need.
- Who might help you – people are also a great resource for learning; could a friend or a tutor be of assistance?
- How you will check that your learning is successful – you need to have a way of seeing if you have made progress. This could be by setting yourself a task or asking the opinion of an appropriate person.

You will need a sheet of paper to write out your plan. This is a very good thing to do because it ensures that you mentally prepare your study and this means you are likely to be more successful.

Example: action plan

Let's look at an example of an action plan:

- What you need to do: *learn to write effective, clear paragraphs.*
- When you will do it: *3–4 hours each day, Saturday and Sunday.*
- Where you will do it: *in the Study Workshop in the university library.*
- What resources you need: *Study Workshop Worksheets 1–5 on paragraphing; book: S. Cottrell, The Study Skills Handbook, pp. 157–60.*
- Who might help you: *Study Workshop tutor; English tutor.*
- How you will check that your learning is successful: *by checking with the key to the Worksheets and in the book; by writing an assignment for the English tutor.*

By having a clearly focused plan, you are preparing yourself for success.

Task 2.14

Think carefully about what you need to learn in the coming week. Set yourself two or three learning goals and make study plans for each of them. Make sure they are realistic and that you have time in your weekly schedule to carry them out. At the end of the week assess your progress.

Learning English

Finally, let's look at learning English. Learning a language is different from other kinds of learning you do at university. You are learning a skill rather than information, and it is a skill that has many different aspects. We use language for everything we do, and so there are many opportunities to learn. This gives you a great deal of freedom about how you study English and it should be easy for you to work in ways that suit your learning style.

THE GOOD LANGUAGE LEARNER

Task 2.15

Read through the statements below and tick any that are true for you:

Strategy	Always	Sometimes	Rarely
I try to think in English			
I take every opportunity I can to use my English			
As soon as I learn something new, I practise it			
If I don't understand, I try to guess			
I listen to the way other people speak and notice how English works			
I find learning a language rather like doing a puzzle			
If I make a mistake it doesn't bother me, but I try to notice my mistakes			
I like trying different ways of learning			
I like speaking to people and I initiate conversation			
I have a regular study timetable and I study English for a period each day			
If people don't understand me, I will try anything to get my point across			
I make a big effort because I know that it is very difficult to learn a language			

It has been shown that good language learners tend to use these strategies. Adopting any of these you do not already use may prove very helpful to you.

Conclusion

To be successful at university you need to be prepared to work independently and to develop good study habits. The other chapters in this book will give you guidance on how to approach each of the different aspects of your learning. Put the ideas you have been given in this chapter and in the others into practice. It is by persistence and practice that you develop any ability – the ability to study effectively is no different.

REFERENCE

Kolb, D. (1984) *Experiential Learning: Experience as the Source of Learning and Development*. Englewood Cliffs, NJ: Prentice Hall.

USEFUL RESOURCES

http://www.und.edu/dept/ULC/rf-stps.htm
   This site from the University of North Dakota gives useful tips on how to study.
http://brain.web-us.com/memory/memory_and_related_learning_prin.htm
   This is a very interesting and useful site on memory and retention of information. It
   includes links to further information on learning and memory.
http://www.fis.edu/eslweb/esl/parents/advice/good.htm
   Accessible site on the Good Language Learner.
http://www.smsu.edu/vlc/Language%20Learning/goodlearner.htm#
   Characteristics of good learners plus a self-check.
http://www.smithworks.org/chinese/articles/goodll.html
   Detailed and interesting site on the Good Language Learner.
http://www.fis.edu/eslweb/esl/students/teanotes/index-fp.htm
   An index of connected sites for improving all aspects of your language learning.

Cottrell, S. (1999) *The Study Skills Handbook*. Macmillan Study Guides. Basingstoke: Palgrave Macmillan.
Rowntree, D. (1998) *Learn How to Study*. London: Time Warner Paperbacks.
Rubin, J. and Thompson, I. (1994) *How to be a More Successful Language Learner*. Boston, MA: Heinle & Heinle.

Sinfield, S. and Burns, T. (2003) *Essential Study Skills: The Complete Guide to Success at University.* London: Sage.

KEY TO TASKS

Task 2.2

Consequences of not taking personal responsibility for your learning:

- If you don't attend classes regularly and arrive punctually, you will miss important information and fall behind in your learning.
- If you don't do all the set work, you will not consolidate your learning or get feedback from the tutor.
- If you don't read background and any other recommended texts, you will not be well prepared and you will have difficulty understanding classes.
- If you don't find out when your assignments are due in, you may miss the deadline.
- If you don't hand assignments in on time, you will be penalized (and may fail the course).
- If you don't find out when and where your exams are held, you may miss the exam (and may fail the course).
- If you don't make sure you arrive for exams in plenty of time and are well prepared, you will arrive at the exam stressed and nervous (and probably won't do your best).
- If you don't ask about anything you don't understand, you may miss important information.
- If you don't take care of your health and well-being, you will become run down and won't work well.

Task 2.3

1 Extrinsic; she is looking forward to an external reward.
2 A mixture; intrinsic because he gets pleasure from succeeding in a difficult subject; extrinsic because he needs this subject in order to do his research.
3 Intrinsic; she gets pleasure from studying the subject itself.

Task 2.8

Every study has a link up with the natural world. The objective of study is to learn and

know the world. So, the ultimate aim of education is to understand the world and yourself better, apart from gaining concrete knowledge.
(Bangladeshi Foundation student)

[Our book is] about what we value in education: curiosity, motivation, caring, excitement, joy and a meaningful life.
(Carl Rogers and H. Jerome Frieberg)

The aim of education should be to teach us rather how to think, than what to think – rather to improve our minds, so as to enable us to think for ourselves, than to load the memory with thoughts of other men.
(Bill Beattie)

Your instructor or teacher is not your 'Daddy.' You are not a child. The parent–child format simply does not work in modern training and education. Each student must take responsibility for his/her own learning by using the instructor as one of the learning tools.
(David Meier)

Education is the most powerful weapon which you can use to change the world.
(Nelson Mandela)

Education either functions as an instrument which is used to facilitate integration of the younger generation into the logic of the present system and bring about conformity or it becomes the practice of freedom, the means by which men and women deal critically and creatively with reality and discover how to participate in the transformation of their world.
(Paolo Freire)

Anyone who stops learning is old, whether at twenty or eighty. Anyone who keeps learning stays young. The greatest thing in life is to keep your mind young.
(Henry Ford)

We do not have precise details of the sources of all of these quotations but many of them were taken from **http://www.wisdomquotes.com/cat_education.html.**

③ Understanding spoken English

Listening is the key

Understanding what we hear is an essential skill for communication. It is perhaps the most important of all skills because we need to understand what people are saying before we can respond in any way. It is also important because we spend a lot of our time listening – it has been calculated that students spend over 50% of their time listening. It is often thought of as being a passive skill but in fact to listen well you need to be very active. There are many different aspects to understanding spoken English. We will explore these in the sections below.

Assess your level

Do you know how good your understanding of English is? Spend 24 hours observing how well you understand all the language around you. Then do the task below.

Task 3.1

Look at the table below and choose the description that best fits your level of understanding:

Description of listening ability	Your level
I can understand simple everyday conversations if they are spoken slowly and clearly. I have difficulty with TV, conversations with native speakers and lectures, even within my field of study. I often have to ask for things to be repeated.	
I can understand clear speech on everyday matters. I can identify the main point of TV programmes on familiar or simple topics. I can identify the main points of a lecture on a familiar topic. I can follow short conversations. I have difficulty when there is background noise, with complex or unfamiliar topics and with understanding native speakers. I have to ask for things to be repeated.	

Description of listening ability	Your level
I can generally follow extended discussion and understand most everyday conversation. I can follow a lecture within my own field if the presentation is clear, and most TV and films. I have difficulty in all these areas if the topic is complex or unfamiliar, if the speech is rapid or colloquial or if it contains regional language. I have some difficulty with native speakers speaking at natural speed.	
I can understand all standard spoken language, even with background noise. I can follow complex presentations and lectures with ease in my own field. I can understand the TV and follow most conversations between native speakers. I have problems with poor conditions, some colloquial language, regional language and specialized language outside my own field.	
It is easy for me to follow lectures, presentations or conversations that use a range of colloquial language, some characteristics of regional language or terminology outside my own field, spoken at natural speed or in conditions which are less than ideal. I can follow conversations between native speakers. I have difficulty with extreme colloquial use or strong accents.	
It is easy for me to follow lectures, presentations or conversations that use a lot of colloquial language, regional language or unfamiliar terminology, even when they are spoken at speed or in poor conditions. My understanding is as good as a native speaker of the language.	

Source: Based on the Common European Framework scales for listening.

Later in this chapter we will look at what you can do to improve your listening ability.

I can't understand! How can I cope?

Everybody speaks so fast and their accent is not the same as the English I learnt at school.
(Korean student)

Some students find it difficult to understand all the English they hear around them, especially when they have just arrived in the country. Some things, such as fast conversations between native speakers or lectures on difficult and abstract topics, can be very hard to understand. The important thing to remember is – don't panic! If you feel stressed and under pressure, you will understand less well. So, relax but remain attentive.

In the long term, the most important thing is to work on improving your listening ability. However, in the short term, you can use some strategies to help you get by.

PAY ATTENTION

If you become distracted, you have far less chance of understanding.

USE EXTENSIVE LISTENING

You are more likely to become distracted if you are overloaded. This will happen if you try to listen for every detail. If you are having difficulty, don't panic, just relax and try to get the main ideas. If you don't get the main idea of a lecture, the details will not be very useful. The same is true of a conversation.

Signpost

See the section 'Ways of listening' later in this chapter for more information on intensive and extensive listening.

POSITION

Place yourself where you can hear well and can see the speaker's mouth (this helps understanding).

LISTEN TO THE MESSAGE

Listen to the message, not the language used. We understand language in the context of the message being communicated. Did you know that nearly 50% of the words in a conversation at natural speed cannot be recognized individually if they are removed from the conversation and heard alone? We naturally process language in meaningful 'chunks'.

USE VISUAL SUPPORT

Very often what is being said relates to something that you can see. In a lecture, it may be a diagram or a picture. In a conversation, it may be something you can see. Look out for anything that will help you guess the meaning of what is being said.

PREPARATION

Prepare for situations in which you will be listening. You can and should prepare for lectures and other classes.

Signpost

See the section 'Listening to lectures' later in this chapter for more information about this.

You can also prepare for other types of listening. Before listening to the news, read a newspaper or look at a news website. Find out a bit about a programme or film you plan to watch. Find out something about people before you meet them. If you can predict what may be said, it will help your understanding.

ASK FOR HELP

Ask for help when you can. Successful listeners ask for clarification when they don't understand. Use expressions such as *'Excuse me? I don't understand'* or *'Sorry, I missed that'*. The first step is to recognize what you don't understand, then to indicate this to the speaker and to tell him or her what information you need. This is what happens in the conversation below:

Student 1:   OK, so we'll meet dead on five outside the flat.
Student 2:   Sorry, I didn't understand the time.
Student 1:   Dead on five, I mean, exactly five o'clock.

You can also ask other listeners for help, such as sharing notes after a lecture or just checking with a friend what he or she thought had been said.

JUST PRETEND

This is the opposite of the last strategy and *should be used with care*. It can sometimes be a useful strategy in social situations, where the conversation is light hearted and there is no important information being exchanged. In such cases it is best not to keep on saying 'I don't understand' because this may interrupt the conversation. Relax and try to follow as much of the conversation as you can. *Never* use this tactic with your teachers – you may miss vital information!

GUESS

Before you give up, take an educated guess at what is being said. If you draw on all the information available to you, you may be right.

What is listening?

EFFECTIVE LISTENING

Good listening is the ability to

1 receive
2 decode
3 interpret

the message the speaker is communicating.

Receiving the message
Obviously, you must first be able to hear before you can understand. If you have normal hearing and the conditions are good, receiving the message should not be a problem. Remember, though, that hearing a foreign language is always more difficult than hearing your own and even very competent speakers may have problems with bad conditions such as high winds, background noise and poor-quality recordings, or on the telephone.

Decoding the message
Hearing the sounds: listening and pronunciation are closely linked. If you are aware of how the pronunciation system of English works, you will find it easier to understand people when they speak.

Signpost

See Chapter 5, 'Speaking English at university', for more information.

Understanding the words: a good vocabulary is a great help in understanding spoken English. If you don't understand the words being used or you don't recognize them because you are not sufficiently familiar with their pronunciation in different contexts, it will be more difficult for you to understand.

Signpost

See the sections 'Vocabulary' and 'Pronunciation' later in this chapter for more information.

Understanding the grammar: It may be difficult for you to understand if grammatical structures are being used which you are not familiar with. Remember that colloquial speech has its own 'grammar' which may be different from the standard grammar you have studied.

Interpreting the message
Once you have heard the words and understood the English, you still have to work out what the person means by what he or she says.

Special meanings: in particular situations language takes on special meanings. If someone is talking about 'a menu' the meaning will depend on whether they are sitting in a restaurant or working on a computer. You also have to decide if the person is speaking literally or using metaphorical language, such as *'He's out to lunch'* or *'That idea is a bit of a dead duck'*. Very often your common sense and the context will allow you to realize which it is, but this can create an extra level of difficulty.

Intonation: it is also important to understand the speaker's attitude to what they are saying. To do this you need to be aware of intonation patterns, which communicate attitude and expectations related to the speaker, to the situation and to what is being said.

Signpost

See Chapter 5, 'Speaking English at university, for more information.

Understanding the ideas: how familiar you are with the ideas being communicated will affect how easy it is for you to understand. Even a person with very good listening skills will find it difficult to follow ideas that are totally unfamiliar to them. If you have some knowledge of the topic, it will help you a lot because your knowledge will compensate for the parts you may miss.

WAYS OF LISTENING

It is also important to remember that there are different ways to listen and that we don't listen to everything in the same way.

Task 3.2

Look at this list of things you might listen to. How do you listen? Which ones do you really listen to carefully, trying to understand every word?

- A joke.
- Someone else's conversation on a bus.
- A lecture.
- A song on the radio while you are tidying up.
- Gossip from a friend.
- A documentary programme on TV that interests you.
- A boring conversation.
- A TV programme that doesn't interest you very much.
- An announcement about your flight.
- Instructions from your teacher.

Intensive listening

If you need to know the details of what you are hearing, you need to listen intensively. We listen intensively to directions to a friend's house, or details of when a train is leaving. This is because specific detailed information is important to us. There may be points in a lecture or a lesson when you need to listen intensively because you need some specific information.

Extensive listening

This kind of listening is when you need to get the general idea of what is being talked about. You listen to get an overall picture of what is being talked about. This is the way you might listen to a radio programme while you are cooking your lunch. You might also listen this way in a lecture when you are trying to get a general grasp of the subject and you are not worried about detail.

It is rare that we listen intensively for long periods of time, because listening intensively is very tiring. We normally have short periods of intensive listening, when we feel it is important to pay attention, within a longer period of extensive listening.

If you are having difficulties in listening and understanding, particularly to lectures, it is better to try to listen extensively, for the general idea, than to strain to pick out details and by doing that miss the overall sense of what is being said. If the lecturer will allow you to tape the lecture, you can always listen again for the specific information you missed the first time.

The factors that affect understanding

Jokes are most difficult things for me to understand. I can't understand at all.
(Turkish student)

It is common that learners of languages often find jokes the hardest thing to understand. This is not surprising, as they tend to combine all the factors that make listening in another language difficult: they often use colloquial language, they draw on shared background knowledge and they play on special meanings in language. On top of that they may be delivered at speed or in a funny voice. It is useful to think about the example of the joke; this helps us see what the factors are that affect understanding.

Listening is sometimes described as a 'passive' skill. This is misleading as it sounds as if the listener has no active role. In fact, a better term is 'receptive'; listening is a receptive skill, and the listener actually has to do quite a lot of active work.

PRIOR KNOWLEDGE

Successful listening means actively constructing our own interpretation of the message. We have to hear the sounds, we have to decode them and we have to interpret the message. This means activating our personal knowledge. We need several types of knowledge to listen well:

- Knowledge of the world – of facts, events, people, etc.
- Knowledge of how and why people speak in certain situations – i.e. what they are doing by speaking (are they warning, advising, being friendly, passing on information?).
- Knowledge of language.

The last, knowledge of language, may seem to be the most important, but this is not the case. In fact, there are times when two native speakers do not understand each other, despite having no difficulties with the language, because they do not share the same background knowledge, or they were not expecting the speaker to say that kind of thing.

How this can affect understanding is explained below.

Knowledge of the world
Remember, knowledge of the world includes facts, relationships, etc.

Being able to draw on your prior knowledge of the topic can help you to predict ideas and language and help you to fill in the gaps if you 'miss' something that is said. This is why it can be very difficult to follow a conversation you join halfway through. As you do not know the topic, it is difficult to apply your knowledge of the world and you have to search for clues until you realize what is being talked about.

Knowledge of the situation
Knowledge of the situation includes where you are, who else is there, what has or has not been said, and knowledge of how people use language (possible topics of conversation in certain settings, how a discussion may be directed or concluded, etc.).

You can interpret what is meant by what is said more easily if you know what the speakers' relationship and status are. Knowing what people are likely to say allows you to predict what may be said in certain settings or at certain points in a conversation or discussion.

Knowledge of language
Remember, knowledge of language includes grammar, vocabulary, phonology, etc.

Of course, the better general level you have in English, the easier it is for you to 'decode' the message but, as we stated above, this is only part of what you need to understand a message. Research has shown that native speakers rely on both linguistic knowledge and other knowledge in order to understand what is said:

> *I tend to understand clearly conversations that are related to my interests while in some other areas I have difficulty sometimes.*
> **(Brazilian student)**

As we said above, knowledge of the world can affect how easy or difficult it is for us to understand what we hear. As is shown by the quotation above, it is much easier to understand when the topic is familiar. We can therefore use two strategies:

1 Take the opportunity to listen to something where the subject is familiar, as practice, wherever possible. This can be very helpful when you are at a lower level of listening.

2   Prepare the topic when you know in advance what you will be listening to. This will make the listening task much easier.

Signpost

For more ideas and advice see the sections 'Listening to lectures' and 'Improving your listening skills' later in this chapter.

VOCABULARY

Young people are more difficult to understand because they use slang.
(Chinese student)

It can be difficult to understand when the person you are listening to uses words that you are not familiar with. If you have arrived in Britain with only school English, you may find the English spoken by young people in the street unfamiliar and confusing. On the other hand, if you have picked up English by mixing with young people, you may be confused by the more formal language used in your university classes.

General vocabulary
As stated above, a large vocabulary will be a great help for understanding, *as long as you recognize the words when they are spoken*. It is important when studying vocabulary to learn how the words sound in different contexts. Most good dictionaries will come with a CD-ROM which gives you the pronunciation of the word, pronounced individually and possibly also within a sentence.

Did you know that there are a fairly small number of words – only 2,500 – that make up about 80% of everything we hear or read? These words are obviously the most important ones to learn thoroughly because they are always present. Nowadays many good dictionaries for learners of English indicate which words belong to this group. This makes it easier for you to know which to study.

Topic-specific vocabulary
Although only 2,500 words make up 80% of all text, if you are listening to a lecture it is probably the other 20% that will be crucial to your understanding! These are the words that are particular to a topic. You need to know and to be able to recognize these words when you hear them. You need to study the vocabulary of your subject. There are many subject-specific dictionaries in English, such as a *Dictionary of Computing* or a *Dictionary of Business,* and these are often designed for learners of English. They are useful because they also describe the main concepts of the subject clearly and simply.

Signpost

For more information on vocabulary and vocabulary learning, see Chapter 4, 'Building vocabulary'.

Linking words

These are conjunctions, like *however, in addition, nevertheless, while,* and adverbs, such as *inevitably, occasionally, generally.* These are particularly important because they signal how the ideas relate to each other. If you miss or misunderstand a linking word, you may get confused over what the speaker really means.

Different ways of referring to one thing

Remember that the same thing can be referred to by a number of different names and expressions. This may be confusing to you, but you have to be prepared for it. You may find it easier to notice this happening in a written text. Look out for different ways of referring to the same thing and practise doing the same in your writing. You may then find it easier to recognize it in speech.

Task 3.3

Look at the text below and pick out the different terms used to refer to the country described:

The Netherlands, also know as Holland, is one of the smallest countries in Europe. The Kingdom of the Netherlands was formed in 1815. However, this low-lying country in Western Europe has a long history which dates back to Roman times when Caesar's invading armies occupied the area. A small, peace-loving nation, the Netherlands remained neutral in World War I but suffered a brutal invasion and occupation by Germany in World War II. The country suffered much damage caused by bombing, and famine devastated the population. After the war, aid from the Marshall plan allowed the ravaged country to rebuild successfully. A modern, industrialized nation, the Netherlands exports food and agricultural products. Today, this politically stable country plays an important role in world politics and economy. The country was a founding member of NATO and the EC, and participated in the introduction of the Economic and Monetary Union (EMU) in 1999.

Key

For suggested answers, see 'Key to tasks' at the end of this chapter.

PRONUNCIATION

With other international students communication can sometimes be hard usually because of their pronunciation or poor vocabulary. It is much easier with British students and trouble-free with teachers.
(Russian student)

Having a good vocabulary is a great help for understanding a language but, as we said above, it will only help you in understanding spoken language if you are able to recognize the words you know when you hear them.

Words are often pronounced differently in fast speech (or even in speech at a normal speed, which can sound fast to a learner) from the way they are pronounced in slow careful speech or when they are said on their own. For example, the words *plant pot* may actually sound like one word *plampo* |ˀ| where the final sound is more like a stop in the throat than a 't'. Some words seem to disappear or be greatly reduced in fast speech, but a native speaker can perceive them. For example, the sentence '*He was there at the corner of the road*' becomes [/hɪwəzðeərətðəkɔːnəvðərəud/]. These are called 'weak forms' and it is very useful to practise recognizing and producing these forms. You will understand better how people speak and improve your own speaking by doing this.

Words in natural speech are not separated out as they are in writing. Each word can be affected by the words that come before and after it. For example, 'Do you know a good book on the subject?' may sound like 'Dju knowa goob boo konthe subjet?' and this can cause problems for understanding if you are not used to it. The end sounds of words can disappear or link to the following word: ('salt and pepper' becomes 'saltan pepper') or two sounds that come together may influence each other ('good girl' becomes 'goog girl'). This is not incorrect English, as some people may think. It is quite normal in natural speech. In addition, each area of the country has its own regional pronunciation and it is helpful if you can familiarize yourself with it.

Rhythm is also an important feature. The rhythm of spoken English is a clear guide to meaning, and words that the speaker chooses not to emphasize are less clearly audible than those which are stressed.

So, in noticing the patterns of stress placement in English, you will be attending to the most important part of the message.

Task 3.4

Listen to the TV or radio with your eyes closed. Notice how some words are emphasized more than others. Try to pick out the words which have most emphasis. News broadcasts can be useful for this sort of practice.

Intonation is another important system that affects meaning. The words 'I'm sorry about that' can be delivered in different ways and may express sincerity, indifference or sarcasm. Also speakers indicate with their intonation if they are sure or unsure about what they are saying, if they have finished or are just pausing and they signal when they expect others to join the conversation. An awareness of this is part of listening effectively. There are no fixed rules that can be taught; you will learn this skill by participating in conversations with good speakers of English and being attentive to how they speak. However, you may find it helpful to practise recognizing certain basic intonation patterns by using pronunciation practice exercises. If you do this, you may find you become more aware of the natural intonation around you.

Signpost

See Chapter 6, 'Giving oral presentations', pages 120–59, for more information.

Task 3.5

Watch a drama or soap opera on TV. Notice how the characters' intonation expresses their feelings and attitudes. Notice what response they get from other characters.

Signpost

See the 'Useful resources' section in Chapter 5 for materials to practise pronunciation.

CULTURAL KNOWLEDGE

To understand English jokes is very difficult for me because people laugh at things that are not funny for me.
(Chinese student)

Learning another language is not just a question of learning language but also learning how another society communicates. We learn how they express social relations, beliefs, customs, ideas, values, etc., so in fact we are also becoming familiar with a different cultural system. If we have gaps in our knowledge of that system, this may cause problems in understanding. Jokes are a very good example of understanding which is culturally determined. Sometimes we understand every word in the joke but we do not 'get it'. We do not see what is funny because we lack the implied cultural knowledge.

It is useful to learn as much as you can about the culture you are studying in. This will help you to understand the people in that culture and to communicate with them more easily. There are different ways of doing this. You can read books which are introductions to the culture or you can 'pick up' knowledge by living in society, by observing the world around you and asking people for explanations of things you find puzzling. It is probably best to do both. You need to keep an open mind and to be a bit of an anthropologist to discover how a culture works, but it should be extremely rewarding.

Signpost

Some helpful books are listed in the 'Useful resources' section at the end of this chapter and there is also information on the Internet.

Questions you could ask yourself when exploring the cultural background of a country are as follows:

- What is important to people in this society?
- What do people find funny?
- How is respect communicated?
- What do they find offensive?
- Who are the most well-known and popular public figures?
- What are the everyday habits of people in this country?
- What is the typical lifestyle?
- What professions do they value most?
- What are acceptable topics of conversation between strangers?

Task 3.6

How many of the questions above can you answer for the society you are studying in? Find the answers for any questions you can't answer. You can do this by asking people or by reading texts about culture and society.

THINGS IN COMMON

> *It is easy to communicate with other international students in that they do not use 'unusual' vocabulary and they talk slower than native speakers. We have common interests and problems and that helps as well.*
> **(Ethiopian student)**

In a way, this is rather like having prior knowledge of the topic, but it also includes having empathy with the person you are speaking to. If you have an understanding of the person, their ideas and points of view, it will help you to understand what they are saying – to interpret their meaning – more easily.

PHYSICAL CONDITIONS

External noise and difficult conditions will obviously make it more difficult for you to understand. If you have difficulty in listening, you should try to make sure that the conditions are as good as possible. Traffic, high winds, poor-quality recordings or public address systems will add to your difficulty, so don't be discouraged if you can't understand in such situations. The telephone can also be difficult, as some of the frequencies of the voice are missing. Naturally, if you have any hearing problems, these can cause you more difficulty than they would in your own language.

If you have any concerns about your hearing, go to the doctor and get it tested. In poor conditions for listening, make sure you find the best position for yourself: in the front of a large lecture hall, far away from disruptive students, where you can see the speaker's face (this helps a lot), etc. Recognize potential problems and plan ways of coping with them.

What makes a good listener?

Remember, you can't learn anything when you are doing the talking.
(Harvey Mackay, author and businessman)

There are certain listening skills which are different from level of listening ability in a foreign language (which we looked at earlier in this chapter), although the two things are connected. These are more general, personal skills and improving them can help your understanding of English greatly.

ABILITY TO CONCENTRATE

When you are listening, whether in conversation or to a lecture, the first thing you must do is eliminate all distractions and pay attention to what is being said. Give the person or the subject your full attention. Switch off from everything else. If you are talking to a person, maintain eye contact. Look at their face. It will help you understand more easily and it shows the other person you are interested in what they have to say.

ATTENTION

Keep an open mind and be receptive to what the person is telling you. Do not prejudge or disagree until you have fully understood. Do not interrupt and start talking yourself, but do ask questions to clarify anything you do not understand (if you cannot ask the person at the time, make a note of your questions and ask them later).

EMPATHY

Try to understand what the person is saying *from their point of view*. This is not easy. You also need to listen for feelings as well as for information. This is a particularly good skill to develop in conversations. In order to understand fully, you may need to summarize what the person has said to make sure you have not missed anything or to ask questions to make sure you understand how they feel.

CHECK

After you have listened, check your understanding. In a conversation, you can do this by responding to what the person has said. After a lecture or class, you can confirm (or correct!) your understanding by talking to another student and seeing if they thought the same.

Task 3.7

How good are your listening skills? Tick the sentences that are true for you. Be honest!

	Nearly always	Sometimes	Nearly never
I am patient when I listen to someone	☐	☐	☐
I concentrate only on the speaker	☐	☐	☐
I ask questions about anything I don't understand	☐	☐	☐
I take notes when appropriate	☐	☐	☐
I do not interrupt	☐	☐	☐
I can predict how the conversation/lecture will develop	☐	☐	☐
I can paraphrase or summarize what I have heard	☐	☐	☐
I understand the other person's point of view	☐	☐	☐

If you have been honest – good listeners tend to underestimate their skills; poor listeners tend to overestimate their skills – and you have all the ticks in the 'Nearly always' box, you have very good listening skills. Congratulations! Even if your ability to understand English is not as good as you would like it to be, you should improve very quickly.

If your skills are not so good, try to make sure you follow the suggestions above. If you can develop general listening skills, your understanding of spoken English will definitely improve.

Listening to lectures

Listening to lectures is a very special skill. It is a skill that even native speakers may not find easy. It requires concentration and the ability to process a lot of information. If you are also making notes, then the task is even more difficult.

Signpost

See Chapter 8, 'Making notes', for more information.

There are several things you can do to help yourself get more out of lectures. Let us go back and look at the things we have discussed before.

PHYSICAL CONDITIONS

Sit where you can hear the lecturer well and preferably also see their face. Make sure you are comfortable to take notes. It goes without saying that you should be in a good condition to concentrate. If you are cold, tired, hungry or very worried, you will not be able to attend to what is being said.

PRIOR KNOWLEDGE

Make sure you know in advance what the lecture is going to be about and prepare the topic. Do some background reading, prepare some questions you would like answered and, if possible, find out what other students know (or would like to know) about the topic. If you do this regularly, you should notice that you understand much more of your lectures and that you learn better. You may find it helpful to read texts at a simpler level as preparation.

LANGUAGE

While you are preparing the topic, you may come across terms and expressions connected to the subject. Make a note of these and make sure you understand them. If you have a dictionary with a CD-ROM, you may find it useful to listen to new vocabulary. (Just because you understand a word when you read it does not mean you will understand it when you hear it.) As well as helping with listening, doing this will expand your vocabulary and this will be useful when you are writing assignments, too.

YOUR ATTITUDE

As you sit down at the front of the lecture room, tell yourself that you will understand better. A positive attitude helps. Pay attention to how the lecturer is organizing the lecture and try to understand the structure. Practise active listening by asking yourself questions and trying to predict what the lecturer will say. Make allowances for the fact that you will probably miss some information. Leave a gap in your notes if you know you have not understood and ask another student once the lecture has finished.

Remember that you should not be listening intensively throughout an hour-long lecture. Some of your listening will be extensive, where you just want to get the main idea of what the lecturer is saying. You will listen intensively when you need to focus on details. During the lecture you will alternate between these two ways of listening.

Task 3.8

Find out the topics of the lectures you will be attending this semester. Make a time in your weekly timetable to prepare for each of them in advance. Ideally, you should allow time for background reading, thinking of questions and discussion with fellow students. At the very least, you should spend some time thinking about the topic before the lecture. After a few weeks of doing this, see if you notice an improvement in your level of understanding.

Improving your listening skills

If you put into practice all the suggestions given so far in this chapter, your listening skills should improve and you should find yourself understanding spoken English more easily. However, there are also certain, specific things you can do if you want to work hard on improving your ability to understand.

To improve listening skills, consistent practice is very important. Try to practise every day. You need only practise for a short time. It is the regularity of the practice that counts.

Remember the two different type of listening: extensive and intensive. To practise intensive listening – where you are listening hard for details – you should choose a time of day when you are fresh and able to concentrate. You can afford to be less fresh for extensive listening, such as listening to a story on tape or watching television for relaxation.

ELT MATERIALS

There are many ELT (English language teaching) resources on the market. You may find them in your college or university library or you can buy them at a bookstore. Start at a level that is reasonably easy for you (i.e. where you are getting most answers right). The book should have a key for you to check your answers. Once you have done this, listen again to try to understand what you missed.

Signpost

Some titles are listed in the 'Useful resources' section at the end of this chapter. There are also a number of ELT websites which have listening practice activities. Some of them are also listed in the 'Useful resources' section.

AUTHENTIC MATERIALS

Authentic resources are those in the world around you. To improve your understanding you can use the following:

Television
This is a good resource as it is easily available and there is a wide range of programmes you can listen to. This range means that you can get practice in listening to many different types of speaking, from documentaries (where the English will probably be quite standard) to dramas and soap operas (where language may be colloquial, regional or spoken at speed). Soap operas can be challenging at first, as their language is quite natural, but they can provide quite good practice as they may be broadcast daily and, if you listen regularly, this allows you to get used to the characters and their ways of speaking.

Videos
These have all the good points of television, with the added advantage that you can replay a difficult section. There may be a selection of useful videos in your college or university library.

Radio
This is generally considered to be slightly more difficult than television as there is no visual support for what you hear. Of course, this makes it a better test of your understanding. Listening regularly to programmes such as the news can help you to improve your understanding. Remember, you can always watch the news on television and then listen to a later broadcast on radio, to see how much you can understand without the pictures.

Cinema
Apart from making an enjoyable outing, watching a film at the cinema can be excellent for improving your listening skills. Sitting in the dark helps your concentration and following a story can aid your understanding.

The Internet
There are many interesting sites that have sound files. Sometimes you can read the text as you are listening. The BBC's website is a particularly good resource and there are many varied texts to listen to. The BBC also has a section dedicated to English language learning.

Signpost

Details of some sites are listed in the 'Useful resources' section at the end of this chapter.

TALKING TO PEOPLE

This is perhaps the best way to practise your listening skills because it is the most natural use of listening, as well as being the most interesting and perhaps the most challenging. Remember, you don't have to speak just to native speakers; you can learn a lot and develop your skills by talking to other foreign students. As well as improving your listening, you will be developing your speaking skills:

> *I didn't go out all last week because I had a bad cold. However, I spoke English every day with my friends of different nationalities. I realized that speaking practice is a very important thing for international students. I need to understand and communicate with people from all countries.*
> **(Japanese student)**

Conclusion

Remember, it is *practice* that improves your ability to understand spoken English, as one student discovered after a semester of hard work:

> *My listening has improved a lot. I heard lots of accents; many students are from different countries, so it was a good opportunity to practise your listening skill. I think it is impossible to hear clear, standard English all the time. In fact, if you listen to many accents, it requires you to have a very good listening skill. I have practised a lot and I feel my listening is better than before.*
> **(Student from the Ivory Coast)**

USEFUL RESOURCES

http://www.listen.org/
> This is the home page of the International Listening Association: 'The International Listening Association promotes the study, development, and teaching of listening and the practice of effective listening skills and techniques.'

http://www.uefap.co.uk/listen/listfram.htm
> This site gives advice about improving your listening skills in an academic context and provides exercises for practice.

http://www.bbc.co.uk/radio4/
> This is the Radio 4 home page of the BBC website. There are many interesting

programmes you can listen to, some of which have transcripts that you can read at the same time.

http://www.englishlistening.com/contents.phtml

This website has a number of listening passages for you to practise your listening. Some are free and others are available on subscription.

http://www.esl-lab.com

Randall's ESL Cyber Listening Lab. This site has listening exercises for you to practise your listening.

Blass, L. and Hartman, P. (1999) *Quest: Listening and Speaking in the Academic World.* New York: McGraw-Hill Higher Education.

Lynch, T. (1983) *Study Listening.* Cambridge: Cambridge University Press.

KEY TO TASKS

Task 3.3

The Netherlands, Holland, one of the smallest countries in Europe, The Kingdom of the Netherlands, this low-lying country, A small, peace-loving nation, The country, the ravaged country, A modern, industrialized nation, this politically stable country.

4 Building Vocabulary

By studying and doing the activities in this chapter you should:

- understand how English vocabulary is different from many other languages;
- understand what it means to know a word;
- be aware of the distinction between formal and informal English;
- learn a variety of ways to study vocabulary;
- learn how to choose and make good use of a dictionary; and
- learn how to use new words in your writing and speaking.

GLOSSARY

These key words will be useful to you while reading this chapter:

Concept: A principle or idea.
Connotation: A feeling or idea that is suggested by a particular word.
Strategy: A detailed plan for achieving success.
Taboo: A word avoided for social reasons because it may be offensive.
Vocabulary: All the words used by a particular person or all the words used in a particular subject or language. Note that this word refers to a *collection* of words and so you cannot say 'a vocabulary' (in the sense of 'a word').

Why is vocabulary important?

I am finding that studying in English is not as easy as I thought. Architecture is a very nice, interesting subject but there are certain things that I am really worrying about because I don't understand the words, so I can't work.
(Greek student)

Ideas are expressed through words so, obviously, having a good vocabulary in English is essential when you are studying at university. You need a solid base vocabulary of the most frequently used words in English and you need to know the specialist vocabulary of your topic. This is a minimum requirement to study successfully.

Vocabulary is the problem most frequently mentioned by students who are struggling with their work:

Despite the fact I have stayed in the UK for 6 months, I can't have good communication in English. It is because my vocabulary is poor.
(Japanese student)

I know what I want to say but I can't always express it with enough vocabulary.
(Chinese student)

I feel that my vocabulary is not enough, so I can't read a journal smoothly.
(Japanese student)

Vocabulary in English

Today there may be as many as a million words in the English language. Some claim that the number is even higher. English has a larger vocabulary than any other language, for historical reasons. However, you should not worry; you do not need to learn such a huge number of words! While an average educated speaker has a vocabulary of about 20,000 words, he or she uses far fewer on a day-to-day basis.

A fairly small number of words – only 2,500 – make up about 80% of everything we hear or read. You can find out what these are by consulting any good dictionary for learners of English, which should indicate which words belong to this group. These are clearly the words you should study. Some dictionaries even use a star rating system to indicate which words are the most common within the group of frequent words.

WHERE DOES ENGLISH GET ALL THESE WORDS FROM?

An interesting aspect of English vocabulary is that many words used in English today are taken from other languages. This means that students from certain countries actually have a big advantage when learning English. It has been estimated that 12% of words in English originally come from Greek. Over half of all English vocabulary comes from Latin, which should be a help to speakers of languages that are derived from Latin, such as French, Spanish, Italian or Romanian.

Task 4. 1

Do you know which languages these words come from?

- education
- typhoon
- sauna
- bungalow
- kiosk
- theatre.

Key

For suggested answers, see 'Key to tasks' at the end of this chapter.

The fact that English has taken so many words from different languages has consequences for language learning. Word formation does not always follow a regular pattern as it does in some other languages. For example, in plural forms the normal plural is formed with an 's' (car – cars) but 'men', 'women' and 'children' are exceptions to this rule. Oddly, the plural of 'house' is 'houses' but the plural of 'mouse' is 'mice'! There are also various different systems at work in the formation of verbs and nouns. Once you understand that there are historical reasons for these 'irregularities', it should be less confusing. The English language of today is a rich mixture of vocabulary and grammar taken from a number of source languages and transformed through use.

HOW MANY WORDS DO YOU NEED TO KNOW?

There is no numerical answer to this question. The only sensible answer is that *you need to know the words you need to perform successfully in the tasks you have to do, in everyday life and in your studies.* There are many native speakers of English who have a poor vocabulary in areas they are not specialists in. This does not mean they are not educated. A doctor may have little knowledge of the language of engineering and an engineer may know few terms relating to medical conditions.

The other thing to remember is that everyone has a larger passive vocabulary (the words you recognize and understand) than their active vocabulary (the words you use). This is normal and you should not be worried if you cannot use all the words you understand.

What does it mean to know a word?

Many people think that they know a word if they look it up in the dictionary and understand the meaning. Is this really 'knowing' a word? Do you know a word if:

- ◆ You cannot pronounce it?
- ◆ You cannot spell it?
- ◆ You understand it but never use it?

Of course, *how* you need to know a word depends on *why* you need to know it.

UNDERSTANDING THE MEANING

If your purpose is mainly reading, it may only be necessary to understand the word when you see it, but it is more likely that you will need to do other things with the vocabulary you learn, such as writing, listening or speaking. An aspect of understanding the meaning that you should also think about is whether the word has particular connotations. Some words may have a negative or a positive meaning attached to them. For example, 'famous' means 'well known' in a positive sense, whereas 'notorious' means the same but in a negative sense. Also some words may be connected with certain things: 'handsome' means 'good-looking' but it is used mainly for men.

Task 4.2

Which of the points below are important in knowing a word? Are some more important to you than others? Look at the statements below and using the key, mark each one 1, 2, 3 or 4:

1 Essential.
2 Very important.
3 Quite important.
4 Unimportant.

◆ Understanding the meaning.
◆ Knowing how to put it into a sentence.
◆ Being able to spell it.
◆ Knowing when to use it.
◆ Recognizing it when you hear it said.
◆ Being able to pronounce it.

KNOWING HOW TO PUT IT INTO A SENTENCE

This is where grammar and vocabulary meet. If you also want to be able to use the words you learn, you must know how to put them into sentences. It is important to know what preposition follows the word or what form the following verb will take. This information can be found in a good learner's dictionary.

Signpost

The 'Useful resources' section at the end of this chapter lists some dictionaries that might be of help to you.

RECOGNIZING IT WHEN YOU HEAR IT SAID

Do not forget how important it is to be able to understand a word when you hear it. Having a large vocabulary will help your listening skills, but only if you know what the words sound like when they are pronounced in normal speech. Most good advise /əd'vaɪz/ *verb* **1** [I or T] to give someone advice: [+ *to* infinitive] *I think I'd advise him* ***to*** *leave the company.* ○ *His doctor advised him* ***against*** *smoking.* ○ *I'd strongly advise* ***against*** *making a sudden decision.* ○ [+ ***that***] *They're advising* ***that*** *children be kept out of the sun altogether.* ○ [+ v-ing] *I'd advise* ***waiting*** *until tomorrow.* ○ [+ question word] *She advised us* ***when*** *to come.* ○ *She advises the President* (= gives information and suggests types of action) ***on*** *African policy.* ○ *You* ***would be well-advised to*** (= It would be wise for you to) *have the appropriate vaccinations before you go abroad.* ✳ NOTE: Do not confuse with the noun, **advice**. **2** [T] *FORMAL* to give someone official information about something: *They were advised* ***of*** *their rights.* ○ [+ ***that***] *Our solicitors have advised* ***that*** *the costs could be enormous.*

A dictionary definition of the word 'advise'
Source: Cambridge Advanced Learner's Dictionary (2003)

dictionaries can be bought with a CD-ROM. This will give you the pronunciation of the word.

BEING ABLE TO SPELL IT

This is important obviously for essays and exams, in preparing visual aids for presentations and also if you ever need to look the word up in a dictionary.

BEING ABLE TO PRONOUNCE IT

You need to be able to pronounce a word you want to use in speaking. If you can read the phonemic script in the dictionary, this will be a great help to you. If not, get a dictionary with a CD-ROM and listen to the word several times and repeat it.

KNOWING WHEN TO USE IT

This is a question of *style* (is it formal or informal?) and *register* (are the words special to a certain subject?).

KNOWING IF IT IS FORMAL OR INFORMAL

The dictionary will also tell you if the word is formal, informal, slang or taboo (very rude). This is important information to know, otherwise you might make the wrong impression. As a young person, it is probably quite important for you to learn a certain amount of slang and taboo language if you are going to mix with home students. Young people typically use this kind of language. You may not wish to use it yourself but you should have some understanding of it. However, you should avoid using very informal language with your teachers or in your university work.

KNOWING IF IT IS COMMON OR UNUSUAL

You may sound strange if you use unusual words unnecessarily, and the way of speaking that is appropriate to speaking in a seminar on your subject will not be suitable for a conversation in the student bar. As one international student pointed out:

> I know formal and academic phrases quite well due to the fact I studied them for a year. However, I don't know general English and I can't speak naturally. For example, I can't say 'It is my personal opinion' instead of 'I think' when I am speaking to my friends, can I?
> **(Japanese student)**

You have to learn to know how to adapt your style to different occasions and situations and knowing the right vocabulary will help you do that. If you are speaking with friends, it is best to use simple, neutral or informal language. If someone uses unnecessarily complex language in an informal situation, he or she will make a negative impression. If you are in a seminar it is very good if you can use the language of your subject appropriately. However, do not look for difficult or unusual words in order to make an impression. The best essay or presentation is not the one with most unusual vocabulary; it is the one that communicates ideas most clearly.

So, there are many different aspects to learning a word properly. While this means you have to do more work, if you do this work, it will help you greatly, in the long term, because you will have a good vocabulary that you can use to learn effectively.

Ways of building your vocabulary

CHOOSING A DICTIONARY

A good dictionary can be a great help in building your vocabulary – if you use it well.

A good dictionary should tell you how to deal with all the aspects of vocabulary learning mentioned above.

It is important to choose the right dictionary for you. The first thing to think about is what type of dictionary you want. There are many different types and they do different jobs. An English-speaking person will need a different dictionary from a foreign learner; a university student will need a different dictionary from a schoolchild; and a person studying linguistics will need a different kind of dictionary from a computing student. So you must think about what you want from a dictionary and choose accordingly. Dictionaries can be divided into two types: specialist (dictionaries of legal terms, computing, nursing, etc.) and general language dictionaries. We recommend buying a specialist dictionary for your subject.

Further, general language dictionaries can be subdivided into monolingual and bilingual.

Monolingual dictionaries (English–English)
These can be divided into those aimed at English native speakers and those aimed at learners. Some students think that buying a dictionary for native speakers, particularly one aimed at children, can be helpful. This is not correct. What an English-speaking child needs to know from a dictionary is very different from what an adult leaner of English needs.

A dictionary designed for native speakers will not contain the kind of information about pronunciation, grammar and use that a learner needs. Explanations may be difficult to understand. A learner's dictionary will provide a lot of helpful information and usually it will contain at the beginning a guide to using the dictionary.

Bilingual dictionaries (English–your language)
These can also be a great help, but you have to use them carefully. Remember that they have to contain twice as much information (because they contain two languages) so they cannot be as comprehensive and detailed as a monolingual dictionary. Very often there is not a one-to-one correspondence between words in two languages so, if you rely too much on a bilingual dictionary, you may produce some very strange English! However, they can be very useful for checking the meaning of an English word you are unsure about. You should be aware, though, that even the best bilingual dictionaries have limitations and may even contain mistakes.

The good thing about using a monolingual dictionary is that reading the explanation in English forces you to think in English, so you are improving your English even as you study.

Electronic and online dictionaries

Lastly, modern technology means that we now also have electronic and online dictionaries. Electronic dictionaries are often bilingual, so you should use them cautiously. Remember that some tutors may not allow their use in class and they are usually banned from examination rooms. Many publishers also make their dictionaries available online. Some of these are learners' dictionaries, which are the best for you to use.

You can access them while you are doing a piece of work at your computer, which is very convenient. Some paper dictionaries now come with a CD-ROM, so you can also use them when working at your PC. Both online dictionaries and CD-ROMs usually have the facility to be accessed straight from the document you are wordprocessing. This allows you to make very active use of the dictionary.

Signpost

See the 'Useful resources section' at the end of this chapter for details about these dictionaries.

Thesauruses

A thesaurus is a dictionary that contains lists of words that have similar meanings. It is a very useful tool for expanding your vocabulary because you can look up one word and find others which are related to it. It does not normally give the meaning of words, but a good learner's thesaurus will indicate how the similar words are used with different meanings or in different situations. The most popular and famous thesaurus in Britain is *Roget's Thesaurus* but you may find it easier to start by using a learner's thesaurus.

Signpost

See the 'Useful resources section' at the end of this chapter for details about thesauruses.

> **clean**
> *adjective* not at all dirty; *I asked the waiter for a clean glass as the one I had been given had some marks on it*
>
> ◊ **hygienic** which is clean and free of germs; *we decided not to eat at the restaurant as the kitchen didn't look at all hygienic*
>
> ◊ **immaculate** perfectly clean and tidy; *the nurses all wore immaculate white uniforms*
>
> ◊ **polished** *or* **shiny** so clean that it is bright and reflective; *the table top was so highly polished he could see his face reflected in it*
>
> ◊ **spotless** very clean, without any marks; *he cleans his kitchen every day, it is spotless*
>
> ◊ **sterile** free from bacteria, microbes or infectious organisms; *the nurse put a sterile dressing on the wound*

A thesaurus entry for the word 'clean'
Source: English Thesaurus for Students (1999) reproduced by kind permission of Peter Collin Publishing, a division of Bloomsbury Reference.

Lastly, it is well worth spending a bit of money to buy a good-quality dictionary. It will be expensive because a lot of work and research has gone into producing it. Your dictionary (or dictionaries) will be a useful tool for you throughout your studies. It is one of the most important investments you will make.

USING THE DICTIONARY

> *I find the CD-ROM with the pronunciation fantastic! I prepare my speeches for the congress using it. I practise the words I don't know until I am confident.*
> **(Spanish postgraduate medical student)**

Refer back to the section 'What does it mean to know a word?' earlier in this chapter. There we had a list of different aspects of knowing a word:

- Understanding the meaning.
- Knowing how to put it into a sentence.
- Being able to spell it.
- Knowing if it is formal or informal.
- Knowing when to use it.
- Recognizing it when you hear it said.
- Being able to pronounce it.

◆ Knowing if it is common or unusual.

A good dictionary should be able to help you with most, if not all, of these. However, you have to know how to find this information in a dictionary.

Task 4.3

Look at the sample dictionary page opposite and see how many of the aspects listed above you can find.

It is very important that you make active use of your dictionary. As well as giving you information about the meaning of a word it can teach you how to use the word in a sentence, how to pronounce it, whether it is formal or informal, common or unusual and when it can be used.

THREE ASPECTS OF VOCABULARY LEARNING

Many students think that the best way to learn vocabulary is to look words up in a dictionary, often a bilingual dictionary, then write down a list of the words they have looked up with their translation next to them. This is one way to try to learn vocabulary, but it is not the only way and it is probably not the best.

There are many different ways of learning vocabulary and it is important to experiment with different techniques. Different words can be learnt in different ways and some learners prefer certain techniques while others find that other methods suit them.

It is useful to understand that there are three aspects of learning a word. The techniques people use to study vocabulary will be based on one or more of these aspects.

Cognitive
This refers to how you use thinking to understand and process new vocabulary. Organizing vocabulary lists, matching opposites and grouping words in various ways are all cognitive activities.

Affective
This refers to how you associate words with feelings and significant events. Having a personal response to a word or using words to express feelings both use an affective approach to learning.

cussed the advisability of building so near to the airport.
adviser /əd'vaɪ.zəʳ/ ⑤ /-zɚ/ noun [C] (ALSO **advisor**) someone whose job is to give advice about a subject: She is the party's main economic adviser. ○ a financial advisor
advisory /əd'vaɪ.zᵊr.i/ ⑤ /-zɚ-/ adj: She is employed by the president in an advisory capacity (= giving advice).
advisory /əd'vaɪ.zᵊr.i/ noun [C usually pl] US an official announcement that contains advice, information or a warning: weather/travel advisories ○ Television companies sometimes broadcast advisories before violent movies.

COMMON LEARNER ERROR

advice

Remember that this word is not countable.
She gave me lots of advice.
~~She gave me lots of advices.~~
If you want to use advice in a countable way, say a piece of advice.
He gave me a good piece of advice.
~~He gave me a good advice.~~

COMMON LEARNER ERROR

advice or advise?

Be careful not to confuse the noun advice with the verb advise.
I advise you to see a lawyer.
~~I advice you to see a lawyer.~~

advisedly /əd'vaɪ.zɪd.li/ adv FORMAL If you say you are using a word advisedly, you mean you are choosing it after thinking about it very carefully: This action is barbaric – and I use the word advisedly.
advisement /əd'vaɪz.mənt/ noun [U] US the process or activity of advising someone about something: a counseling and advisement center ○ Contact Dr. Gray about academic advisement. ○ student/graduate/career advisement
● **take** sth **under advisement** US to consider something such as advice or information carefully: Thank you for your input, Mr. Walters – I'll take what you've said under advisement.
advocate [SUPPORT] /'æd.və.keɪt/ verb [T] to publicly support or suggest an idea, development or way of doing something: [+ v-ing] She advocates taking a more long-term view. ○ He advocates the return of capital punishment. **advocate** /'æd.və.kət/ noun [C] He's a strong advocate of state ownership of the railways. **advocacy** /'æd.və.kə.si/ noun [U] She is renowned for her advocacy of human rights.
advocate [LAWYER] /'æd.və.kət/ noun [C] a lawyer who defends someone in a court of law
adze, US USUALLY **adz** /ædz/ noun [C] a tool like an axe with the blade at an angle of approximately 90° to the handle, which is used for cutting and shaping wood
aegis /'iː.dʒɪs/ noun FORMAL **under the aegis of** sb/sth with the protection or support of someone or something, especially an organization: The project was set up under the aegis of the university.
aeon /'iː.ɒn/ ⑤ /-ɑːn/ noun [C] MAINLY UK FOR **eon**
aerate /eə'reɪt/ ⑤ /er'eɪt/ verb [T] **1** to add a gas to liquid, especially a drink: aerated water **2** to allow air to act on something: Earthworms help to aerate the soil. ○ aerated soil **aeration** /eə'reɪ.ʃᵊn/ ⑤ /er'eɪ-/ noun [U]
aerial [RADIO] /'eə.ri.əl/ ⑤ /'er.i-/ noun [C] (US ALSO **antenna**) a structure made of metal rods or wires which receives or sends out radio or television signals ⊃See picture Car on page Centre 12
aerial [AIR] /'eə.ri.əl/ ⑤ /'er.i-/ adj in or from the air, especially from an aircraft: Meanwhile, the massive aerial bombardment/bombing of military targets continued unabated. ○ aerial photography
aerie /'ɪə.ri/ ⑤ /'ɪr.i/ noun [C] MAINLY US FOR **eyrie**
aero- /eə.rəʊ-/ ⑤ /er.oʊ-/ prefix of the air or of air travel: aerodynamics ○ aeronautics
aerobatics /ˌeə.rəʊ'bæt.ɪks/ ⑤ /ˌer.oʊ'bæt̬-/ plural noun skilful changes of position of an aircraft, such as flying upside down or in a circle: The crowd was entertained

with a display of aerobatics. **aerobatic** /ˌeə.rəʊ'bæt.ɪk/ ⑤ /ˌer.oʊ'bæt̬-/ adj: an aerobatic display

aerobics /eə'rəʊ.bɪks/ ⑤ /er'oʊ-/ noun [U] energetic physical exercises, often performed with a group of people to music, which make the heart, lungs and muscles stronger and increase the amount of oxygen in the blood: She does aerobics. ○ I go to aerobics (= to a class where we are taught such exercises) once a week. ○ an aerobics instructor/teacher **aerobic** /eə'rəʊ.bɪk/ ⑤ /er'oʊ-/ adj: aerobic exercise
aerodrome /'eə.rə.drəʊm/ ⑤ /'er.ə.droʊm/ noun [C] UK OLD-FASHIONED FOR **airfield**
aerodynamics /ˌeə.rəʊ.daɪ'næm.ɪks/ ⑤ /ˌer.oʊ-/ noun [U] the science which studies the movement of gases and the way solid bodies, such as aircraft, move through them **aerodynamic** /ˌeə.rəʊ.daɪ'næm.ɪk/ ⑤ /ˌer.oʊ-/ adj: aerodynamic principles ○ an aerodynamic design/car **aerodynamically** /ˌeə.rəʊ.daɪ'næm.ɪ.kli/ ⑤ /ˌer.oʊ-/ adv: aerodynamically designed/efficient
aerogramme, US ALSO **aerogram** /'eə.rəʊ.græm/ ⑤ /'er.ə-/ noun [C] an airletter
aeronautics /ˌeə.rə'nɔː.tɪks/ ⑤ /ˌer.ə'nɑː.t̬ɪks/ noun [U] the technology and science of designing, building and operating aircraft **aeronautic** /ˌeə.rə'nɔː.tɪk/ ⑤ /ˌer.ə'nɑː.t̬ɪk/ /ˌeə.rə'nɔː.tɪ.kᵊl/ ⑤ /ˌer.ə'nɑː.t̬ɪ-/ adj: aeronautic design/engineering **aeronautical** /ˌeə.rə'nɔː.tɪ.kᵊl/ ⑤ /ˌer.ə'nɑː.t̬ɪ-/ adj
aeroplane /'eə.rə.pleɪn/ ⑤ /'er-/ noun [C] (US **airplane**) UK a vehicle designed for air travel, which has wings and one or more engines: She has her own private aeroplane. ⊃See picture Planes, Ships and Boats on page Centre 14
aerosol /'eə.rə.sɒl/ ⑤ /'er.ə.sɑːl/ noun [C] a metal container in which liquids are kept under pressure and forced out in a spray
aerospace /'eə.rəʊ.speɪs/ ⑤ /'er.oʊ-/ adj [before n] producing or operating aircraft or spacecraft: the aerospace industry ○ an aerospace company
aesthetic, US ALSO **esthetic** /es'θet.ɪk/ ⑤ /-'θet̬-/ adj **1** relating to the enjoyment or study of beauty: The new building has little aesthetic value/appeal. **2** describes an object or a work of art that shows great beauty: furniture which is both aesthetic and functional
aesthetics, US ALSO **esthetics** /es'θet.ɪks/ ⑤ /-'θet̬-/ noun [U] the formal study of art, especially in relation to the idea of beauty **aesthetically**, US ALSO **esthetically** /es'θet.ɪ.kli/ ⑤ /-'θet̬-/ adv: I like objects to be both functional and aesthetically **pleasing**.
aesthete, US ALSO **esthete** /'iːs.θiːt/ noun [C] a person who understands and enjoys beauty: The ugliness of the city would make an aesthete like you shudder.
AFAIK, **afaik** INTERNET ABBREVIATION FOR as far as I know: used when you believe that something is true, but you are not completely certain
afar /ə'fɑːʳ/ ⑤ /-'fɑːr/ adv from or at a great distance: People came from afar to see the show. ○ HUMOROUS I've never actually spoken to him – I've just admired him from afar.
affable /'æf.ə.bl̩/ adj friendly and easy to talk to: He struck me as an affable sort of a man. ○ She was quite affable at the meeting. **affably** /'æf.ə.bli/ adv: He greeted us affably. **affability** /ˌæf.ə'bɪl.ɪ.ti/ ⑤ /-ə.t̬i/ noun [U] FORMAL
affair [MATTER] /ə'feəʳ/ ⑤ /-'fer/ noun [C] **1** a situation or subject that is being dealt with or considered; a matter: She organizes her **financial** affairs very efficiently. ○ He's always **meddling in** (= trying to influence) other people's affairs. ○ What I do in my spare time is my affair (= only involves me). **2** a matter or situation which causes strong public feeling, usually of moral disapproval: The arms-dealing affair has severely damaged the reputation of the government. ○ The President's **handling** of the affair has been criticised.
affair [RELATIONSHIP] /ə'feəʳ/ ⑤ /-'fer/ noun [C] a sexual relationship, especially a secret one: She's **having an** affair with a married man. ○ The book doesn't make any mention of his love affairs. ○ an extramarital affair
affair [EVENT] /ə'feəʳ/ ⑤ /-'fer/ noun [C] an event: The party turned out to be a quiet affair.

A sample page from a dictionary
Source: Cambridge Advanced Learner's Dictionary (2003)

Physical

This refers to learning the sound and stress pattern of the word, and also the form in writing. Saying the word or beating out the number of syllables is a physical activity. Another type of activity is to respond physically in some way to a word you see or hear.

Apart from being aspects of vocabulary learning, these are three approaches to learning in general. While each is useful on its own, when they are used together they can be a very powerful tool for gaining new knowledge.

You can associate thinking (cognitive), feeling (affective) and movement (physical) with the words you learn to make your way of learning more powerful.

Task 4.4

Look at the different ways of learning vocabulary described below. Which approach is taken in each case?

1 One student follows another student's instructions to carry out actions: for example in learning names for parts of the computer: Touch the *screen*; press the *hash key*; turn off the *caps lock*, etc.

2 A student studies vocabulary by organizing it into a table like the one below:

Noun	Verb	Adjective	Opposites	Notes
Education	Educate	Educative, educational educated	Uneducated	Adjectives have different meanings
Conclusion	Conclude	Conclusive	Inconclusive	
Bullshit, Bullshitter	Bullshit		True, genuine	Informal/rude!

3 An architecture student makes a mind map of vocabulary:

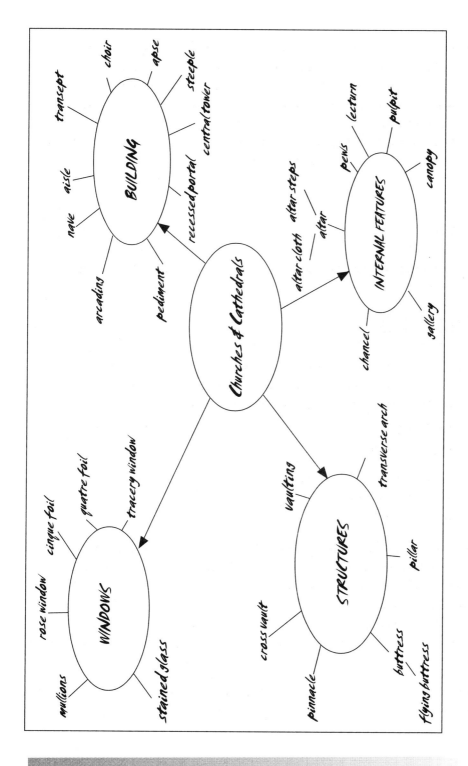

A mind map.

4 Two students look through some pictures or photographs of people and try to find a word that sums up each person. (e.g. 'eccentric', 'lively', 'stern', etc.). They see if they agree with each other.
5 A student listens to the pronunciation of words on a CD-ROM and then repeats the words on to a tape.
6 Two students play a game using vocabulary cards which have the meaning on one side and the word on the other.

Key

For suggested answers, see 'Key to tasks' at the end of this chapter.

Task 4.5

Look back over these activities for learning vocabulary. Which do you think are most useful for you? Why? Choose one to use to learn new vocabulary and try it out for the next two weeks.

GATHERING WORDS

Although I make a plan for collecting vocabulary (news, dictionary etc.) yet the harvest is not ideal. What should I do?
(Chinese student)

You need to be an active collector of words in order to build up a good vocabulary. Collecting the words is the first stage. You will find new words as you study your subject, by hearing words in classes and reading them in texts. You will also come across words during your everyday life. These are also important. Some learners collect items such as tickets, packets or advertisements which contain new vocabulary. It is helpful to have a word in its context. This can help both your understanding and your memory.

A good strategy for selecting words is to choose those that seem very important to the text you are reading or listening to, or those that come up again and again. If you are studying words for your subject then sometimes it is worth looking through a subject dictionary (e.g. *English for Computing*) for the key concepts. You might also choose to look at a thesaurus in order to find exactly the right word for what you want to say. For example, instead of saying something is 'clean' you might look in the thesaurus and discover that the word 'hygienic' expresses your idea more exactly. However, reading the dictionary is generally not a recommended way of studying vocabulary. It is much better just to use the dictionary to look up the words you have found.

The important thing, especially if your level of English is not high, is to choose which words you are going to study carefully. However hard you work, there is a limit to what you can learn. If you try to learn too many words, you will simply forget them or get confused. Of course, if you have good study techniques and you learn very actively, you will be able to learn more but, nevertheless, there is still a limit. It is much better to learn five words a day and actually learn them properly than to try to learn twenty words a day and fail to learn most of them.

Task 4.6

How do you record the new words you find? Tick any of the following methods that you use:

Word + translation	☐
Word + picture	☐
Word + an example sentence	☐
Word + definition in English	☐
Word + pronunciation	☐
Word + information about style and register (informal, formal, medical, legal, etc.)	☐
Word + opposite or synonym	☐
Word + information about grammar	☐
Word + the text it came from	☐

Think about what we said earlier about what it means to know a word. Any aspects you feel are important should be included in your way of studying new words and this starts with the way you record them.

ACTIVE STUDY

Once you have found the words you need to study and you have recorded them, you actually have to study them actively. Some students think that studying vocabulary is simply recording it, but this is only the beginning!

Task 4.7

Here are 20 ways of studying vocabulary. Some are very active, while others are fairly passive. Tick the ones you use:

1   Underlining or highlighting words in a text   ☐
2   Using a dictionary to find the meaning of a word   ☐
3   Using pictures or diagrams in the text to help you
    understand unknown words   ☐
4   Keeping word lists and reading through them regularly   ☐
5   Using a vocabulary workbook to do exercises   ☐
6   Using an interactive vocabulary exercise on the computer   ☐
7   Using pictures or colours to make words more memorable   ☐
8   Organizing new vocabulary in mind maps or tables   ☐
9   Collecting examples of new words, such as tickets,   ☐
    advertisements, letters and packets, and making a display   ☐
10 Carrying cards with new words on them in your pocket   ☐
11 Recording new vocabulary on to a tape and listening to it   ☐
12 Repeating new words to yourself many times   ☐
13 Learning a poem or a song with new vocabulary in it   ☐
14 Labelling items with their name in English   ☐
15 Asking someone to explain a word to you   ☐
16 Using a dictionary or thesaurus to find new words on a
    topic   ☐
17 Asking a friend to test you   ☐
18 Working out the meaning of a word for yourself before   ☐
    checking with the dictionary   ☐
19 Writing paragraphs using new vocabulary   ☐
20 Explaining the vocabulary you have learnt to a friend   ☐

You have probably noticed that the ways of learning become more active as the list progresses. It is good to use a combination of activities and you should definitely be using some from the bottom of the list. Choose at least one activity which is new for you and try it out for two weeks.

MAKING WORDS WORK FOR YOU

The final stage in really knowing a word is to be able to use it correctly and fluently when you need to. It takes time for words to pass from your passive to your active vocabulary. This is natural, and how long it takes depends on how actively you study the word. Remember, even educated native speakers use far fewer words than they understand.

Signpost

In order to make your knowledge of words really active, you may have to use a number of the techniques listed above in Task 4.7.

One other technique that may help you is mental rehearsal. This means you practise by imagining yourself using the word. You might speak out loud in front of a mirror. It is important to practise using the word in a context. Imagine the word you have just learnt is 'nevertheless' (a linking word to show that something is done or happens despite a fact or idea that has been mentioned). You imagine yourself in a seminar saying: 'The government had been warned that its fiscal policy was failing. *Nevertheless*, it continued with this policy.' Of course, you have studied the word thoroughly and you know it is rather formal. You want to be able to express the same idea in an informal way, so you also imagine yourself speaking to friends and using the word 'anyway' with the same meaning: 'I told him the party wasn't on but he came round *anyway*.'

You may also find it easier to use new words in writing than in speaking, as when writing you have longer to think about what you want to say.

THE LANGUAGE OF YOUR SUBJECT

Although we said above that only 2,500 words make up 80% of all text, the other 20%, which are the more specialist words, will be very important to your understanding, as these will be the words connected with your subject. You need to know and to be able to use these words. You should study the vocabulary of your subject *in depth*. This means:

* actively collecting words;
* recording them in a clear and accessible way;
* using active methods of studying them;
* making an effort to use them when appropriate.

There are many subject-specific dictionaries in English, such as a *Dictionary of Computing* or a *Dictionary of Business*. These are often designed for learners of English and they very are useful because they also describe the main concepts of the subject clearly and simply. So, by using them, you are teaching yourself some key concepts in your subject as well as expanding your vocabulary. Remember, many dictionaries are available on the World Wide Web now and you may find it helpful to use an online dictionary as well as a paper-based dictionary.

Conclusion

You have to decide how much vocabulary you want or need to learn and how you are going to learn it. The important thing is to choose the way of working that suits you and is most effective. The way to do this is to try different techniques with an open mind. As learning vocabulary is a long and continuous process, it helps to be systematic. Try to study some words every day.

At the beginning you may feel you have enough to cope with just trying to understand all the new words you find in your reading and lectures. As you progress, however, you may be able to take a more proactive approach by predicting what vocabulary you will need in a situation and learning it in order to use it. When you reach this stage, you can feel that you are really making words work for you.

REFERENCES

The information about the number of words in the English language comes from http://hypertextbook.com/facts/2001/JohnnyLing.shtml

USEFUL RESOURCES

http://www.warwick.ac.uk/EAP/study_skills/dictionaries/index.html
This site for international students from Warwick University teaches you about choosing and using dictionaries.
http://www.antimoon.com/other/activevocab.htm
The Antimoon Team 'Don't worry about your active vocabulary' site.
http://towerofenglish.com/vocabulary.html
A site with links to vocabulary practice pages.
http://towerofenglish.com/idioms.html
This site provides a list of links to pages dealing with slang and idiomatic language.
http://www.uefap.co.uk/vocab/vocfram.htm
This site from the University of Hertfordshire provides useful practice in vocabulary for academic purposes.

DICTIONARIES

Cambridge Advanced Learner's Dictionary (2003). Cambridge: Cambridge University Press.
   This dictionary is available with a CD-ROM, which includes a thesaurus. It is also available online at **http://dictionary.cambridge.org/**. This is a free online dictionary, with online worksheets and activities to practise your vocabulary.
Collins Cobuild English Language Dictionary for Advanced Learners (2004). London: Collins.
   This dictionary also provides help with grammar and word-building, and is available with a CD ROM, which includes a 5 million word-bank. An accompanying workbook is also available.
Dictionary of Law (2000). London: Peter Collin Publishing (Bloomsbury Reference).
   This specialist dictionary is also available free online at **http://www.petercollin.com/lawcom.html**.
Easier English Student Dictionary (2003). London: Peter Collin Publishing (Bloomsbury Reference).
   For intermediate and upper-intermediate students.
English Thesaurus for Students (1999). London: Peter Collin Publishing (Bloomsbury Reference).
Hoad, T.F. (ed.) (1993). *The Concise Oxford Dictionary of Etymology*. Oxford: Oxford University Press.
   This dictionary gives you the origins of words.
Macmillan English Dictionary for Advanced Learners (2002). Basingstoke: Macmillan.

This has a companion *Workbook* to help you learn more vocabulary and develop your dictionary skills. There is an online dictionary with a pronunciation feature available at **http://www.macmillandictionary.com/online/** after registration for which you will need a copy of the dictionary.

Oxford Advanced Learner's Dictionary (6th edn). Oxford: Oxford University Press.

Also available online at **http://www.oup.com/elt/global/products/oald/lookup/**. This is a free online dictionary, with online worksheets and activities to practise your vocabulary.

Oxford Dictionary of Business English for Learners of English (1993). Oxford: Oxford University Press.

Oxford Dictionary of Computing for Learners of English (1996). Oxford: Oxford University Press.

Trappes-Lomax, H. (1997) *Oxford Learner's Wordfinder Dictionary*. Oxford: Oxford University Press.

This is a clear and simple learner's thesaurus.

VOCABULARY WORKBOOKS

There is a large range of vocabulary practice books available on the market. There are too many to list here. However, it is worth mentioning that Peter Collin Publishing (Bloomsbury Reference) produce a range of workbooks on different specialist topics, such as medicine, law, finance and banking, among others.

KEY TO TASKS

Task 4.1
- education (Latin, via French)
- typhoon (Chinese)
- sauna (Finnish)
- bungalow (Gujarati)
- kiosk (Turkish)
- theatre (Greek)

Task 4.4
1 This is a physical approach. This is a very good way of ensuring you remember the word and its meaning but, of course, it is only suitable for vocabulary which can be related to by physical movement.

2   This is a cognitive approach. It is an active way to organize new vocabulary and is good for those who like to think logically. There are many ways of using tables and more information could be put in – such as pronunciation. The way this student has used the table is particularly good if your language has a completely different grammatical system and you get confused between the different forms of nouns, verbs and adjectives.

3   This is cognitive because it involves grouping words and making logical links, but it is also visual. This is also a good way to study actively and can help you to remember words more easily.

4   This is an affective approach as the students are having a personal reaction to something and then putting it into words. Working with another person can make the learning more memorable. It also has an element of physical learning as the students are handling the photographs.

5   This is physical and is focused on the sound shape of the word. The stages listen (to the CD)–record–listen (to yourself) are particularly effective. It is an auditory notebook.

6   This is a mixture of cognitive (words and meanings linked) and affective (because it is a game). It is good to learn with a bit of fun, and an activity like this, done with a fellow student, can be very effective in getting new words into your memory. The time it takes to prepare the cards is a good investment if it means you really learn.

5 Speaking English at university

By studying and doing the activities in this chapter you should:

- think about what it means to communicate in another language;
- develop your communication strategies;
- be able to participate effectively in a seminar;
- develop your skills for group work; and
- learn how to develop your English-speaking skills.

These key words will be useful to you while reading this chapter:

Assertive: Someone who behaves confidently and is not frightened to say what they want or believe.

Challenge: Something needing great mental or physical effort in order to be done successfully and which therefore tests a person's ability.

Challenging: Difficult, in a way that tests your ability or determination.

Convey: To express a thought, feeling or idea so that other people understand it.

Discourse: Communication in speech or writing.

Dynamics: Forces or processes that produce change inside a group or system.

Interlocutor: Someone who is involved in a conversation.

Rewarding: Bringing benefits, especially by making you feel satisfied that you have done something important or useful, or done something well.

Submission: Giving in a piece of work.

Succinct: Said in a clear and short way; expressing what needs to be said without unnecessary words.

Communicating in another language

While you are studying at university in the UK you will be spending much of your time communicating in English. This gives you the opportunity to learn to speak English really well, a skill that will be useful for the rest of your life. However, it can be quite a challenge to communicate successfully in another language. Communication is a complex process and involves knowledge of the language at a number of levels. To communicate effectively a person has to have a good command of each of these levels. In our own language we are not normally aware of these levels as we use them without thinking. Speaking in another language is different because things do not necessarily come naturally, the way they do in our own language. Let us have a look at what is involved:

- *Phonological level*: this involves making the sounds of the language in the right way and also speaking with the right rhythm and intonation.
- *Lexical level*: this means using the vocabulary of the language to express meaning.
- *Grammatical level*: this is the system of combining words into phrases and sentences.
- *Discourse level*: this is the way the other elements are combined to create continuous pieces of language – that is, written text or dialogue.

You need to operate effectively at all these levels in order to be a really good communicator. It is important to be aware of each level and to develop your abilities in each.

Signpost

If you know you need to make improvements in some areas of your language, you should make a study plan. Turn to Chapter 2, pages 34–5, 'Being an effective learner', for ideas on how to do this.

Here are some other parts of this book that could be helpful:

- For pronunciation, see the section, 'Developing your speaking skills', later in this chapter.
- For vocabulary, see Chapter 4, 'Building vocabulary'.
- For discourse, see Chapter 9, 'Writing'.

Task 5.1

Complete the table below as honestly as you can to indicate where you need to make improvement:

	None/very little improvement needed	Some improvement needed	A lot of improvement needed
Pronunciation: Can people understand my speech easily?			
Vocabulary: Do I have the right word for each occasion?			
Grammar: Are my sentences correctly formed?			
Discourse: Can I link ideas effectively, in order to communicate, including linking my ideas to those of others?			

It is important to remember that you can compensate for any difficulties you have by being aware of the problem and trying to use other ways of putting your message across. For example, if you know your pronunciation is poor but you have a large vocabulary, then when you see that someone doesn't understand something you have said, you can substitute another word with a similar meaning.

Saying the right thing

As well as being correct in the sense of using the right vocabulary and grammar, it is also important to say the right things, to the right person and to speak in the appropriate style – that is, with the right level of formality. If you use very formal language in relaxed social situations, you will sound odd and perhaps unfriendly. If you use informal language at the wrong times, you may sound rude or as if you are not taking things seriously. So it is important to think about what kind of language to use in each situation. It is also important to be aware of what you can and cannot say or ask. For example, you might ask a fellow student for their home telephone number, especially if you were working on a joint project with them, but it would not be appropriate to ask your teacher for their telephone number. People from different cultures have different ideas about what is acceptable to talk about, and you will have to be sensitive to discover what these are for your fellow students and for the society in which you are living:

> *In my country, people discuss money very openly but I find here that my friends do not like it if I ask how much money they have or how much money their parents earn.*
> **(Chinese student)**

> *I don't normally have problems communicating with other students or teachers, but sometimes there are problems with international students because we come from different cultures and our jokes and the way we see things is different.*
> **(Turkish student)**

Levels of formality vary according to the situation, the speakers and their relationship. A lecture, especially a large, public lecture, is likely to be more formal than a seminar, and a conversation between students is obviously less formal than a conversation between a student and a teacher. Of course, a lot depends also on what is being talked about and how well the people know each other, and there are a number of factors that determine the level of formality appropriate in any particular situation.

Formality in English is expressed by the following:

- The vocabulary used (e.g. 'return' rather than 'come back').
- The grammatical structures (e.g. the passive – 'the houses have been demolished' rather than 'they've demolished the houses').

Task 5.2

Look at the quiz below and decide:

- Is it acceptable to say such things at all?
- Is the language right for the occasion?

Tick the box that best describes the use of the language in that particular situation:

	Completely appropriate	Acceptable	Inappropriate
A student says 'this is bullshit' in a presentation	☐	☐	☐
A student calls her teacher (Mary Smith) 'Mrs Mary'	☐	☐	☐
A student calls her teacher (Mary Smith) 'Smith'	☐	☐	☐
A student calls her teacher (Mary Smith) 'Mary'	☐	☐	☐
A student writing to apply for a course begins the letter 'Highly Esteemed Professor'	☐	☐	☐
Student to teacher in a seminar: 'I can't agree with you on that point'	☐	☐	☐

Student to another student in a seminar: 'I can't agree with you on that point'	☐	☐	☐
A student corrects another on a mistake of fact he or she has made in a seminar: 'I'm sorry to correct you but General Motors were not the market leaders at that time'	☐	☐	☐
A student corrects another on a mistake in his or her English in a seminar: 'Excuse me, but it isn't "putted", it's "put"'	☐	☐	☐
A group of English friends are talking and use one word ('paradigm') repeatedly. You don't understand. Should you ask them to explain?	☐	☐	☐
Your teacher speaks too fast. You say: 'Slow down. We can't understand you'	☐	☐	☐
A student thanks a teacher who has been particularly helpful and friendly by saying 'Cheers, mate'	☐	☐	☐
A student says to a teacher: 'I want you to change the mark you gave me for my essay'	☐	☐	☐

Key

For comments on this task, see 'Key to tasks' at the end of this chapter.

- ◆ The level of personalization ('It is believed' rather than 'I think').
- ◆ The use of tentative language (*might, would, could*).
- ◆ The length and complexity of sentences.

Differences in style can be due to the following:

- ◆ *The relationship between the speakers.* For example, speaking to a friend you might say: 'I didn't catch a thing you said. Just slow down and speak up.' To someone you didn't know so well you might say: 'I'm sorry but I can't understand what you're saying. Could you speak a little slower and louder, please?'
- ◆ *The formality of the situation itself.* Talking to friends while preparing a presentation on change within a company you might say: 'It's incredible. They changed the system five times in four years. What a mess. No wonder the people who worked there were pissed off.' In the presentation you would be more likely to convey the information in a more formal style: 'Many changes to the system were introduced in a short period of time, with five new methods of operating brought in within a four-year period. Naturally, this caused confusion and some discontent in the workforce.'

English does not tend to use a lot of flowery language, such as 'Highly Esteemed Colleague, your most worthy and illustrious institution', etc.; this is regarded as old-fashioned and awkward. Even formal English tends to be quite simple and direct but it avoids the use of slang and colloquial language.

It is not a question of formal or informal language being easier or more difficult – it all depends what you are used to. Some students find speaking to young people who use slang and informal language much easier than speaking using more formal English. For others it is the opposite:

The common words used by young people are more familiar to me and it is not difficult to communicate with them. I feel easy with them. With older people you have to think before you speak.
(Greek student)

Young people tend to speak faster and use more slang. Older people tend to speak more clearly and are more formal. It is easier to speak with them.
(Korean student)

It is important to be able to communicate using both formal and informal language appropriately.

Signpost

For more information on formal and informal language, see Chapter 4, 'Building vocabulary'.

TALKING TO YOUR TUTORS

The tutors here are very helpful and friendly and they treat you in a friendly way. I call my tutor by her first name. But I still don't speak to her as I speak to my friends. However, it is not so formal as in my country.
(Korean student)

Often students find it difficult to determine exactly how to speak to their teachers, as the relationship between teachers and students in English-speaking universities may seem less formal than in their own countries. The key is to be friendly without being familiar. Do not be surprised if your teachers expect you to call them by their first name and are quite happy to provide help and guidance in a fairly informal way. They will not expect there to be a big distance between staff and students and will treat you in many ways as an equal. In return, they will expect you to be respectful and to be conscientious in your work. In order to have happy relations with your tutors here are some helpful guidelines:

- Check how they would like you to communicate with them – by phone, by email or in person.
- Find out if it is necessary to book tutorials in advance or if they have a drop-in system. If it is the second, find out the times and stick to them. Do not disturb your tutor outside tutorial hours unless the matter is urgent.
- Make sure your tutor has a way of contacting you if they need to. If your telephone number or email address change, let your tutor know.
- Ask your tutor any questions you need to in advance of deadlines. Do not leave it until the day before submission to get help with a piece of work and do not expect your tutor to provide you with a reference without notice. (You should always ask a tutor's permission before giving their name as a referee.)

Speaking in seminars

WHAT IS A SEMINAR?

Generally, classes at college or university fall into three types: lectures, seminars and tutorials. Let us look first at what lectures and tutorials are in order to see how they are different from seminars.

Lectures

Lectures are talks given by teachers or guest speakers, who have particular expertise on the topic, to groups of students, usually large groups. There may be as many a several hundred people present in a lecture. There may be time for questions and discussion at the end of the lecture but, generally, the role of the lecturer is to present knowledge and information, and the role of their audience is to listen and absorb what is being said.

Tutorials

Tutorials are classes where a small group of students discuss a subject or subjects with a tutor. Some tutorials may consist of the tutor and only one or two students. These classes may be less formal and may centre on topics the students have suggested or problems they are having with their work.

Seminars

A seminar is a class at a college or a university in which a group of students discuss a subject with a teacher. The size of the group may vary (usually between 10 and 20 students) but generally a seminar will have more participants than a tutorial and fewer than a lecture. The dynamics are different from either of the other two types of classes as well. Students are expected to be active participants – that is, they are expected to speak up, unlike in a lecture. On the other hand, the class is more formal than a tutorial, as it centres on focused discussion of a topic that the members of the seminar group are expected to have prepared. A seminar often allows students to discuss in depth issues that have been presented in a lecture and which they will have explored through their reading. It is a very valuable part of the teaching and learning experience.

What makes a good seminar?

A really good seminar is one in which ideas are actively explored in depth. Participants leave with a feeling of satisfaction that they have learnt something new, that they have been able to express their ideas, that they have listened to other people's views and have perhaps expanded or changed their own views as a result.

Active participation

The value of a seminar is in direct proportion to the contributions of the participants. It is important that all the students taking part in the seminar are able and willing to contribute. This means they must be *willing to speak* (see below), and they must have *something to say*. It is also important that all the students participate. If the seminar is dominated by a few of the more confident and talkative students, it will be much less interesting for everyone. Having a range of different views and approaches to the topic makes the seminar more interesting and a better learning experience. It is important to remember that even quite a small or apparently minor point may start off a really good discussion. Each person's contribution, however small, helps the rest of the participants to develop their ideas. This may be because it supports their own thoughts or, on the other hand, because they are in disagreement and it forces them to think more clearly about what they believe. So, remember: don't be shy – by sharing your thoughts you are helping the whole group to participate.

Having something to say
It is important to prepare for seminars because it is more difficult to come up with ideas and to express them clearly without any preparatory work. At the very least, you should:

- find out what the topic of the seminar is in advance;
- do some thinking about it;
- consider what you already know about the topic;
- think about what you do not know;
- do the reading your teacher has recommended; and
- think of questions to ask.

You might find it helpful at this point to work with another student who is in the same group as you. Together you can share what you already know and brainstorm ideas around the seminar topic or question (some seminars focus on a question). You should use the library, the Internet or other resources to do some research on the topic. This will mean that you go to the seminar with some knowledge of the subject, which will help you to feel more confident.

Example: preparing for a seminar

We could consider what thinking we could do before going to this seminar on a first-year Business and Management course, where the following task has been set:

Consider the main functions, in relation to the provision or administration of tourism, of any public sector organization, e.g. regional tourist authority, national tourist board, district council.

Questions that could be considered in this case are: 'What are these organizations exactly?', 'How far do their functions overlap?' and 'Whose interests are they promoting?' How could the student find the answers to these questions? Possible sources of information are recommended textbooks, the websites of the various organizations or even a telephone call to the organizations themselves. For example, a visit to the website of the Zambian National Tourist Board will provide you with a detailed list of its functions (http://www.zambiatourism.com/zntb/).

Task 5.3

Find out what the topic of your next seminar is. Write the title of the seminar at the top of a piece of paper. Underneath list anything you know about the topic. Then think about what you don't know and write some questions. Speak to a fellow student and see if they agree with your list and if they can answer any of the questions. Then write down at least three resources you could consult to research this topic and commit yourself to looking at them before your seminar.

Students are usually asked to read particular texts in preparation for a seminar. Very often your tutor will be happy to recommend extra reading you can do to prepare yourself for classes and most courses give lists of recommended readings for teaching sessions.

HOW CAN I BUILD UP MY CONFIDENCE?

I find speaking groups difficult. Sometimes I don't manage to say anything in my seminars.
(Korean student)

Be prepared

As we noted above, the first step to build up your confidence is to prepare. The way to do this is to:

- make sure you know the topic of the seminar;
- reflect on what you know/don't know;
- think of questions you would like to ask; and
- read around the subject.

Being prepared should give you more confidence to speak and make it easier for you to understand other students' contributions. You will find that you are not only more familiar with the ideas related to the topic but also with the language you will need:

If you have prepared beforehand it is easy to describe something or to understand the vocabulary used. I have more difficulties in explaining what I cannot understand in the subject.
(Brazilian student)

Analyse the difficulties
Sometimes it can be difficult to manage to speak, even if you want to and have something to say. The way conversation works differs greatly between cultures, so it may be difficult to participate even if you understand what is being said and you are informed about the topic. In order to feel comfortable about speaking in class in an English-speaking environment, you may need to adopt a different approach to discussion. Two aspects to consider are 'wait time' and level of emotional expression.

Wait time

The time left between one person finishing speaking and the next person beginning to speak.

Some students find it difficult to enter the discussion as there never seems to be a pause long enough for them to take their turn. This may be because of shyness but it may also be because of different cultural expectations about the appropriate amount of time to wait after one person has finished speaking before the next person begins to speak.

Wait times can vary considerably between cultures (including between different cultures within the same country). People who have a very short wait time often start to speak as soon as their interlocutor has completed his or her final word. British, American, Australian and many European cultures tend to have short wait times. They often use a pattern of overlapping speech, which for them is a sign of involvement and interest. However, speakers who come from cultures where a significant pause between speakers is needed may perceive them as over-assertive or dominant. Speakers from cultures with long wait times may get frustrated at being interrupted and find themselves unable to join in a discussion. A teacher with short wait time may think a student has completed a response when the student only intended to pause.

For people from certain cultures it is natural to express emotional involvement in a discussion, for example by expressing personal convictions or raising their voice, whereas other cultures consider this to be inappropriate. If members of a group involved in discussion come from different cultural backgrounds, this can have an impact on their communication. Students for whom assertive communication comes naturally may tend to dominate in a conversation with students from more reserved cultures.

No one particular way of speaking is right or wrong but, for seminars to work well, those involved need to find a way of communicating comfortably without misunderstanding. It is important to devise strategies for effective participation that will allow you to listen attentively to other students and to speak effectively to communicate your views.

DEVISE STRATEGIES FOR PARTICIPATION

Getting an opportunity to speak
If you are a shy student, or you come from a culture with a longer wait time, you may need to make an extra effort to make sure you are heard in discussion. Making eye contact with the person who is speaking or the chair of the discussion, leaning forward slightly or slightly raising a hand are all ways to signal you wish to speak.

Try to speak early on in the seminar. This will get you into the habit of speaking and let the others know you are willing to participate.

The phrases below are useful ways of entering a conversation. You may have to raise your voice more than you feel at first is appropriate. Don't be shy – assertiveness is valued in English-speaking educational institutions as a sign you are attentive and keen:

- Could I just make a point?
- Could I say ... ?
- Ah – I'd like to say ...
- Yes, that's quite right and I'd like to add ...
- May I add something?

- ◆ May I come in here?
- ◆ Can I ask … ?

You might even simply ask someone to repeat what he or she has said or to explain it a bit more.

If you find it easier to speak to just one other person at a time, you should make an effort to practise joining in conversations with groups of people. This is generally more difficult, even in one's own language, so be prepared to find it challenging. You have to listen to several people and follow more than one idea. If you can practise as often as possible in informal situations, you will build your confidence and skills to cope in the classroom.

Task 5.4

Arrange to meet with a group of people you feel comfortable with to discuss topics of interest to you all. You might like to form a study group to continue discussion of seminar topics outside class. Practise being appropriately assertive and try to use the expressions listed above to make sure you participate fully in the discussion.

Giving opportunities to speak

If you are from a culture with a short wait time, if you are a confident, fluent speaker and if you have lots of experience of speaking out in groups and you know that it is not a problem for you, you can have a crucial role in helping other students to speak. Remember that having a range of different views and approaches to the topic makes for a better seminar. It will benefit everyone if the quieter students participate. There are various things the more confident members of the group can do:

- Make your point succinctly – don't continue talking for longer than necessary.
- Speak clearly, explaining vocabulary if necessary, so you are sure everyone understands.
- Address everyone in the group rather than just the seminar leader or one or two other students.
- Encourage others to talk by making eye contact or asking questions.
- Listen attentively while other students are speaking.
- Have an encouraging manner, showing that you welcome other people's ideas.

Task 5.5

Set yourself the goal of getting one other student to participate in your next seminar discussion by using any or all of the strategies above.

Asking questions

Asking questions can be a very positive way to contribute to a group discussion. It is a good strategy for active but limited participation and so this is a particularly useful way to begin to build up your confidence. This is where the questions you prepared in advance can be very helpful. Questions that require an elaborated response (i.e. those beginning with 'why', 'how', 'what', 'when', etc.) tend to stimulate better answers than questions that can be answered by 'yes' or 'no'. Other speakers will welcome your questions as they give them a chance to participate as well.

Task 5.6

Look at these seminar topics. (Degree programmes that such a seminar might be related to are given in brackets after the topic.) How many questions can you think of for each topic? If you do not know much about the topic, don't worry; you will probably have more questions! You may like to do this exercise with another student:

- Globalization and its effect on the labour market (International Studies/ Business).
- China's financial markets and Chinese economic reform (International Studies/Business).
- The effects of climate and climate change on fish and fisheries (Environmental Sciences/Biology).
- The place of European law in the English legal system (law).
- The European Union, enlargement and reform (European Studies/ Politics).
- The impact of tourism on the environment and society (Social Studies/ Business).
- The political participation of ethnic minorities in multicultural cities (Sociology/Politics).

Key

You may want to compare the questions you have thought of with those suggested in the 'Key to tasks' section at the end of this chapter.

Signpost

If you have not already looked at Task 5.3 above, you could try it now.

Responding to other people's views

You can also ask questions in response to what other people say in the seminar. This allows you to clarify what they have said and gives them the chance to expand on or elaborate their views.

Example: asking questions in a seminar

In a degree programme in Environmental Science, there might be a seminar, 'The Antarctic peninsula: a vulnerable ecosystem'. A student expresses the view: 'All commercial and most scientific activity in the Antarctic peninsula should be stopped, due to its impact on the ecosystem'. Before getting into a debate on whether this is right or wrong, it would be interesting to ask more questions, such as:

- What do we know about the impact of these activities on the ecosystem?
- Is the research reliable?
- Should activity be stopped indefinitely?
- What would the consequences of that be?
- What kind of scientific activity would be excluded from the ban?
- How would a ban be enforced legally?
- Who would ensure this was done?

These questions could be answered by the original speaker or by others in the seminar. This kind of interaction makes the seminar more dynamic

Task 5.7

Now think of one or two questions that could be asked in response to the arguments stated below:
- It is economic common sense that multinational companies should locate production in areas where labour costs are low.
- The benefits of tourism are greater than the negative effects.
- Growth in membership of the European Union will be a positive thing because it will bring diversity.
- Ethnic minorities are inevitably at a disadvantage when it comes to participating in politics.

Key

For suggested questions, see 'Key to tasks' at the end of this chapter.

Tell me more

You can also participate by inviting the speaker to expand on his or her point. This is a useful strategy if you feel you need more information or you have not fully understood what the person means. You should feel able to ask for further explanation if you have not understood a point.

Useful expressions are as follows:

- Could you tell us more about … ?
- That's interesting, can you say more?
- I'm sorry, I didn't get that, could you go over it again?
- I don't really understand your point, could you explain further?
- That's quite difficult to understand, can you give us more explanation/some more examples?

This can be a way of getting information even if you do not have a precise question to ask. Make sure you use one or more of these expressions in your next seminar to get someone to expand on their point.

Working in groups

All that we have said about speaking in seminars can be applied to speaking in less formal groups, such as when you are a member of a study group or when you are preparing a piece of group work with other students. You may also be asked to work in groups within a classroom setting.

The important thing to remember is that, for a group to work together successfully, all members have to be willing and able to participate. You will be working with people who come from other areas of the world, and their English and their ideas about studying may be different from yours. This means it is especially important to make an effort to communicate effectively.

There are tremendous benefits to working in groups: you can share ideas and knowledge, give each other support and confidence and be constructively critical of the work produced, leading to a higher standard of work. There are also challenges, and cross-cultural communication can be one of them. It is important for you to use your listening and your speaking skills well.

Signpost

For extra information about this, see the section 'What makes a good listener?', pages 57–9, in Chapter 3, 'Understanding spoken English'.

Simple rules for successful group work are as follows:

- Be organized – make sure you arrange meeting times and that you have each other's contact details.
- Include everyone – make sure all members of the group get the chance to contribute.
- Consider everyone's feelings – be encouraging of contributions, especially from quieter members.
- Allow time for discussion – make sure you understand everyone's point of view.

Group work is often a good opportunity for you to develop your speaking (and listening) skills, as the situation is less formal and less stressful than a seminar. If you take the opportunity to participate fully in group work, you may find that you are more able to take an active role in your seminars.

Developing your speaking skills

SPEAKING CLEARLY

You will feel more confident and be able to contribute more effectively to seminars if you are clear and easy to understand when you speak. You may feel that you are at a disadvantage because you have an accent when speaking English but this, in itself, is not necessarily a problem. Everyone speaks with an accent, including English native speakers, who have their own personal or regional accent. The important thing is to articulate sounds clearly so that you can be understood and to use rhythm and stress to convey your meaning effectively.

PRONOUNCING SOUNDS

Certain sounds in English may not exist in your language or may be slightly different. A typical example is the 'th' sound in words like 'think' or 'truth' /θ/ which does not exist in a number of other languages such as French or Turkish. Some languages do not make the same distinctions that English does between vowel sounds, such as /I/ (the vowel sound in 'ship') and /i:/ (the vowel sound in 'sheep') or between consonant sounds such as /r/ (in 'right') and /l/ in ('light'). An added complication is that English has a large number of vowel sounds (20 vowels and diphthongs) and distinguishing between them causes problems for many students (Japanese, for example, has only 5 vowel sounds). However, with careful study and plenty of practice, these distinctions can be learnt. English has certain combinations of sounds that do not occur in some other languages such as those that appear at the end of 'crisps' (/sps/) or 'grounds' (/ndz/).

If you find that particular sounds or sound combinations are difficult for you, you can help yourself by using pronunciation exercises available on tape and in books, which you should find in the language laboratory or the language centre of your college or university.

Signpost

If you are not sure which sounds to practise, you can consult a book such as *Learner English* or *Sounds English* (see the 'Useful resources' section at the end of this chapter). These books will tell you the sounds that speakers of your language have problems with in English. A dictionary with a CD-ROM (see the 'Useful resources' section at the end of Chapter 4) will give you the pronunciation of the sounds of English, and you can use this to check which sounds are difficult for you.

STRESS, RHYTHM AND INTONATION

These are three areas that contribute greatly to clear speaking and so are useful areas to work on in English. If you have not learnt to use the English system of stress, rhythm and intonation, English native speakers will find you difficult to understand and you may also find it difficult to understand what they are saying.

Task 5.8

Look at the phonemic chart taken from *Collins Cobuild English Language Dictionary* and, working from your own knowledge or with the help of one of the books mentioned above, make a note of the sounds that you find difficult:

Vowel Sounds

ɑ:	calm, ah	ɒ	lot, spot	
ɑ:ʳ	heart, far	oʊ	note, coat	
æ	act, mass	ɔ:	claw, maul	
aɪ	dive, cry	ɔʳ	more, cord	
aɪəʳ	fire, tyre	ɔɪ	boy, joint	
aʊ	out, down	ʊ	could, stood	
aʊəʳ	flour, sour	u:	you, use	
e	met, lend, pen	ʊəʳ	lure, pure	
eɪ	say, weight	ɜ:ʳ	turn, third	
eəʳ	fair, care	ʌ	fund, must	
ɪ	fit, win	ə	the first vowel in about	
i:	feed, me	əʳ	the first vowel in forgotten	
ɪəʳ	near, beard	i	the second vowel in very	
		u	the second vowel in actual	

Consonant Sounds

b	bed, rub	s	soon, bus
d	done, red	t	talk, bet
f	fit, if	v	van, love
g	good, dog	w	win, wool
h	hat, horse	ʰw	why, wheat
j	yellow, you	x	loch
k	king, pick	z	zoo, buzz
l	lip, bill	ʃ	ship, wish
ºl	handle, panel	ʒ	measure, leisure
m	mat, ram	ŋ	sing, working
n	not, tin	tʃ	cheap, witch
ºn	hidden, written	θ	thin, myth
p	pay, lip	ð	then, bathe
r	run, read	dʒ	joy, bridge

Now choose the one you think is the most important and set yourself the goal of improving your pronunciation of that particular sound.

Stress

When a word or syllable is pronounced with more force than the surrounding words or syllables.

A feature that is very important in English is 'stress timing'. This means that the rhythm of speech depends on the number of stressed and unstressed syllables in the sentences. Many languages stress the syllables fairly equally, which produces a regular rhythm. English speakers stress the words that carry most meaning so that listeners know what to pay attention to. They make these words clearer by using a different pitch and by making them longer and louder. The less important words receive less emphasis and so a rhythm is created of strong and weak beats, like music (e.g. 'I remembered to post the letters'). Stress typically falls on nouns, verbs, adjectives and adverbs, as these are the sorts of words likely to communicate the meaning of what someone is saying.

In addition, you should remember that the stress is always on a particular syllable in a word. To know which syllable this is, you can look at a dictionary. The stress will be marked on the phonemic transcription of the word. The symbol | is commonly used by dictionaries to indicate that the following syllable is stressed. For example:

---

adversity /əd'vɜː.sə.ti/ ⑩ /-'vɝː.sə.ti/ *noun* [C or U] a difficult or unlucky situation or event: *She was always cheerful in adversity.* ○ *The road to happiness is paved with adversities.*

A dictionary definition of the word 'adversity'
Source: Cambridge Advanced Learner's Dictionary (2003)

However, some dictionaries may underline the stressed syllable instead:

---

ec|lec|tic /ɪklɛktɪk/ An **eclectic** collection of objects, ideas, or beliefs is wide-ranging and comes from many different sources. [FORMAL] ❏ *...an eclectic collection of paintings, drawings, and prints.*

A dictionary definition of the word 'eclectic'
Source: Collins Cobuild English Language Dictionary (2004)

So this is another way the dictionary can be of great help with pronunciation. If the dictionary has a CD-ROM, listen to the recording of the word. Some dictionaries have a facility for you to record your voice and compare your pronunciation with the original word.

Task 5.9

Look at the passage below, which has the stressed syllables marked by capital letters. Try reading it aloud to get a feel for the rhythm. Remember not to put emphasis on the unstressed syllables:

The IBErian LYNX is on the VERGE of exTINCtion. Its NAtural HAbitat is the CORK forests of SPAIN and PORtugal but these FORests are now under THREAT because the deMAND for CORK is FALLing. There has been an INcrease in the USE of SCREW-top and PLAStic STOPpers by WINE proDUcers.

Task 5.10

Now look at the passage below and highlight or underline the words you think a speaker should stress. It may help you to read the text aloud as you do this. If there are any words where you are not sure of the syllable where the stress falls, consult a dictionary:

Recent figures show that there are one hundred and fifty Iberian lynx left. Of these, thirty are breeding females. The lynx has been classified as 'critically endangered'. The World Wide Fund for Nature has given warning that unless something radical is done, the lynx will become extinct within a decade.

Key

For suggested answers, see 'Key to tasks' at the end of this chapter.

INTONATION AND PAUSING

To speak clearly and be understood easily you need to use English rhythm. The rhythm of speech is affected not just by stress but also by where you put pauses and whether your voice rises, stays level or falls (this is intonation).

Generally, pauses come between ideas, with longer pauses ‖ marking the end of an idea and shorter pauses | marking breaks between related ideas, rather like full stops and commas in punctuation:

> I'm going shopping ‖ I'll buy meat | tomatoes | eggs | and spaghetti ‖ and then I'll come home and cook.

Intonation is an important guide to meaning in English. Intonation patterns are not fixed according to grammar or vocabulary but are used flexibly to communicate what the speaker wants to say on a particular occasion. However, there are some simple, approximate guidelines that you can follow to help you. Your voice should fall ↘ to show that an idea is complete or that you are certain of something. It rises ↗ to show that an idea is incomplete or there is uncertainty. It stays level → to indicate an item in a list:

> I'm going shopping ↘ I'll buy meat → tomatoes → eggs → and spaghetti ↗ and then I'll come home and cook ↘
>
> Are you going out? ↗ Yes, ↘ and if you wait ↗ I'll take you with me ↘

(*Note*: The *amount* the voice rises or falls is determined by how the speaker feels about the information he or she is communicating. The voice rises most in surprise or disbelief and falls most to show complete certainty or that an idea is totally finished.)

So, by using a rising or falling intonation, you can use your voice to show how you feel about what you say and that you have or have not finished what you want to say.

Example: Intonation

In the first sentence below the speaker is expressing one idea. In the second this becomes the first part of a more complex idea and the voice shows there is more to come:

Developed countries should be prepared to take responsibility for global warming ↘

Developed countries should be prepared to take responsibility for global warming ↗ but developing countries also need to play their part ↘

Task 5.11

Look at the text below (which is unpunctuated) and mark where you think the voice rises and falls and where the pauses are. You may find it helpful to read the text aloud as you do this:

In my talk today I'd like to explore three regimes of pre-school education I shall look at the situation of children educated in their home language that of those educated in the national language and that of those educated in bilingual programmes while it is still too early to draw definite conclusions there are indications that these different regimes are not equally effective in promoting bilingualism

Key

For a suggested answer, see 'Key to tasks' at the end of this chapter.

All this information on pronunciation is only a very basic guide. You should consult any of the books suggested to understand the subject in more depth and to find exercises to help you practise. You can practise by:

- using a book such as *Speaking Clearly* to develop effective stress, rhythm and intonation;
- speaking aloud on a topic to a friend and asking him or her to say how clear you are; and
- speaking on to a tape and then playing it back to yourself.

You may also find it useful to listen at the same time as you read a text. There are websites that have these facilities (the BBC's Reith Lectures are a good example of this) and this allows you to notice the stress, intonation and pausing of good speakers.

Signpost

Details of *Speaking Clearly* and the BBC's Reith Lectures can be found in the 'Useful resources' section at the end of this chapter.

Conclusion

There are many different aspects of developing your speaking skills and, by putting the ideas in this chapter into practice, you can become a more effective speaker.

One last thing you should think about is the principle of co-operative communication. This was described by a linguist named Grice and was simple:

Say what is necessary to say, in the most appropriate way, for that particular point in the conversation (or discussion).

He clarified this into four 'rules', which are called 'Grice's maxims'. Here they are below in a simplified form:

1 *Be clear*: this means to speak in a way that your interlocutors can understand you. This may mean you have to work on your level of English.
2 *Be truthful*: this means you must not say that which you know to be false and you must not say things that you lack evidence for.
3 *Be brief*: do not say more than you need to (but don't say less than is necessary either!).
4 *Be relevant*: do not go off the point. Make sure what you are saying is related to the general direction of the conversation or discussion.

Much of this is common sense. However, if any of these 'rules' are broken the result is poor communication and frustration for the interlocutors.

One more 'rule' we should add is: *be confident!*

Confidence is key to success in speaking. So remember to be confident in your own abilities and be willing to do whatever is necessary to make sure you are understood. Shyness does not help in communication! Prepare before, when you can, and then speak up and get your message across!

REFERENCE

Grice, H.P. (1975) 'Logic and conversation', in P. Cole and J. Morgan (eds) *Syntax and Semantics*. Volume 3. New York, NY: Academic Press.

USEFUL RESOURCES

General

http://www.uefap.co.uk/speaking/spkfram.htm

This is part of the website for the University of Hertfordshire and it gives helpful advice on aspects of speaking in academic contexts.

http://pweb.sophia.ac.jp/~j-yamamo/page4.html

This site is written for Japanese learners of English but the advice it gives is sensible and helpful for students of all nationalities.

Anderson, K. and Lynch, T. (1992) *Study Speaking*. Cambridge: Cambridge University Press.

Swan, M. and Smith, B. (2001) *Learner English*. Cambridge: Cambridge University Press. Although this book is written for teachers of English rather than students of English, you should find helpful indications of where your language is different from English and what you should therefore study.

Pronunciation

http://pronunciation.englishclub.com/sentence-stress.htm

This site gives a clear and simple guide to where emphasis goes in the sentence.

http://pronunciation.englishclub.com/word-stress.htm

This site gives a clear and fairly comprehensive guide to word stress in English.

http://www.bbc.co.uk/radio4/

This is the Radio 4 home page of the BBC website. There are many interesting programmes you can listen to, some of which have transcripts that you can read at the same time. You will also find the link to the Reith Lectures (recommended above) here.

Baker, A. (1981) *Ship or Sheep*. Cambridge: Cambridge University Press.

Hancock, M. (2003) *English Pronunciation in Use*. Cambridge: Cambridge University Press.

Haycraft, B. (1994) *English Aloud 1 & 2*. Basingstoke: Macmillan ELT.

Headway Pronunciation Course (four levels: elementary to upper intermediate). Oxford: Oxford University Press.

O'Connor, J.D. and Fletcher, C. (1989) *Sounds English*. Harlow: Longman.

Rogerson, P. and Gilbert, J. (1990) *Speaking Clearly.* Cambridge: Cambridge University Press.

KEY TO TASKS

Task 5.2
- It would be totally inappropriate to say 'this is bullshit' in a presentation. This is vulgar, informal language that would only be used in very informal situations with people you know well, probably students of your own age. More appropriate expressions could be: 'This is wrong/untrue/misleading/false. I don't agree with this', etc.
- Generally, the appropriate way to address a member of staff you know is by his or her first name, so 'Mary' would be the right way to address the teacher. It is unacceptable to call a teacher by his or her surname only, although Ms Smith for a female teacher or Mr Smith for a male teacher you do not know well is fine. Titles such as Ms or Mr are not used with the first name. Although not likely to cause offence, it sounds very odd.
- The correct way to begin a letter to a person you know is 'Dear + his or her name'. If you do not know the name then use 'Dear Sir or Madam'.
- There is nothing wrong with a student openly disagreeing with a teacher or another student in a seminar as long as the disagreement is expressed respectfully and backed up by argument. Disagreement can often be the basis of some stimulating discussion.
- A student corrects another on a mistake of fact he or she has made in a seminar. This is perfectly acceptable and in fact helpful if the first student is wrong.
- A student corrects another on a mistake in his or her English in a seminar. Unless the mistake leads to misunderstanding, correcting someone's English is unnecessary and could lead to embarrassment, so it is better not to do it.
- A group of English friends are talking and use one word repeatedly you don't understand. Should you ask them to explain? If the word is repeated several times it is probably important and so worth asking about. However, in general it is best not to ask people to explain things too often as this can disrupt the conversation.
- It is good to ask the teacher to slow down, but this is not the most polite way. 'Excuse me, could you speak more slowly, we are finding it difficult to understand.' would be better.
- 'Cheers, mate' is too informal. 'Thank you very much' is neutral and appropriate.
- It is totally inappropriate to ask a teacher to change a mark. Marks are given

based on a teacher's professional judgement, not on what a student wants or expects. The only thing the student can do is ask to know why they got the mark they did, and hopefully the student will then be able to apply what the teacher says in order to do better in their next essay.

Task 5.6

These are some possible questions. The list of questions is not supposed to be complete.

Globalization and its effect on the labour market (international studies/business):

* What are the main effects?
* Are the effects felt equally all over the world?
* Are they regarded as positive or negative? By whom?
* Are the effects likely to be long lasting?

China's financial markets and Chinese economic reform (international studies/business):

* Where are China's main financial markets?
* What kind of reforms have there been/are there planned?
* How long-term is the reform?
* What else is affected by the reforms?
* Who is most affected by these reforms?

The effects of climate and climate change on fish and fisheries (environmental sciences/biology):

* What climate change has taken place? In which areas?
* Are all fish equally affected?
* Are the effects negative or positive?
* Are the changes permanent or temporary?
* How have fisheries adapted so far?

The place of European law in the English legal system (law):

* In which areas are there most differences between European law and English law?
* How far does European law complement English law?

◆ How do English legal bodies/the British government feel about the relationship between European and English law?

The European Union, enlargement and reform (European studies/politics):

◆ How has the EU responded so far to enlargement?
◆ What future enlargement is planned?
◆ How do the member states feel about this?
◆ In what areas is reform needed?
◆ Are member states in agreement on reform?

The impact of tourism on the environment and society (social studies/business):

◆ Which parts of the world are being considered?
◆ Is the impact the same in different places?
◆ Are some areas more vulnerable? Why?
◆ Are the effects of tourism positive or negative?
◆ How is the impact measured?
◆ Who makes the assessment?

The political participation of ethnic minorities in multicultural cities (sociology/politics):

◆ Which cities are considered to be multicultural?
◆ What is the definition of multicultural?
◆ How is political participation measured?
◆ Which factors have most influence on their political participation?

Task 5.7
Here are some questions we have thought of. There could be many more.

It is economic common sense that multinational companies should locate production in areas where labour costs are low:

◆ Do you think there are other factors that should be considered?
◆ What is the effect on the areas where production starts up/closes down?
◆ What are the long term/short term effects?

The benefits of tourism are greater than the negative effects:

* What are the benefits/negative effects?
* Are they affecting the same people?
* Are they of the same type?
* How are they measured?
* Are they long- or short-term?

Growth in the European Union will be a positive thing because it will bring diversity:

* How will this diversity express itself?
* Is diversity always positive?
* What will the concrete effects be?

Ethnic minorities are inevitably at a disadvantage when it comes to participating in politics:

* Is this shown in all cases?
* What are the major obstacles?
* Are there any ways of avoiding or lessening the disadvantage?

Task 5.10
REcent FIGures SHOW that there are ONE HUNdred and FIFty IBERian LYNX LEFT, Of THESE, THIRty are BREEDing FEmales. The LYNX has been CLASSified as 'CRITically enDANgered'. The WORLD WIDE FUND for NAture has given WARNing that unLESS something RADical is DONE, the LYNX will become exTINCT within a DEcade.

Task 5.11
In my talk today↗ | I'd like to explore three regimes ↗ of pre-school education ↘ || I shall look at the situation of children educated in their home language ↗ | that of those educated in the national language ↗ | and that of those educated in bilingual programmes ↘ || while it is still too early ↗ to draw definite conclusions ↗ | there are indications ↗ | that these different regimes ↗ are not equally effective in promoting bilingualism ↘ ||

6 Giving oral presentations

AIMS

By studying and doing the activities in this chapter you should:

- learn how to plan and prepare oral presentations at university;
- develop strategies for making yourself understood in English;
- consider how to use your voice and body language expressively;
- understand the benefits of using audio-visual aids;
- know how to build your confidence and reduce nerves;
- be able to deal with questions from the audience; and
- consider how to approach group presentations.

GLOSSARY

These key words will be useful to you while reading this chapter:

Adrenaline: A hormone produced by the body when you are frightened, angry or excited, which makes the heart beat faster.

Articulate: Pronounce words clearly.

Colloquial: Informal and more suitable for use in speech than in writing.

Context: The situation within which something exists or happens, and that can help explain it.

Dynamic: Having a lot of ideas and enthusiasm; energetic and forceful.

Prompt: Words which help when you have forgotten what you are going to say.

Pull your weight: To work as hard as other people in a group.

Slang: Very informal language that is usually spoken rather than written, used especially by particular groups of people.

Spontaneous: Happening or done in a natural, often sudden way, without any planning or without being forced.
Stimulant: A substance, such as a drug, which makes the mind or body more active.

Oral presentations at University

During your studies at university you will be asked to give oral presentations. This may be in class, in a seminar or for an assessment. It will involve preparing information on a particular topic and presenting this information formally to your tutors and classmates. You may be asked to present the findings of some research, to persuade your audience of a particular viewpoint or to present an analysis of information. Often at the end of the presentation there will be an opportunity for your audience to ask you questions about what you have said.

Oral presentations can be very interesting both for the audience and the speaker. You can learn a lot from listening to other students' presentations and often students feel a real sense of satisfaction after they have given their talk. Many students like having the opportunity to express themselves through speaking rather than writing. Once

they have presented a few times, they realize it is often easier to get high marks for an oral presentation than for a written essay:

I really had great pleasure in doing my presentation, I felt very confident.
(Russian student)

Being an international student I can say that oral presentations are very important to improve listening and speaking skills and there is a chance to prove ourselves in front of each other.
(Bangladeshi student)

It is amazing how much you can learn in so little time listening to presentations.
(Colombian student)

Planning your presentation

It is essential that you ask yourself four basic questions when you begin to plan your presentation:

1. What do I want/need to say?
2. Why do I want/need to say it?
3. Who do I want/need to say it to?
4. How much time to I have/need to say it?

You should bear these questions in mind while you are looking for information for your talk.

Signpost

See Chapter 7, 'Reading', for more information on how to research effectively.

WHAT DO YOU WANT TO SAY AND WHY DO YOU WANT TO SAY IT?

The content is the most important part of your presentation. You need to decide exactly what it is you want your audience to know. A good university presentation will have a clearly defined topic and a clear purpose or aim. Your tutor may give this to you or you may have to think of it on your own. You must make sure that your topic and aims correspond with what you have been asked to do. Always check with any subject guidelines, module handbooks or your tutor at the planning stage to make sure you are doing the right thing.

It is important to be able to distinguish between your topic and your aim. Very simply, your topic is *what* you want to talk about and your aims are what you want to achieve by communicating with your audience – in other words, *why* you want to talk about it.

Topic and aim: example 1

You are studying IT (Information Technology). You are giving a presentation on a specific computer software program because you would like the audience to understand how it works. Your *topic* is the computer software program. Your *aim* is to inform.

Topic and aim: example 2

You are studying business and you are giving a presentation on world trade because you want to convince your audience that globalization has a negative impact on developing countries. Your *topic* is world trade. Your *aim* is to persuade.

It is usually quite easy to know what your topic is, but being clear about your aim is more difficult. It helps if you can write down a sentence which explains exactly what the aim is. Because the main point of any presentation is for your audience to understand or learn something, it is often particularly useful to think about your aim from the point of view of the audience. So, for our first example we could say:

Topic: computer software program X.

Aim: by the end of my talk, the audience will understand how computer software program X works.

This statement of aims is often called an SPS (specific purpose statement) because it states exactly what you want to achieve by the end of your presentation. It is very useful to try to write your SPS as soon as you start planning. Then you can refer to it as you continue to plan and prepare your talk. This will help to ensure that all the information you include is relevant because it helps you to achieve your aim.

Task 6. 1

Complete the specific purpose statement (SPS) for example 2:

Topic: world trade
Aim/SPS: by the end of my talk, the audience will ...

Key

For a suggested answer, see 'Key to tasks' at the end of this chapter.

If you have researched and understood your topic well, it can be very tempting to try to say everything you know about it in your presentation. However, it is much better to choose one aspect and explain it clearly and in detail than to talk briefly on lots of different aspects of your topic. If you do not have a clear focus, your audience will find it very difficult to follow what you are saying. If you try to give them too much information, they will not be able to remember it.

WHO ARE YOU TALKING TO?

It is essential that you communicate with your audience in an oral presentation. Communication is a two-way process. If you speak to your audience but they do not listen to you or do not understand you, you have not communicated with them. You need to think carefully about who your audience is. Then you will be able to decide what information will be relevant to them and find ways of making what you want to say understandable to them.

Task 6.2

Consider these two groups of people:

- A group of 30 surgeons at a medical conference.
- A group of 6 women aged 50+ at a local community centre.

Imagine you will be presenting a talk on breast cancer. How might your talk change, depending on which group you are speaking to? What would you have to take into consideration when planning your talk?

Write your ideas down.

Key

For a suggested answer, see 'Key to tasks' at the end of this chapter.

Who you are speaking to, and in what context, can therefore greatly affect how you present your information. Of course, the more information you have about your audience, the more you can ensure that you give a talk that is relevant to their needs. At the planning stage you should ask yourself the following questions about the audience:

What do they already know about the topic?
It will not be very interesting or informative for the audience to hear information they are already familiar with. However, you may decide that a reminder of some basic information might be useful:

> *He explained ... but I think he should have mentioned this only briefly because it was not a very important point and because everybody knew it.*
> **(Japanese student)**

What do they need to know?
Will your audience have to do anything with the information you give them? If so, you will have an attentive audience. Make sure you provide them with the content they will need in order to take any action.

What would be interesting or useful for them to know?
The most interested and attentive audience will be the one that is intrinsically motivated.

If you think about who the people in your audience are and then provide them with information that is relevant and meaningful to them, they will want to listen to every word you say.

Signpost

See Chapter 2, 'Being an effective learner', for more information about motivation.

What opinions or experience could you expect them to have in this area?
If your aim is to persuade your audience of a particular point of view and you predict that some of them may hold an opposing view, you will probably have to think more carefully about how you present your ideas, anticipating their objections. If your audience has any experience in this area, they will find your talk more relevant if you refer to this experience.

MAKE THE PRESENTATION INTERESTING FOR YOUR AUDIENCE

Listening is a difficult skill.

It will help your presentation to be successful if you make it interesting for your audience:

Signpost

See Chapter 3, 'Understanding spoken English', for more information about listening.

I like presentations because I can listen to so many different topics, but sometimes it is boring and I can't listen.
(Korean student)

It will be much more interesting for them if:

- the content is relevant to them;
- it tells them what they want or need to know; and
- it takes into account their experiences and/or opinion and views.

What kind of language will they understand?

You will be speaking in English, but what kind of English will your audience understand? For example, imagine that while researching your presentation, you struggled to understand the meaning of a new word. If you use this word in the presentation, can you expect your audience to understand it, or would you have to give them an explanation? If you use vocabulary that is specific to your topic, would you expect your audience to share this vocabulary or would you have to explain it to them first? For example, a specialist in education might understand a word such as *'pedagogical'* whereas a non-specialist might not. You want your audience to understand you as easily as possible, so always choose vocabulary you think they will know, or explain specialist terms to them when you use them.

How many people are there?

Giving a presentation to a small group of 5–10 people can feel very different from speaking in front of 40–50 people. You should consider this so that you can prepare yourself. The number of people may also affect other aspects of your presentation, such as the amount of audience participation you can expect, how long it will take to distribute a handout or how loudly you will have to speak in order for everyone to be able to hear you.

HOW MUCH TIME DO YOU HAVE?

Timing is very important in oral presentations. You will be told how long your presentation should be and you will be expected to stay within this time limit. If your presentation is too short, you have not said enough. If your presentation is too long, you have said too much. If you go over the time limit, it is quite usual for your tutor to stop you from talking any longer. Therefore it is essential that you know how long your presentation is going to take:

While I was giving the presentation I forgot about time limits – I recognized that my time was nearly finished only 2 minutes before the end and I still had so much to say.
(Latvian student)

The best way of doing this is to practise and time yourself. It often takes longer than you think to explain your points to an audience.

It is very important to consider timing when you are gathering your information. You want to make sure you do not have too little or too much content. If you are speaking for 5 or even 10 minutes, you will not be able to go into a lot of detail about a wide subject. That is why presentations often focus on one very specific point.

Preparation

Now you can begin to prepare the structure of your talk and the way you are going to deliver it. You want to be sure that your audience will understand your content:

> *The most important thing is preparation: reading/choosing topic/info, composing preparation, oral training before presentation, keep confidence and smile.*
> **(Latvian student)**

> *Plan and have deep knowledge in certain subject. Plan well and structure the presentation well and present without any fear.*
> **(Sri Lankan student)**

STRUCTURING YOUR PRESENTATION

Organizing your ideas
When you have finished researching the information for your talk, you may find that you have a lot of information but that you are not sure which points you should include and which you should leave out.

Now you need to decide on the order that you will present your ideas in, and how you will link those ideas together. Your talk will need to be clearly divided into:

- introduction
- body
- conclusion.

It is essential that there is some kind of logical structure. If there is not, it is too easy for you to lose your place and become confused about what you are saying. It will also be

Task 6.3

1 Take a blank sheet of paper. In the centre of the page write the topic and SPS of a talk you are preparing. On the rest of the page write down *anything* you can think of about your topic. Do not worry about writing in sentences or following any kind of logical order at this stage. Just write down as many things as you can remember about your topic. This is called brainstorming (see Chapter 8 on note-making for more information on brainstorming).

2 Look at your notes. Have you written down the same idea twice? If so, cross out the repetition. Are there any ideas that are connected to your topic but are not directly relevant to your SPS? These need to be crossed out. Be ruthless!

3 Look at the ideas you have left. Which are the most important points? Write these down as subheadings on another piece of paper. Do any of your other ideas fit beneath these subheadings? If so, write them down. If you have any ideas left, check they are relevant to your talk. If they are, write them down as smaller subheadings; these are separate points, but not your most important points.

4 Take each subheading in turn. Is there any information missing? If so, add it. Is there any information there that you do not really need? Cross it out. Can you think of any examples or illustrations that will help you explain any of these ideas? Write them down.

Remember to think about your audience when choosing your examples and illustrations; the ones they can relate to will be the most meaningful to them.

confusing for your audience. They will find it much easier to follow and understand your talk if they can follow your structure. Here are one Japanese student's comments about two student presentations she listened to:

It was well organized which made it easy to follow her talk.

Her presentation was simple and clear, going step by step so it was really easy to understand.

INTRODUCTIONS AND CONCLUSIONS

Effective talks have a clear introduction and conclusion. The introduction puts your talk into context and the conclusion reminds your audience of the main points. You might want to prepare these parts of your talk after you have prepared the body.

The introduction

The introduction is probably the most important part of your presentation. If your audience does not understand your introduction, they may find it very difficult to follow the rest of your talk. Imagine listening to a lecture without knowing first what subject the lecture was on. Even if you could hear the tutor's words clearly, it would probably be difficult to understand their meaning without knowing what the topic is.

The introduction is also your chance to make a good first impression. The first thing you should do is introduce yourself. This is face-to-face communication between real people. They can see you and you can see them, so it is useful to try to establish some sort of relationship.

Next, you should introduce the topic of your talk and explain the aims. You need to make sure you speak loudly, slowly and clearly because, if your audience miss this part, they may be confused throughout your whole presentation. Some people find that they speak more quietly or quickly at the beginning of the talk because they have not yet 'warmed up', so you need to make a special effort to be clear. It might be a good idea to write down your first sentence in full on your notes so that you do not forget your important opening words. You could even add little reminders to yourself on your notes, such as 'Remember to speak slowly and loudly!'

Explaining your aims will help your audience to understand what the focus of your talk will be and it will give them a reason for listening. It is a good idea to try to explain the aims from the point of view of the audience. Rather than telling them what *you* hope to achieve by giving your talk, tell them what *they* can learn by listening to you. Point out why the information you will give is going to be useful or interesting to them. Give them a reason to listen.

There are certain strategies you can use to attract your audience's attention.

While you may already have their attention because your topic is relevant to them, listening is difficult and requires a lot of concentration so you should use all the strategies at your disposal to help.

Rhetorical questions: this is when you ask your audience a question but you do not want them to reply because you are going to supply the answer yourself:

'So, what are the three most important aspects of ... ? Well, the first one is ...'

Even though they do not need to respond out loud, your audience will probably start to work out the answer to your question in their heads. This means they are actively engaged with your talk. They will want to find out the answer to your question, so they will listen attentively to find out what it is.

Audience participation: you may decide that you do want the audience to answer your question out loud. You could use their responses as the basis for further discussion or as examples to illustrate your ideas. This can be very engaging for your audience who are now actively involved in your talk. It also shows that you are linking your content to your audience's ideas and experiences.

If you want audience participation, you need to think about how you are going to control it. Will you ask a particular audience member or will you allow anyone to shout out an answer? Remember, your audience can be unpredictable – you may get answers that you are not expecting, or not get any answers at all! Nevertheless, well thought-out audience participation can make your presentation dynamic and interesting.

Of course, you can use these strategies for making your talk interesting at other stages of your talk as well, not just in the introduction.

The final part of your introduction should indicate the structure of your talk. If your listeners know which point is coming first, second and so on, it will be easier for them to follow you when you begin the main part of your talk. Remember, listening is not like reading. If your listeners miss something, lose their concentration or do not understand straightaway, they cannot go back and hear that part again because you will already have moved on to the next part of your talk. They are having to listen, process and remember the information all at the same time, while you continue to talk! By providing them with an outline you will help them to follow what you are saying.

So, your introduction is very important. Remember:

+ Speak slowly, loudly and clearly.

- Introduce yourself.
- Introduce your topic and explain your aims.
- Attract your audience's interest – give them a reason to listen.
- Provide an overview of your talk.

The conclusion

We said that the introduction was *probably* the most important part of your talk. This is because some people argue that your conclusion is the most important part. The conclusion is the last part of the talk the audience hears, so what you say here may be the information they remember the most clearly.

Some students I have spoken to are aware that their presentation should end with a conclusion, but are not sure exactly what this conclusion should be. Because of this their talks end rather abruptly, with comments such as 'That's it, I've finished!' Your conclusion should leave your audience feeling that your talk has come to a logical end and should remind them not only of what they have heard but also of how your talk has achieved its aims.

Here are some suggestions for bringing your talk to a successful end:

- Let the audience know you have finished the main part of your talk and are about to conclude by using the appropriate linking language, for example 'In conclusion …' or 'To sum up …'
- Summarize the main points of your talk. Make sure that the points your audience are going to go away and remember are the most important points.
- Do not give any new information.
- Refer back to the aims you made in the introduction and show how these have been achieved. This brings your presentation neatly to an end.
- Be dynamic! This is the part of your talk your audience will remember, so finish positively.

THE BODY OF YOUR TALK

This section contains all the important information. You will have decided on the order of your points at the planning stage. As well as making sure that you follow this structure, you need to ensure that your audience can follow it too.

One way to do this is to introduce and summarize each point you make: tell them

Example: signalling language

Look at the following sentences:

- 'Many people believe that China joining the WTO (World Trade Organization) has been a very positive step for China. *However,* ...' The linking word 'however' signals that the speaker is about to say something that contrasts with the preceding sentence. Its function is to introduce a contrasting point.
- 'Many people believe that China joining the WTO (World Trade Organization) has been a very positive step for China. *This is because,* ...' 'This is because' signals that the speaker is about to give us reasons why people have that belief. Its function is to give a reason or reasons for something.

Task 6.4

Look at the signalling language on the left below and match it with one of the functions on the right. The first one has been done for you (in italic).

Signalling language

1 *I'd like to begin by ...*
2 That's all I have to say about ...
3 Let me turn now to ...
4 Let's look at this in more detail ...
5 A good example of this is ...
6 Finally, let's recap some of the main points
7 First ... secondly ... then ... next ... finally ...

Function

a giving an example
b sequencing
c summarizing/concluding
d reaching the end of a point
e *introducing the first idea*
f moving on to the next point
g developing a point

Key

For suggested answers, see 'Key to tasks' at the end of this chapter.

what you are going to say, say it, and tell them what you have just said! For example, introduce each point before you make it: 'First, I'd like to talk about X ...' Then make your point: 'X is ...' Finally, remind your audience of what you have just said, and introduce the next point: 'So, we have seen that the main attributes of X are a, b and c. Now let's compare this with Y.' This will give your audience time to process the information to prepare themselves for the next point.

Linking ideas
Using linking words and phrases is another way of making sure that your structure is clear. This is often called 'signalling language' because the words and phrases are signs or signals that tell us what is coming next.

Communicating with your audience

Your presentation is almost ready. Now you need to think about how you are going to deliver your talk on the day. First of all, let us consider how you are going to remember everything you want to say. Look at the three options below and try to decide which you think is the best advice to follow:

1 Write out your presentation word for word to read out on the day.
2 Write out your presentation word for word and memorize it.
3 Write notes on the main points of your presentation to remind you of what to say on the day.

WRITE OUT YOUR PRESENTATION TO READ OUT ON THE DAY

Many students like to do this to make sure they say exactly what they have planned to say, without forgetting anything or making any mistakes. It can be comforting to have every word written down so that you do not have to worry about making English language mistakes. However, it is not a good idea to write out your presentation word for word and read it to the audience.

Don't read it out!
If you do, it is as if you are reading an essay aloud rather than speaking to your audience. Written English and spoken English are not the same. Eye contact is a very important part of spoken English. It shows that both speaker and listener are engaged in the

communication. It is very difficult to listen to somebody who is not looking at you. If you are reading, you will be looking at the words on the page instead of at your audience. If you do try looking up, you may find that you lose your place on the page and repeat a sentence, or miss something out.

In written English we use punctuation to help our readers understand us. A full stop or a paragraph indicates when we have finished a point and are moving on to the next; question marks indicate a question. When we are speaking we use our voice, facial expressions and gestures to do this job. We pause to indicate that we have come to the end of a sentence, or use our voice to show that we are questioning something or that we are very sure of a point. When we read aloud written work, we often forget to use our voice and body language to communicate. This means that our audience will not understand a lot of what we say, even if the English itself is perfect.

Signpost

See Chapter 5, 'Speaking English at university', pages 108–113, for more information on using your voice to show meaning.

Reading out a written presentation is rarely successful. Most people, other than practised and skilled speech readers or actors, find it very difficult to read written work aloud expressively and with eye contact. A flat, monotonous voice and a speaker who is not looking at us is very boring to listen to and, if we are bored, we may stop listening altogether!

> *My tutor explained why I had failed the presentation. It is because I read it instead of speaking it.*
> **(Chinese student)**

It is better to have confidence in your spoken English. It is actually easier to understand somebody speaking English if they make few grammatical mistakes but are expressive than if the grammar is perfect but they do not use their voice as well as their words to communicate.

Later on we will look at how you can build confidence in your spoken English and how to use body language. However, first, let us continue to think about how to remember what you want to say on the day.

MEMORIZING YOUR PRESENTATION

Some students prefer to memorize their presentation. This can be effective as you are always talking to your audience rather than looking at your notes. However, some people find it easier than others to memorize large amounts of information. For many people it is stressful to try to remember everything perfectly so, if you are worried that you might forget something, it might be better to use notes. In addition, a memorized talk will be less spontaneous and will not be adapted to any response the audience may make.

MAKING NOTES

There are different ways you can make notes. You could just write down key words which will remind you of what you want to say. Your spoken English will be very natural because it has not been written out in full sentences. However, it is much more difficult to speak spontaneously if you are not speaking in your first language:

> You express yourself easier in your own language. But in English, I want to say something,
> I know what to say, but I can't express it in English. It's very frustrating.
> **(Cypriot student)**

This is why some students find it useful to write out their talk in full first, and then practise reading it aloud until they can remember most of what they want to say. Then they can make notes of the main points (which they will take into the presentation with them) that will remind them of what they had practised saying.

Whichever method you decide to try, here are some tips for making good notes:

◆ Write your notes on small cards. Give each card a heading and write two or three key words on each card to act as memory prompts. Number each card so that you know what order your points are in. Only write on one side of the card. This should be more effective than having all your notes written on one large piece of paper. You will not lose your place and you will not hide your face with your notes!

Example: writing notes on small cards

2 Making Notes

- *Use palm cards*
- *Write a heading and key words*
- *Number cards*
- *Write only on one side*

- Write your opening and closing sentences in full so that you do not forget how to begin and end your talk.
- Write down your linking words to help you remember how to move from one point to another.
- Write down information you find difficult to remember, such as people's names, dates, statistics or quotations.
- You can also use your notes to remind you to do things. For example, write down when you want to use a visual aid or when to pause. If you tend to speak quickly, write yourself a reminder to slow down. If there is a particular word you find difficult to pronounce, write it down phonetically.
- You do not have to use palm cards. If you are going to display your main points on an overhead projector or use PowerPoint slides, these can also act as your notes.

Signpost

See Chapter 5, 'Speaking English at university, for more information about pronunciation.

Remember, the important thing is to communicate effectively with your audience, so memorize your talk or use notes. Do not just read aloud!

Speaking in English

Communicating with your audience in a meaningful way is much more important than being grammatically correct in an oral presentation. Obviously you need to be understood, but it does not matter if you make a few minor language mistakes when you are speaking – many native English speakers do, too! Do not worry that speaking with an accent will detract from your presentation. There are many varieties of English, and everybody who speaks English has an accent, whether it is national or regional. People enjoy listening to different accents. The important thing is that you have confidence in your spoken English and that you find ways of making yourself understood:

> Don't be afraid of making English mistakes. And if you do make a mistake, don't worry. You can say it again better.
> **(Chinese student)**

The best way of being confident about the language you are going to use in your presentation is to have prepared what you want to say carefully before you speak. Do not try to use long or complex sentences if you find them difficult. Use short simple sentences; not only is this simpler for you to say but it also easier for your audience to understand. If you are using new words, make sure you have looked them up in a dictionary and, if possible, practised using them with an English speaker so that you are sure you are using them correctly.

SAYING THE RIGHT THING

Signpost

In Chapter 5, 'Speaking English at university', we look at the importance of using appropriate language in different situations. If you need to revise this, look at this chapter now.

What language is appropriate for oral presentations? To a certain extent this will depend on your specific context: who you are talking to and in what situation (see Task 6.2). However, there are some general guidelines to help you select the most appropriate English.

The level of formality

The language used in academic oral presentations is usually less formal than a written essay but more formal than conversation.

Task 6.5

Read these sentences from student presentations. Decide whether the language used is appropriate. Tick ✓ the box which best describes the use of language.

	Appropriate	Too formal	Too informal
1 I'm gonna introduce three main points	☐	☐	☐
2 I'd like to talk to you today about agricultural developments in South East Asia	☐	☐	☐
3 I have great pleasure in speaking to such a distinguished audience about Japan's economic reform	☐	☐	☐
4 Unfortunately, this turned out to be a load of crap	☐	☐	☐
5 So, basically, like, there are more good points than bad, yeah?	☐	☐	☐
6 I extend my gratitude to my esteemed audience for listening to my speech	☐	☐	☐
7 Now, let's look at the effect this had on the environment	☐	☐	☐

Key

For suggested answers, see 'Key to tasks' at the end of this chapter.

Do not use very formal or overly polite language, such as 'my esteemed audience'. Do not use slang or colloquial expressions, such as 'kids' instead of 'children'. Avoid using features of conversational English, such as repetition, hesitations and fillers.

Repetition, hesitation and fillers

When we are speaking spontaneously, chatting to friends or responding to questions, we often repeat words, hesitate or use 'fillers' – words that do not really mean anything. This is normal in spontaneous speech because, unlike when we write, we do not always have enough time to decide on exactly which words we want to use before we say them aloud. Repeating words, hesitation and use of fillers such as 'um' and 'actually' give the speaker *thinking time.* They fill the silence while we search our minds for what we want to say next.

However, an oral presentation is not really spontaneous speech. It should be prepared, reducing the need for such strategies used to create thinking time. When people use too many fillers during an oral presentation it can be distracting and even irritating for the audience. One student told me about a lecturer they had at college who would repeat the word 'right' so often during a lecture that, instead of listening to what he had to say, the students would try to count how often he said 'right' in one session!

HAVE CONFIDENCE IN YOUR ENGLISH

Make sure the language you are using is your own English. In other words, do not take large chunks of material from your sources and memorize it. Your tutors are much more interested in what you have to say about a topic than what somebody else has already said or written. It is fine to use a quotation, if you think it is relevant, as long as you give the name of the person who originally said it. However, if you use somebody else's words instead of your own throughout the presentation, without referencing them, your tutor may think you have plagiarized or copied your talk. This is a very serious offence.

Signpost

For further discussion about plagiarism, See Chapter 9, writing.

When you have prepared what you want to say, practise saying it so that you are comfortable with the language and can speak reasonably fluently. Make your notes as helpful as possible so that, if you do have difficulty expressing your ideas in English, you have some prompts to help you.

PRONUNCIATION

Speaking clearly is not just about knowing how to pronounce the right sounds. Using the appropriate word and sentence stress, rhythm and intonation and pausing correctly will all help to ensure that your audience can understand you.

When you go to a dictionary to check the meaning of new words that you want to use in your presentation, make sure you also find out how to pronounce them. You should check the pronunciation of words that you have seen written down but never heard spoken. Remember to check both the sounds and the word stress. When you are practising your talk, remember to use rhythm, intonation and pausing.

Signpost

In Chapter 5, 'Speaking English at university', there is advice and tasks on all these aspects of speaking clearly. There are also suggestions for further reading and practice that you can do in this area. Go to this chapter now if you want to revise this.

STRATEGIES FOR MAKING YOURSELF UNDERSTOOD

If you are still having difficulty with some aspects of pronunciation when you have to give your presentation, do not worry; there are other things you can do to make sure that you are understood:

- *Slow down*: make sure the audience has time to hear and understand your words.
- *Articulate*: practise moving your mouth so that you pronounce each individual sound. Sound the end of each word clearly – do not allow them to run together. This will make your speech clearer and will also help you to speak more slowly.

◆ *Use visual aids*: this is a very useful strategy if you are worried about being understood. Your audience can see the word or phrase as well as hear it so they are much more likely to understand it. However, make sure that the written English is accurate.

Being expressive

We do not just use words to communicate. We also express ourselves using our voice and body language.

VERBAL COMMUNICATION: HOW YOU SAY IT

Intonation
The way you say something is as important as the words you say. Intonation – moving the voice up and down – helps to convey meaning and feelings, and to engage and

Task 6.6

Practise saying the short sentences below out loud. Try to use intonation to convey the message in brackets beside it. If possible, work with a partner and ask him or her to guess which emotion you are trying to express:

◆ 'It's snowing' (you are surprised – it never snows!).
◆ 'It's snowing' (you are not surprised – it has been snowing every day for a week).
◆ 'What time is it?' (You are being very polite.)
◆ 'What time is it?' (You are feeling bored.)

Now practise saying the following sentences with as much emotion as possible:

◆ 'I am happier than I have ever been in my life!'
◆ 'I don't care what anyone says, I'm going to win this race!'

interest your audience. It is much more interesting for the audience to listen to a speaker who is displaying emotion than to a flat, monotonous voice. It is also easier to understand him or her. So, for example, if you are telling your audience that a certain point of view is very interesting, move your voice so that you sound interested! They are much more likely to believe you and to be interested themselves! If you want to convey the fact that a certain conclusion is surprising, sound surprised!

Voice projection
Can your audience hear you? Some people's voices are naturally louder than others. You need to check that you are speaking loudly enough for your audience to hear you, without shouting at them. If you can, it is always a good idea to practise in the same room you will be speaking in. Ask a friend to stand at the back of the room and listen. They can tell you if you need to speak louder or more quietly. If you find it difficult to speak loudly, practise at home. You could write out a few simple sentences in English and practise reading them out as loudly as you can. Over time you will train your voice to travel further.

Are you speaking too quickly?
When you are presenting, you should not speak as quickly as you do when you are having a conversation. Your audience needs time to hear and understand your ideas. Most people speak more quickly than they think, which makes the job of listening very hard indeed! Slow down and pause for a moment at the end of each idea. Standing in front of an audience for a moment without saying anything may feel strange, but your audience will welcome a brief pause so they can process all the information you are giving them. However, do not slow down too much. You should keep the presentation lively to keep your audience interested.

NON-VERBAL COMMUNICATION: BODY LANGUAGE

The way you say something is important, but so are the messages that you are sending with your body. Go back to the sentences in Task 6.6. Repeat the task, but this time in front of a mirror. Notice how your facial expressions change as you convey emotions. You may find you are also moving your head, your hands or your body to communicate your feelings. Body language can effectively reinforce the message you are sending. It also makes the talk more interesting to watch.

Making effective use of body language
Here are some points to consider:

- *Posture – how you hold your body*: a speaker who stands up straight, looks at their audience and smiles will appear much more confident than one who looks at the floor, and they will probably feel more confident as well!
- *Eye contact*: some people avoid eye contact with the audience because they feel nervous or they look only at the tutor or at a friend. However, having eye contact with everyone in your audience is very important. It will encourage them to look at you and listen to what you are saying, and they will feel involved in the communication. It also makes you appear more confident.
- *Facial expressions*: a speaker who looks interested in and enthusiastic about what they are saying will be much more interesting to listen to.
- *Head/body movements and gestures*: make sure your gestures reinforce the point you are making rather than distracting the audience. For example, if you tap your pen against your leg, pace up and down or play with your hair, you may find that your audience is looking at what you are doing instead of listening to what you are saying!

Use your voice and your body language to help you express your message. As Nicki Stanton states in *Communication* (1990), 'Non-verbal channels are the ones of which we seem to be least aware if in ourselves, but most aware of in others'. Your audience will take as much notice of how you say it as what you say.

Understanding your audience's body language
As well as using body language yourself, you should also look out for your audience's body language. It may help you to see whether or not they have understood a point, if they agree with you or if they find your talk interesting. For example, if they look puzzled or confused, you might want to check they have understood your point. If they look bored or are not looking at you at all, you might decide to focus on your intonation or to ask a rhetorical question in order to regain their interest. An audience that is looking at you attentively will boost your confidence because you know they are paying attention to your talk.

Using audio-visual aids

Good audio-visual aids (AVA's) can really make a difference to presentation. They support your talk by allowing your audience to see what you are talking about, as well as hear it. They can take the pressure off you and make you feel more confident. Well produced visuals make your presentation look more professional and interesting.

Task 6.7

Three of the most commonly used AVA's are listed below. Do you know what they are?

- ◆ Overhead projector (OHP).
- ◆ Whiteboard.
- ◆ Flip chart.

Key

For suggested answers, see 'Key to tasks' at the end of this chapter.

Task 6.8

Can you add any more to the list?

Key

For further suggestions, see 'Key to tasks' at the end of this chapter.

HOW AVA's CAN HELP YOU

AVA's which are used well can do the following:

Make your presentation much more interesting, and memorable
Showing photographs, charts and diagrams, key points or moving images can really bring your presentation to life. They can have a big impact, get people's attention and provide variety by giving the audience something to look at other than you! Many people, particularly visual learners, find it much easier to remember information visually, and everyone finds information they have heard and seen more memorable.

Signpost

See Chapter 2, 'Being an effective learner', for more information about different types of learner.

Help your audience understand complex ideas

Reinforcing your explanation of complex ideas with a visual can be very effective, particularly if you show an example or illustration. Most people find it easier to understand statistics by looking at a chart or diagram rather than listening to a list of numbers. Sometimes it easier to show your audience something rather than trying to describe it to them. However, do not simply display the visual instead of presenting the information yourself, and do not just read the words on the visual aloud.

Help your audience (and you) to follow the structure of your talk

If you provide an overview of your talk visually as well as orally, it will help your audience to follow you. If you show your key points, you can point to or reveal each one as you make it. Your audience will find this much easier to follow, and you could use them as your notes as well to remind your audience of what you want to say and in what order.

Act as a backup

If you are worried about the clarity or accuracy of your spoken English in general, showing images or examples of what you are talking about can help your audience to understand you. If you are concerned about the pronunciation of specific words, writing them down as well can make them clearer. If you are worried that your audience won't recognize some of the words you are using (for example, specialist vocabulary, names of places or people they may not know or difficult-to-remember dates and numbers), displaying these visually as well as explaining them will help.

However, AVA's that are badly designed can make your presentation worse. At best, they add nothing but, at worst, they can distract or mislead.

Task 6.9

Go back to the list of AVA's you made in Task 6.8. Choose at least three, and write down any problems or difficulties that a presenter might have while using them. When you have finished, check your ideas with the advice below.

MAKING YOUR AVA's WORK

Choose the information that you want to display. You cannot show everything – your audience does not want to read your presentation! However, it is useful to show:

- your overview, or plan, of the talk to help them follow your structure;
- the most important points, to help them remember; and
- examples or illustrations of particularly difficult points.

Use your AVA's – and get your audience to use them, too:

- Do not just leave a visual sitting there without ever referring to it; your audience will not know when they are supposed to look at it or how it fits in with the rest of your talk.
- Point to the information you are talking about.
- Only allow them to see it when you are referring to it.
- Give the audience enough time to read the words or understand the diagram before you go on to talk about another idea.

Choose the appropriate way to display your information. You might like to go back to the suggested answer keys for Tasks 6.7 and 6.8 at this point to remind yourself of the different AVA's that might be available to you. Below are some tips about using some of the more common AVA's effectively:

- Only use the whiteboard as a backup if other technical equipment does not work, for very small pieces of information or for collecting ideas from the audience. Writing on a whiteboard is time-consuming, and you have to turn your back on the audience in order to do it. It can also look untidy.

- If you are using technical equipment such as the OHP or PowerPoint, make sure you have checked the equipment and that you know how to use it.
- A flip chart can work very well in small groups but is often not big enough for larger groups to be able to see.
- Using video images can be useful and interesting, but not if they go on for too long! Only use very short extracts so that your presentation does not lose pace.

Prepare your AVA's effectively. Make sure that whatever information you are displaying is big enough for your audience to be able to see. Do not crowd too much information on to one slide or handout. Leave space round the edges, and only use key words or brief quotations. Make sure your grammar and spelling are correct. Do not leave the preparation until the last minute. Give yourself time to prepare them well, especially if you might need help with technical equipment you are not familiar with:

- Practise using them.
- Include reminders on your notes of when you should be showing a slide or giving a handout.
- Practise using any technical equipment before you present.
- Make sure do not stand in front of your AVA and obscure it. (Tip: if you are using an OHP and you want to point to the idea you are talking about, point to the image projected on to the wall that your audience can see rather than the image on the transparency. That way you know you are not obscuring their view.)

Practice, practice and practice!

When you are giving your talk you are giving a performance. Everyone needs to practise before they perform in front of an audience. This is the final stage of your preparation, but it is very important. Do not forget about it!

The best advice is to practise in front of your friend or in front of a mirror.
(Chinese student)

When I'm preparing I practise as much as I can, it really improves my speaking.
(Cypriot student)

If you can practise in front of friends, they can give you lots of advice about what you are doing well and what improvements you could make. For example, are you speaking too quietly or too quickly? Can they understand you? Is your structure clear? Is your body language distracting? Are you standing in front of your visual aid? Practising with an audience means you become used to talking in front of other people which can build your confidence. Take every opportunity to speak out and present ideas in class, as this really is the key to becoming a more skilled and confident speaker.

Even if you do not have an audience to practise with, practising on your own can still help your confidence and your performance on the day. You will be more familiar with your content, the language you are using and your visual aids. Also, you will be much less likely to forget what you want to say. Practise in front of a mirror so that you are aware of your body language:

> *Practising once is not enough. You need to keep practising. I practised 4 or 5 times in front of a mirror and it made me feel much more confident.*
> **(Bangladeshi student)**

Many students we have spoken to said they learnt a lot from watching other students present. If you have the chance, try to watch other student or tutor presentations in class, or presentations by people outside the university. You could offer to act as the audience for friends or colleagues who want to practise their presentations.

What do I do if I feel nervous?

> *I tend to get less nervous once I start the presentation and afterwards I feel I have achieved a lot. I feel happy.*
> **(Nigerian student)**

Oral presentations are usually exciting and rewarding experiences, but some students feel nervous about presenting information in front of others. Some people are naturally more confident speakers than others. Students may feel worried and nervous if they have never presented before, or feel nervous about having to speak in English:

> *We never give oral presentations in Bangladesh. It is totally new for me.*
> **(Bangladeshi student)**

> *In fact I have never made a presentation in my own language, but I think the problem in*

both languages is that personally I am not a talkative person, so I don't feel confident enough to speak in front of some audience.
(Chinese student)

NERVES CAN BE GOOD FOR YOU!

Whatever your experience, many people will feel a degree of nervousness. This is often a good thing. It can improve your presentation as the adrenaline you feel helps you to present the information in a more dynamic and interesting way. Being nervous is also a sign that you care about the presentation and that you will therefore be prepared to put effort into making it successful. If you have researched and prepared well, you are less likely to feel nervous because you can be confident about what you are going to say. However, you may still feel nervous about standing in front of an audience. You will probably start to relax as the presentation gets underway, but there are strategies you can use to build your confidence and overcome the signs of nerves.

What do you do when you are nervous?
First of all, you need to be aware of how nerves affect you. Here is what some students said happened to them when they felt nervous during oral presentations:

I was really nervous before giving my presentation, and I was shaking.
(Bangladeshi student)

I memorized all the things that I was going to talk about and in the right order, but I felt stressed standing out there and this 'decreased' my memories.
(Chinese student)

After the presentation my tutor told me I was always slapping my leg. I didn't know it. I think it's because I am nervous.
(Sri Lankan student)

Task 6.10

Take a moment to think about what you do when you are nervous. Think back to a situation when you had to give a talk. If you have never spoken in front of an audience, think back to a situation where you felt nervous.

How did your nerves affect you? For example, was your performance more dynamic? Did you forget to say or do anything? Did your hands shake? Did you laugh? Look at the ideas in the list below. Tick the ones that apply to you and add any that are not there:

- Shaking.
- Laughing.
- Using distracting body language (for example, pacing up and down, playing with your hair, speaking with your hand over your mouth).
- Forgetting what you were going to say.
- Using English that you did not know you knew!
- Sweating.
- Speaking too quickly.
- Forgetting to use visual aids.
- Using repetition, hesitations and fillers (for example, 'er', 'basically', 'well now' and 'you know').
- Feeling excited.

Now read the strategies for reducing the symptoms of nerves and decide which ones might be useful for you.

Avoid stimulants
It is probably a good idea to avoid drinks which act as stimulants before you give a presentation. For example, drinking coffee or Coca-Cola can make you feel on edge or cause your hands to shake.

Take deep breaths
Another good idea is to practise breathing deeply. Take a few long, deep breaths just before you go up to speak. This can really help to make you feel calm.

Drink water
If it is appropriate to your situation, drinking water during your talk can help you if you are feeling hot or if your mouth and throat become dry, making it difficult for you to speak. It can also help you to slow down and pause between ideas.

Be comfortable
Do not wear clothing that is going to make you feel uncomfortable, hot or restrict your breathing or movement. Instead, wear whatever is comfortable and appropriate to the

situation. Some people like to make an effort to look smart when giving a presentation because they know that people are going to be looking at them. This can be a good idea as your physical appearance does have an effect on the audience. It also has an effect on you: often if you feel that you look good then you feel more confident.

Be in control of your body language
If they feel nervous about performing, some people try to hide themselves by looking at the floor and folding their arms to make themselves seem smaller. This all sends messages to your audience that you feel uncomfortable and nervous. However, if you stand up straight, put your shoulders back and hold your head high, looking directly ahead of you and smiling, you will look confident, even if you have butterflies on the inside! If you find that your hands are shaking, try holding them behind your back until you relax.

Use memory aids
Students can be well prepared but still forget important points on the day because they feel nervous. Using notes and/or visual aids can be a useful way of helping you to remember to say what you planned to say.

Here are some ideas that students have had:

Learn from other classmates and practise. Don't be nervous, believe in yourself.
(Chinese student)

I think it gets easier after the first time. You need to find interesting information, practise several times. It is quite important not to be nervous: speak slowly, let everyone understand what you mean.
(Chinese student)

Take deep breaths to calm yourself down if you feel nervous; try to be confident while speaking – of course, good preparation helps a lot!
(Chinese student)

Do not be afraid of your audience. The people you are talking to will usually be interested in what you are saying and will want you do to well. They will want to learn from what you are telling them so they will be trying hard to listen to you and to understand what you are saying.

Remember, feeling a little bit nervous when you are speaking in front of an audience can actually make your presentation better! If you use some of the strategies we have discussed in this section, you can reduce the visible effects of nerves and concentrate on the positive energy they may give you.

Dealing with questions

You should tell your audience right at the beginning of your talk whether you will deal with questions as they arise or whether you prefer to answer them at the end of the talk. Most people prefer to deal with them at the end of the talk. This can be a very informative and enjoyable part of the presentation because interesting ideas can be developed in more detail. You have the opportunity to show what you know about your topic, so try to answer the questions fully, avoiding one-word answers. Many people find they speak more fluently when answering questions because it is less formal and more like conversational English, although it is very important that you always respond politely. Take one question at a time, and do not let it turn into a lengthy discussion between you and one member of the audience. If this seems to be happening, suggest that the two of you continue the discussion at another time.

WHAT IF I DON'T UNDERSTAND A QUESTION?

Do not worry. Explain politely that you do not understand and ask the person to repeat or rephrase the question: 'I'm sorry, I'm afraid I don't understand your question. Could you say it again for me, please?'

WHAT IF I DON'T KNOW THE ANSWER?

If you have researched and prepared your topic well, you probably will! But if you don't, do not worry. You are not expected to know everything. Explain that this is not an area you covered in your research, and maybe offer to find out the answer and get back to them. It is always better to admit that you do not know than to give an incorrect answer.

If you are asked lots of questions, it is usually a sign that your presentation has been successful.

Group presentations

You may be asked to give a presentation in a group. This can be a lot of fun, and many students prefer it to an individual presentation because they enjoy having each other's support. However, working in a group is different from working alone. You have to communicate with each other and provide support for your group members. You all need to contribute and should take equal responsibility. If your presentation is being assessed, it may be that you receive a group mark rather than an individual one, so it is important that you all work equally hard.

Signpost

See Chapter 5, 'Speaking English at university', for information about how to work together successfully as a group.

You should go through the same planning and preparation process as for an individual presentation, but you will also need to consider the following points:

MEETING AND COMMUNICATING

Make sure you know how to contact each other. You will need to arrange regular meetings and inform the group if you cannot attend. You will need to contribute to the meetings, making sure that you know what you have to do for the next one, and making sure that you do it.

WORK TO YOUR GROUP'S STRENGTHS

Identify the various strengths and weaknesses of the group members and assign tasks and roles accordingly. Here are some questions you could consider:

- Who knows the most about the topic?
- Who is good at attracting the audience's attention at the start?
- Who is good at explaining detail?
- Who can put forward a point of view strongly?
- Who is good at using audio-visual aids?
- Who is good at dealing with questions?

PRACTISE TOGETHER

It is important that you all know what each member of the group is doing on the day so that you can support each other. Make sure you find out if all the group members have to speak. If they do, try to ensure that you all speak for about the same length of time. You will need to decide who is going to say what, and how you are going to hand over from one speaker to another. When you are not actually speaking, remember that the audience can still see you. Do not do anything that could distract them or other members of your group.

You can learn a lot from working together as a group and it can be very enjoyable, as long as everyone contributes.

Conclusion

Having read this chapter, we hope you feel confident about giving a talk to an audience. When you begin to put these ideas into practice, your confidence and skills will grow. Oral presentations are an opportunity for you to learn more about your subject while gaining confidence in your speaking skills. You are also practising a skill that is highly valued, not only in academic institutions but also in the workplace.

REFERENCE

Stanton, N. (1990) *Communication*. Basingstoke: Macmillan.

USEFUL RESOURCES

http://speaking.englishclub.com/presentations.htm

This site is aimed at learners of English and has advice on giving presentations, including a useful section on language.

http://www.asc.ku.ac.th/Downloads/Blah.PDF

This link takes you to a PDF file of a coursebook on public speaking written by Steve Smith at the Australian Studies Centre in Thailand. It is aimed at helping international students improve their public speaking and debating skills and focuses on helping you to use the English language you already know as effectively as possible.

www.canberra.edu.au/studyskills/learning/oralpres.html

This link takes you to the oral presentation section of Canberra University's Academic Study Skills Online. It includes concise and easy-to-use checklists for preparing, organizing and delivering presentations, as well as using visual aids and dealing with nerves.

http://people.hsc.edu/faculty-staff/cdeal/mainsections/student.html

This is part of the website for Hampden–Sydney College and gives advice on how to become a confident public speaker. It includes a section on how to make nerves work for you and an online tutorial on how to prepare and deliver your presentation.

http://www.uefap.co.uk/speaking/spkfram.htm

This is part of the website for the University of Hertfordshire and gives helpful advice on aspects of speaking in academic contexts for international students.

http://www.unisanet.unisa.edu.au/learningconnection/learnres/learng/index.htm#Oral

This link takes you to two learning guides. The first, 'Making the most of oral presentations', includes advice on planning, preparing and delivering presentations. The second , 'Managing question time', gives advice on how to deal with questions from the audience. The learning guides are in the form of Word documents.

Burns, T. and Sinfield, S. (2003) *Essential Study Skills*. London: Sage.

Pages 209–23 are dedicated to oral presentations.

Comfort, J. and Utley, D. (1995) *Effective Presentations*. Oxford: Oxford University Press.

This is a video that demonstrates the language and practical skills required for giving business presentations in English.

Cottrell, S. (1999) *The Study Skills Handbook*. Basingstoke: Palgrave.

Pages 100–3 are dedicated to oral presentations.

KEY TO TASKS

Task 6.1

Topic: world trade.

Aim/SPS: by the end of my talk, my audience will *believe that globalization has a negative impact on developing countries.*

Task 6.2

There is not one correct response to this task, but here are a few of the things that you could have thought about:

Your content would be different because of your audience's background knowledge and because of their needs: you might expect the group of surgeons to have a lot of background knowledge, perhaps gathered from sources such as academic studies, specialist journals and conferences. It would probably be quite detailed and factual knowledge of breast cancer and the surgical procedures related to it. Therefore they would be interested in adding to their body of professional knowledge and becoming better surgeons, wanting precise information about recent research, new treatments and new surgical procedures.

On the other hand, the group of women would probably have a more general and basic knowledge about breast cancer, perhaps gathered from sources such as informal conversation, TV and magazines or personal experience. The information they have might be less precise and less reliable, perhaps even contradictory. They may be looking to clarify their current knowledge and fill in any gaps. They may want advice on self-diagnosis, emotional support available for those suffering from breast cancer, or advice about how to support a friend or family member who has the disease.

The language you use and your style of delivery would also be different: you may expect to be able to use more specialist medical vocabulary with the group of surgeons than with the group of women. Your tone and style would probably be much more formal and professional when talking to the surgeons, whereas with the women you might be more informal and personal.

Task 6.4

1 (e)	3 (f)	5 (a)	7 (b)
2 (d)	4 (g)	6 (c)	

Task 6.5

1 Too informal.
2 Appropriate.
3 Too formal.
4 Too informal.
5 Too informal.
6 Too formal.
7 Appropriate.

Task 6.7

- *Overhead Projector (OHP)*: a device with a light, which makes large images from a flat transparent sheet and shows them on a white screen or wall.
- *Flip chart*: a board standing on legs with large pieces of paper fixed to the top, which you can write or draw on, and which can be turned over.
- *Whiteboard*: a board with a smooth, white surface, often fixed to a wall, on which you can write and draw using special pens.

Task 6.8

Here are a few more suggestions:

- *PowerPoint*: presentation software that allows you to create slides which can be projected on to a wall or screen. This can look very professional and has the advantage of being able to use colour and moving images easily.
- *Handout*: a document given to students or reporters which contains information about a particular subject.
- *Poster*: a large printed picture, photograph or notice which you stick or pin to a wall or board.
- *Realia*: the real thing! For example, in a presentation about the sense of smell, a student was using the smell of coffee as an example. Instead of just talking about it, she actually brought in some real coffee for her audience to smell.

7 Reading

Gist: The most important pieces of information about something, or general information without details.
Leaning: A preference for a particular set of beliefs, opinions, etc.
Margin: The empty space to the side of the text on a page.
Objective: Based on facts and not influenced by personal beliefs or feelings.
Prediction: When you say what will happen in the future.
Selective: Intentionally choosing some things and not others.
Subjective: Influenced by or based on personal beliefs or feelings, rather than based on facts.
Survey: To look at or examine all of something.
Terminology: Special words or expressions used in relation to a particular subject or activity.
Tip: A useful piece of information, especially about how to do something.

Reading at university

It is essential for students to be able to read well to study. If you can't read, you can't do anything.
(Chinese student)

Reading is one of the most important skills you will need at university and you are expected to read a lot! If you learn to be an effective reader, you will probably be a more successful student. There are a number of ways that developing good reading skills will help you in your studies.

READING TO EXPAND YOUR KNOWLEDGE

You are at university because you want to learn and expand your knowledge. Reading is one of the best ways of doing this. At university you will read to:

- learn about and understand the basic facts and theories of your subject;
- deepen your knowledge in a number of aspects of your subject by reading more detailed texts; and
- be aware of controversial theories and ideas about your subject and be able to make up your own mind about them.

The best way to do this is to take it step by step. You will not be able to question and criticize a new piece of research unless you have first understood the basics.

READING FOR LECTURES AND SEMINARS

You also learn a lot from listening to your tutors and other students. You will gain much more from your lectures and seminars if you have prepared for them. Reading the appropriate section in your coursebook, or from a book recommended on your reading list, *before* the class, will make it much easier for you to understand what your tutor or classmate is saying. You may not have completely understood every idea you have read, but you will have already started to think about the topic and so will be prepared to have your questions answered or points that are not clear explained to you.

READING FOR ASSIGNMENTS

Whether you have to write an essay or give an oral presentation you will need to read first in order to gather the information that you are going to write or speak about. Before you sit an exam, you will need to revise things that you have read before and read notes that you have made.

Signpost

See Chapter 8, 'Making notes', for more advice on revising from notes.

READING TO IMPROVE YOUR ENGLISH

Reading is one of the best ways of increasing your vocabulary. You will find many new English words when you read. You will see how they work in different contexts and in combination with other words. You will also see how pieces of writing are constructed in English, at sentence, paragraph and text level. Although you might think that your level of English is preventing you from reading, actually, if you read in the right way, reading will help you to improve your English.

HOW DO YOU READ?

The good news is that you probably already read more than you think!

Task 7.1

Write down a list of all the things you have read in the last 24 hours. Include everything you have read, not just the reading you have done for your studies. For example, you may have read an email from a friend, an advertisement in a magazine or the destination on the front of a bus.

Were you surprised at how much you read and understand every day?

You probably already use different reading strategies effectively, depending on what you are reading and why you are reading it.

Task 7.2

Consider how you would read the three texts below. Would you read some more quickly or slowly than others? Would you read some more carefully than others? Would you read them all from beginning to end?

1 A fiction book.
2 A magazine.
3 A dictionary.

Key

For suggested answers, see 'Key to tasks' at the end of this chapter.

ACADEMIC READING

What strategy should you use when you are reading in English for your studies? In your academic reading you need to be *reflective*. This means *thinking deeply and carefully* about what you are reading. You will need to identify and remember points that you can use in the future. To be a good reflective reader, you need to be selective about *what* you are reading and to be very clear about *why* you are reading it.

There is so much to read!

BEING SELECTIVE

Many students find that there are so many books in the library, and such a long list of books on their reading lists, they do not know where to start. They feel there will never be enough time for them to read it all!

You are expected to read a lot, but you cannot read everything. The important thing is to be selective. You will probably be given a reading list for each course that you are studying. If you do not have one, check in any course guidelines or with your tutors. The most important books for you to read, the core texts, should be highlighted on the reading lists. All the students on your course will want to read these books, so they will be in demand! It might be worth buying your own copy or checking to see if the core texts are kept in a special part of the library which restricts the amount of time each student can use them.

WHY AM I READING?

The important thing is to have a reason for reading – you should not start reading without knowing what you are going to use the information for. You may not have to read all the books on the reading list. Ask yourself: are you reading in order to prepare for a lecture? Is it part of your research for an essay? Do you need information to help you participate in a seminar? Choose the books that seem relevant to your purpose.

Task 7.3

Look at an extract of the reading list for the course 'Social and Academic English'. Imagine you are preparing for an assignment where you have to give an oral presentation. Which of the texts listed would you want to read to help you prepare for this?

Comfort, J. and Utley, D. (1995) *Effective Presentations*. Oxford: Oxford University Press.

Cottrel, S. (1999) *The Study Skills Handbook*. London: Macmillan.

Hamp-Lyons, L. and Heasley, B. (1987) *Study Writing: Written English for Academic and Professional Purposes*. Cambridge: Cambridge University Press.

Jordan, R.R. (1999) *Academic Writing Course*. Harlow: Longman

McCarter, S. (1997) *A Book on Writing*. Ford, Midlothian: IntelliGene.

Waters, M. and Waters, A. (1995) *Study Tasks in English*. Cambridge: Cambridge University Press.

Key

For suggested answers, see 'Key to tasks' at the end of this chapter.

HOW DO I KNOW IF IT IS RELEVANT UNTIL I'VE READ IT?

It can be frustrating to spend time reading a book that you thought would help you with your studies, only to find that it was not useful at all. To save time you should survey the book before you start to read it. You do not always have to read the whole book from cover to cover. It may be that there are just small parts of the book which will be useful to you. Surveying the book first can help you decide which part of the book you need to study.

Task 7.4

For this task, either choose a book from one of your reading lists or use this book. Answer the questions below as quickly as you can by finding the information in the book. There are some tips on where you might find the information.

1 What is the title of the book?
2 Who wrote it? (*Tip:* look at the front cover.)
3 When was it published?
4 Has it been updated since it was first written? (*Tip:* look just inside the front of the book.)
5 What is the main idea of the book and who is it aimed at? (*Tip:* look at the back cover.)

6   What specific areas are covered in the book, and in what order?
    (*Tip:* is there a contents page?)
7   Has the author written an introduction? What does this tell you?
    (*Tip:* look near the front of the book.)
8   How many sources did the writer use?
9   Does the book have an index? If so, why might this be useful? (*Tip:*
    look near the back of the book.)
10 Has the author used illustrations or examples?

Key

For comments on this task, see 'Key to tasks' at the end of this chapter.

A few minutes spent surveying the book – deciding if it is useful to you, or if parts of it may be useful – is a much better use of time than reading every word from beginning to end, before realizing that you cannot really use the material.

Making the most of the library

Your university library is your best resource, but it is easy to spend a lot of time there without making full use of all it offers:

> Using the library is unavoidable in learning, but using the library well and using all of the material that is available in it is something quite different.
> **(Iranian student)**

It may seem difficult to know where to start looking for information:

> It is difficult to find the book from the specific shelf because there are hundreds of books on many big shelves.
> **(Bangladeshi student)**

However, just like anything else, once you are familiar with the library and how it works, you will find it very useful. Make sure you know:

- where the general inquiries desk is;
- where the books and other resources relevant to your subject are kept; and
- whether there is a librarian who specializes in your subject and, if so, how to contact him or her.

Do not be afraid to ask if you are having any difficulties using the library or finding what you want to read! The sooner you get to know the library the more useful it will be.

OTHER SOURCES OF INFORMATION

You will not only be reading books. There are many other good sources of information, such as newspaper or magazine articles.

Collection of essays

This looks like a book but has an editor rather than an author. If you look at the contents page you will see that each chapter is actually an essay that has been written by a different author. The editor has collected essays written on distinct aspects of the same topic and put them together in one book. There will usually be a short introduction written by the editors explaining the main idea of the book.

Journal article

A journal is a collection of serious academic articles on a specialist subject, which is published regularly. This can be very useful if you are looking for very up-to-date information about a specific topic.

Periodicals

Periodicals are magazines or newspapers, especially on serious or specialist subjects, that are published regularly. Again these are useful for very up-to-date information but may contain less specialized and shorter articles than those found in journals.

Electronic sources

There is an enormous amount of information available online. It is like one big global library open 24 hours a day, which you can access from almost anywhere! The information may be in the form of specialist websites or journals and periodicals that are available in electronic form. It is probably where you will find the most up-to-date information because it is very quick and easy to publish information on the web.

Despite all these advantages, however, you need to be extremely careful about what you choose to read. Anyone can publish information on the Internet, so you must think very carefully about the credentials of the author or website. Is the author an expert of some kind? Is the organization the website belongs to respected and trustworthy? Would you expect the writer or website to be biased?

Signpost

See pages 173–5 in this chapter for further discussion about bias.

Task 7.5

Go to your university library and find the following information. You may need to read signs or leaflets in the library, or to ask the library staff to help you:

1 Write down the opening times of the library.
2 Write down the name of your subject librarian (if there is one) and the times he or she is available.
3 Find the section with the books for your subject. Write down the part of the library it is in (for example, which floor or which section).
4 Find the section with journals and periodicals for your subject. Write down the part of the library it is in.
5 Tick any of the following that are available in your library:

♦ Newspapers
♦ Area for group work
♦ Access to computers
♦ Printing facilities
♦ Language laboratory
♦ Area for key texts
♦ Online library catalogue
♦ Access to the Internet
♦ Photocopying facilities

6 Are there any others?

Getting ideas from your reading

Effective reading is not measured by how much you read but by how much you learn and understand.

YOU DO NOT HAVE TO UNDERSTAND EVERY WORD

You will find reading in English easier if you have a fairly good range of vocabulary.

Signpost

See Chapter 4, 'Building vocabulary', for more information about extending your vocabulary.

Nevertheless, you will often find there are words that you do not know. It is quite usual for native speakers of English to encounter words they do not know when reading. However, they would not look up every single unknown word in a dictionary as they read, and neither should you. It is far too time-consuming and, more importantly, means that you concentrate on the meaning of the individual words instead of the meaning of the sentence.

An important skill when reading is to be able to guess the meaning of a word from the context and to try to understand the main ideas without necessarily understanding every single word. When you have understood the gist, or the main idea, you will know which of the new words it will be useful for you to look up and learn.

When we write in English we write from left to right, so this is also how we read. If you are used to following text in a different direction in your first language, you may have to practise this. Our eyes do not stop at every individual word to examine it. Instead, they look at chunks of text at the same time. This is faster and is also more effective, as we often cannot understand the main ideas being expressed until we have understood the whole sentence:

> *I have seen that it is not necessary to understand every word while reading, rather you should continue reading.*
> **(Nigerian student)**

SQ3R: A REFLECTIVE READING STRATEGY

This is not as technical as it sounds! It is an effective way of approaching a text actively and reflectively.

Skim
Question
Read
Recall
Review

Task 7.6

The newspaper article below has a lot of words missing. Look at it carefully and see if you can answer the questions that follow:

BRITISH COUPLE HURT IN EARTHQUAKE

_____ British couple _____ injured _____ earthquake _____
Greece _____ walking _____ cliffs _____ island _____
Lefkada _____ earthquake struck, _____ rocks _____on them.
_____ tremor, _____ 6.4 _____ Richter scale, _____early
hours. _____ hospital _____ Mr Steen _____ blood transfusion
_____ breaking _____ leg. _____ wife _____ head injuries.

1 Where was the earthquake?
2 Was anyone hurt?
3 What were they doing when the earthquake struck?
4 How big was the tremor?
5 What treatment did Mr Steen receive in hospital?
6 What injuries did his wife receive?

Key

For suggested answers, see 'Key to tasks' at the end of this chapter.

How many did you answer correctly?

We often get meaning from a text by reading just the key words. Read the next part of the article and underline what you think the key words are:

At least 22 other people were hurt, including four rock climbers who fell into the sea and two Italian tourists hit by falling rocks. A bridge linking the island with the mainland was clogged by traffic as people tried to flee. (From *Metro*, 15 August 2003)

Key

For suggested answer, see 'Key to tasks' at the end of this chapter.

Skim: read to get the main idea

This is when you run your eyes over the whole text very quickly. You are not interested in detail but are trying to understand the gist of the text – what is it about?

Task 7.7

Give your self a few minutes to skim read a newspaper or magazine article, or a short chapter in a book. First read the headline or title and try to predict what you think the text will be about, and then skim read the text quickly to see if your prediction was correct.

Key

For comments on this task, see 'key to tasks' at the end of this chapter.

Question: know why you are reading

Before you start reading for detail, you need to decide what questions you want your reading to answer. This is essential if you are going to get the most out of the text.

Task 7.8

Write down at least one question that you would like answered by reading the text you looked at in Task 7.7.

Read: in order to find the answer(s) to your question(s)

If your questions refer to the gist of the text (for example, 'What is the author's opinion about genetically modified food?') skim reading will help you. If they are looking for specific details (for example, 'In what year did the French Parliament open?') *scanning* will help you.

Scanning

This is when you are looking for specific detail rather than an overall idea. Again, it should be done quickly.

Identify the key words in your question and run your eyes over the text looking for those words. When you find the word, or a word, that has the same meaning, stop. Read this small section in detail to see if it contains the answer you are looking for. If it does not, continue to scan.

Think back to our example of reading a dictionary in task 7.2 . This is an example of scanning.

Sometimes you are looking for words, phrases or figures that can be found quickly by scanning for them in the text. For example, look at this question again: 'In what year did the French Parliament open?' Here, your key words to scan for are *French* and *Parliament*, but you also know that your answer must be a year, which is usually written in figures and therefore easy to find. The same is true of people's names or place-names that begin with capital letters.

Think while you read!
Making connections: Try to make connections while you are reading:

- Is there anything that is particularly relevant to your purpose; a quotation you could use, for example?
- Does anything you read remind you of something you have read or heard before?
- Does anything you read make you think of another question you would like answered?
- What is your personal reaction to what you read?

Make sure you underline relevant parts of the text and write your connections in the margins as you read – on a photocopy if the book is not your own!

Being critical: academic reading often requires you to read critically – in other words, to form opinions or make judgements about what you read. This involves the following:
- Identifying the writer's purpose for writing: does he or she want to inform you of the facts, or is he or she trying to persuade you of something?

- Being aware of any bias: is the writer being objective or is he or she writing from a particular viewpoint?
- Distinguishing between fact and opinion: how much of the information can be proven and how much is simply the writer's point of view?
- Evaluating the writer's argument: if the writer is trying to persuade you of a point of view, is his or her argument logical and convincing?

Signpost

See Chapter 9, 'Writing', for more information on argument.

Here is an example of a Japanese student's thoughts on two newspaper articles that she read about the new traffic congestion charge in London. What she says shows that she was thinking while she was reading:

> Then we read articles about the congestion charge. One was for the charge and the other was against it. I found the one that supported the congestion charge quite detailed and descriptive. What he said in the article was based on specific data and was reasonable. He successfully convinced me that the charge is not so bad. On the other hand, the writer who complained about the charge was just saying his opinion, which was strongly coloured. It was almost like he wanted to threaten people. He wrote about many possibilities but they were not reasonable and not based on proof.

Task 7.9

Think critically – try to answer the following questions. Consider:

1 *The source:* which would you expect to be more objective, a scientific report or a newspaper article?
2 *The author:* would you expect a marketing manager for fast-food chain McDonald's to write objectively or subjectively about the nutritional value of hamburgers?

Key

For suggested answers, see 'Key to tasks' at the end of this chapter.

One way of recognizing what is fact and what is opinion is to look at adjectives or adverbs. These are more likely to show someone's opinions. For example 'exciting', 'boring'.
(Korean student)

Recall
You need to make sure you can recall, or remember, what you have read and your thoughts about it, so you should make notes of the important ideas and your connections. Make notes from what you have underlined and noted in the margin. Write the notes in your own words.

Signpost

See Chapter 8 for more detailed information on note-making.

It is also useful to write a short summary of what you have read. This helps you to be clear about what you have understood and also gives you practice in expressing this in your own words.

Remember, if you cannot express what you have read in your own words, it is probably because you have not understood it properly.

Review
If there is anything you still do not fully understand, or cannot remember clearly, go back and read it again to check. Look up the words that you need in a dictionary.

KEEP A RECORD OF WHAT YOU READ

It is essential to keep a record of where the information came from so that you can go back and find it again if you need to, and so that you are able to write references for any ideas you are going to use.

Signpost

See Chapter 8, 'Making notes', for ideas about how to record this information.

Reading in English

It can be very frustrating to struggle to understand English texts about ideas and concepts that you already know, or that you know you would find a lot easier to understand if you read about them in your own language:

> It is a bit hard for me because I have to learn all the definitions and terms in English. I am sure that if I learnt them in Russian it would be much easier for me to understand the financial information.
>
> **(Russian student)**

SHOULD I READ TEXTS WRITTEN IN MY FIRST LANGUAGE?

Sometimes you may find it useful to back up your reading or check your understanding by reading texts written in your own language. However, it is a good idea to read in English as much as you can.

The more you read in English, the more English you will learn. Not only will this help you to do the English reading you have been set in your studies but also to express your ideas about what you have read in English, as you will be asked to do in seminars, assignments and exams.

TRANSLATING FROM ONE LANGUAGE INTO ANOTHER

If you read in your own language, at some point you will need to translate what you read into English so that you can use it. Translating is a very difficult skill. People study for many years to become good translators so, although the initial reading and understanding might be easier, you may find that you have problems when you come to use the material.

We are not suggesting that you never read information in your first language, especially at first, but you should try to read in English as much as you can:

> *I think the most difficult part for me is to read faster because English is not my mother language. I take a long time to translate it back into Chinese so I can understand the article.*
> **(Chinese student)**

Reading in English and translating it into your first language so that you can understand it is an approach that many international students use. It may be useful for you to do this sometimes, particularly when you are first beginning to read in English, but it is a very difficult strategy to do well and is time-consuming. A big problem with this approach is that students read and translate word by word. We have already seen that this is not a quick or effective reading strategy because understanding occurs at sentence or paragraph level.

Let us look at some of the difficulties involved in translating texts word for word and then consider some strategies you can use.

Words that look the same but have different meanings

Example

Example: words with more than one meaning

Compare the following two sentences:

1 'The government aims to *double* the number of students in higher education within 25 years.'
2 'Go through the *double* doors and turn left.'

> In the first sentence 'double' is a verb meaning to make something twice as much or many. In the second sentence it is an adjective, meaning twice the amount or consisting of two similar things together. These are not the only two ways to use 'double'. It can also be a noun that means 'a person who looks exactly the same as someone else'.

In this case, the meaning of the word changes when it is used as a different part of speech. But some words also change meaning because of the context they are used in.

Task 7.10

Look up the word 'register' in a good learner's English–English dictionary:

1 How many different meanings of the word can you find?
2 When does the word change meaning because it is used as a different part of speech?
3 When does the word change meaning because of the context?

Key

For suggested answers, see 'Key to tasks' at the end of this chapter.

Signpost

See the 'useful resources' section in Chapter 4 for a list of learners' dictionaries.

False friends

A 'false friend' is a word that is often confused with another word in another language because the two words look or sound similar, but which have different meanings. For example, the French word *'actuellement'* and the English word 'actually' are false friends. They look and sound very similar but *'actuellement'* means 'nowadays' and 'actually' means 'in fact' or 'really'.

Example: false friends

Here are some other examples of false friends:

- The Finnish word '*kaniini*' means 'rabbit' but sounds and looks very similar to the English word 'canine', which means 'of or relating to dogs'.
- The Swedish word '*affär*' means 'shop' but sounds and looks similar to the English word 'affair', which means 'a situation or subject that is being dealt with or considered'.
- The German word '*konsequent*' means 'consistently' but looks and sounds similar to the English word 'consequently', which means 'as a result'.
- The Spanish word '*decepción*' means 'disappointment' but looks and sounds very similar to the English word 'deception', which means 'when people hide the truth, especially to get an advantage'.

Are any words in your first language false friends with an English word?

Varieties of English

Because of its history there are many varieties of the English language: British English, American English, Australian English, Canadian English, Indian English and West Indian English, to name just a few. Although you will not necessarily encounter all these in your academic reading, you do need to be aware of them. American and British English may be two of the varieties that you come across the most frequently in your academic reading.

Task 7.11

Write AE next to the definitions that you think are American English and BE next to those you think are British English:

1 *Elevator:* a small room which carries people or goods up and down in tall buildings.
2 *Subway:* an underground passage which allows people on foot to cross a busy road.

3 *Gas:* a liquid obtained from petroleum, used especially as a fuel for cars.

Key

For suggested answers, see 'Key to tasks' at the end of this chapter.

Cultural differences

The way we express our ideas through language is affected by culture. This means the following:

- Sometimes we are unable to express an idea in another language. For example, it would not be possible to translate the English sentence 'The aeroplane soared through the sky like a bird' into the language of the Hopi Native Americans because in their language there is only one word for anything that flies in the sky!
- Sometimes people from different cultures express ideas in different ways. We need to understand the culture and the context as well as the words in order to interpret the meaning. For example, most native English speakers would understand the sentence 'He felt blue' to be an informal way of saying that he felt sad. Try translating this word for word into your own language. Does it still have the same meaning?

Task 7.12

See if you can find out the intended meanings of the following idioms:

1 'If the team is winning, *don't rock the boat.*'
2 'In a government scandal, there's always *more than meets the eye.*'

Key

For suggested answers, see 'Key to tasks' at the end of this chapter.

- Idioms are expressions that have a different meaning from the meaning of each word as it would be understood on its own. For example, to 'have bitten off more than you can chew' is an idiom that means you have tried to do something which is too difficult for you. People who share the same culture usually share an understanding of these expressions. However, they can be difficult for learners of a language to understand because translating each word in the expression will not help you understand the intended meaning. There are special idiom dictionaries which list frequently used English idioms with their definitions.

- Sometimes people react to the content of a text in different ways. For example, a group of international students were given a text about the negative impact of cars on society. Many students found this argument easy to follow and agreed with it, perhaps because they came from countries where cars have been common for a long time and where traffic congestion and pollution caused by cars are common problems. However, some students found the argument very difficult to accept because they came from countries where cars were just beginning to be a major method of transport and were seen as a positive sign of technological and economic development.

- Sometimes authors, especially in journalistic or more informal texts, refer to 'famous' people, places or incidents in their writing. However, they may only be 'famous' to people within that country or culture.

Example: 'fame'

Look at the following example from a newspaper article about a man who wanted to join the army:

All Tom Wrigley, 17, wanted to do was become a soldier but with a 46 inch waist and a nickname of Thomas the Tank Engine, he failed to get past the recruiting sergeant. (Taken from 'Army blues of the super slim recruit' by Stephen Hull, *Metro*, 15 August 2003)

What do you think the nickname 'Thomas the Tank Engine' means?

'Thomas the Tank Engine' is a character from a children's television programme and series of books that are very popular in England. Having this as a nickname implies that Tom Wrigley looked like the character – in other words, he was fat. You would not know this unless you were familiar with the television programme or the books.

STRATEGIES FOR READING IN ENGLISH

Do not approach a text word by word

If you do, you will read slowly and will probably find it difficult to make sense of what you read. Instead, approach the text paragraph by paragraph. Read a paragraph and try to understand the main idea.

Task 7.13

Read the list of questions below and then read the paragraph taken from the article 'Six billion and rising' by Emily Moore. Which of the questions would be an appropriate heading for the paragraph?

1 Why do people in poor countries have more children than those in richer countries?
2 Are all the countries growing at about the same rate?
3 Can the world support six billion people?
4 Why has the population grown so much?
5 What kinds of problems does the world's growing population bring?

Richer countries with ageing populations face the challenge of providing support and medical care for the elderly. Poorer countries with growing birth rates, such as those in sub-Saharan Africa, face the problem of having too many mouths to feed and not enough resources. In general, more people on the planet increase the pressure on our environment – for example forests being chopped down, in order to use the wood and farm the land. However, before poor people are blamed for the world's problems, remember that it is the richer, developed countries which consume the bulk of the world's food, fuel and water and cause the most environmental damage. (From the *Guardian Education*, 12 October 1999)

Key

For a suggested answer, see 'Key to tasks' at the end of this chapter.

You may find it useful to write a one or two word heading in the margin for each paragraph you read. This will help you to think about what the main idea of each paragraph is.

Start with easy texts

> *I found it difficult to understand completely, because I didn't have any background knowledge and so I didn't know the words for this.*
> **(Korean student)**

If the subject is new to you, the language used to describe it will be, too. Start off with easy texts to help familiarize yourself with the main ideas about your subject and the English.

If you are familiar with the subject but not with the English used to describe it, starting with easy texts will be a good way of learning the English and revising your knowledge of the subject.

Move on to more difficult texts as your understanding of both the language and the subject grows.

Keep a record of new words
Try to distinguish between new words which are specific to your subject, new words which are used mainly in academic writing and new words which are used in general English. Record those you think you need to learn.

Signpost

See Chapter 4, 'Building vocabulary', for more information about extending your English vocabulary.

Terminology which is specific to your subject may not always be found in a general learner's dictionary, but there are specialized dictionaries and vocabulary workbooks that you can look at, such as workbooks for banking and finance, computing, law, marketing and medicine or dictionaries of accounting, business, ecology and environment, and science and technology, to name just a few.

Signpost

See the 'Useful resources' section at the end of this chapter and at the end of Chapter 4 for more detailed information about these.

Read with your friends

Collaborative reading can be a very useful strategy. If you and another student have been set the same text to read or are researching a similar topic, try understanding the text together.

Task 7.14

Choose a suitable text (an article in a journal or periodical, or a short chapter in a book about your subject). Complete the task below with another student or a small group of students:

1 Look at the title of the text together. Look at the source and any other headings or pictures. Try to guess what the text is about.
2 Skim read the article quickly, without using a dictionary, to check your ideas. Discuss these together.
3 Read the text again carefully and reflectively, underlining and making notes in the margin.
4 Discuss any difficult vocabulary together. Look up the words you need to in a dictionary. Discuss parts of the text that you do not understand. Try to understand it together.
5 Now put the article to one side. With your partner try to decide what you think the main point of the article is. Write it down. Then, together, try to decide on the points you think are important.
6 Discuss your own opinions about what you have read.

How did you find reading in this way? What do you think are the advantages of reading collaboratively?

Reading together means that you can:

- share vocabulary;
- share knowledge of the subject;

- share cultural knowledge;
- help each other to understand parts of the text that are difficult;
- discuss the aims and argument of the article; and
- share different views about what the author has written.

This sharing of ideas and active engagement with the text can lead not only to a better understanding of the written English but also to a deeper understanding of the topic itself.

Make a habit of reading

I had a tutorial with my tutor about my problems with reading. She told me I have to get into the habit of reading. She advised me to read something that is not too hard, that does not have too many difficult or technical words. I should read on my way to and from university, in my free time and before I go to sleep. I found a book written for tourists in London. I'm going to read it to improve my reading and my knowledge about what to do in London.
(Iranian student)

Think about the kind of reading you enjoy in your first language – make a list. It could include anything from comics or fashion magazines, to autobiographies or detective novels.

Now try reading the same kinds of texts in English – but start with easy ones first. You will not need to read reflectively because you are reading for fun, not for your studies. Do not worry if it is difficult to understand at first or if you cannot understand every detail. Avoid looking up every word in a dictionary – keep on reading and try to understand the main ideas. The more you read, the easier reading in English will become. You will soon find that you can understand texts in English without having to translate them.

Conclusion

Read wherever you can – on the bus, on the train, in bed before you go to sleep.
(Chinese student)

Reading can be improved by practising all the time.
(Korean student)

In this chapter we have looked at the importance of reading at university and discussed strategies to help you read actively, reflectively and critically, and to cope with reading in English. Hopefully, you will feel confident about approaching the reading you need to do for your course. Do not put it off! The important thing is to start reading straightaway and to read selectively and reflectively. You will feel more motivated if you try to read about things that genuinely interest you. Your knowledge of the subject, your understanding of the subject language and of academic English – and your reading skills – will all increase the more you read. So, reading for your studies will become easier and more enjoyable!

USEFUL RESOURCES

http://www.uefap.co.uk/reading/readfram.htm
This is part of the website for the University of Hertfordshire and it gives helpful advice on aspects of reading in academic contexts for international students.

http://www.une.edu.au/tlc/aso/reading.htm
This site has a number of links to web pages with advice on active and effective academic reading strategies.

http://www.unisanet.unisa.edu.au/learningconnection/learnres/learng/#Reading
This link takes you to a learning guide 'Getting the most from your academic reading', which is in the form of a Word document.

Burns, T. and Sinfield, S. (2003) *Essential Study Skills*. London: Sage.
Chapter 3, 'How to research and read academically'.
Cottrell, S. (1999) *The Study Skills Handbook*. Basingstoke: Palgrave.
Chapter 6, 'Research skills', and Chapter 9, 'Critical analytical thinking'.
Fairbairn, G. and Fairbairn, S. (2001) *Reading at University*. Buckingham: Open University Press.
This book includes tasks to help develop academic reading strategies.
Glendinning, E. and Holmstrum, B. (1992) *Study Reading: A Course in Reading Skills for Academic Purposes*. Cambridge: Cambridge University Press.
This is aimed specifically at international students studying in English.
Roseberry, R. and Weinstock, R. (1992) *Reading, Etc.* Englewood Cliffs. New Jersey: Prentice Hall.
This is aimed at international students studying in English and includes varied active reading tasks.
Waters, A. and Waters, M. (1995) *Study Tasks in English*. Cambridge: Cambridge University Press.

A practical and task-based book for international students studying in English. Unit 4, 'Finding information', deals with finding information in libraries, books and other sources. Unit 6, 'Coping with extended English', looks at reading actively and effectively and includes a section on dealing with unfamiliar vocabulary.

USEFUL DICTIONARIES

Collin, P. (2001) *Dictionary of Business*. London: Peter Collin Publishing (Bloomsbury Reference).
Collins Cobuild Dictionary of Idioms (1995) London: HarperCollins.
Collins Cobuild Idioms Workbook (1995). London: HarperCollins.
   This is a workbook based on the Collins Cobuild dictionary above.
Encarta World English Dictionary (1999). London: Bloomsbury.
   This dictionary brings together all the main varieties of English.
English Study Dictionary (2000). London: Peter Collin Publishing (Bloomsbury Reference).
   This dictionary includes terms relevant to university students.
Stephens, A. (1996) *Dictionary of Agriculture*. London: Peter Collin Publishing (Bloomsbury Reference).

See the 'Useful resources' section in Chapter 4 for more dictionaries.

KEY TO TASKS

Task 7.2
A fiction book: You would probably read this all, from beginning to end (although not necessarily in one go!). You would usually read at a fairly steady pace, perhaps even quite quickly. You would read to understand, but would not read particularly carefully as you are not interested in studying the content in detail or being able to remember it.

A magazine: you would probably not read this from cover to cover but, rather, skim through the magazine very quickly, looking at headlines and photographs until you see something that interests you. Then you might stop and read that section in a similar way to reading a book of fiction.

A dictionary: you would certainly not read the whole dictionary! You would know exactly what you were looking for before starting to read. You would go straight to the section that contained words beginning with the same letter as the word you were looking for. You would run your eyes very quickly over the list of words until you found it. Then you would stop and read the definition slowly and carefully, maybe even making a note of it.

Task 7.3

The books you would probably want to consult are Comfort and Utley (1995), Cottrell (1999) and Waters and Waters (1995). The most relevant of the three is *Effective Presentations* (Comfort and Utley), as the whole book deals with oral presentations. However, you may expect to find a chapter or section on presentations in the other two books. The remaining books on the list refer specifically to writing and so would not be relevant for this particular assignment.

Task 7.4

You may not find all this information in every book you read because there are variations in the way they are presented. However, you should be able to find most of it:

1 The title will indicate the general topic of the book.

2 You might recognize the name of the author or editor as someone mentioned on your reading list or in a lecture.

3 You should find the date of publication just inside the front of the book. If the book was published a long time ago, the information may be out of date.

4 Information about whether the book has been updated should be near the publication date. If its says 'second (or third, etc.) edition' it means the book has been updated. You should always try to read recently published texts or the latest edition of a book.

5 The publisher's 'blurb' is a short description of the book, usually found on the back cover. It should give you information about what the book covers, who the author is and what kind of audience it is aimed at. The publisher's blurb should also tell you about the author's credentials.

6 The contents page will tell you exactly what kind of areas are covered in each chapter. This can help you decide which parts of the book you need to read, and which you do not.

7 There is often an introduction at the start of the book, written by the author. This is sometimes called a 'preface' or 'foreword'. It will explain the author's aims, approach and the scope of the book – that is, the author's intentions, what he or she has covered and what is not included.

8 The bibliography or list of references, usually at the end of the book (or at the end of each essay or article) and before the index, will show you how extensive the author's sources are. Importantly, it can also give you ideas about where else you can go for more information on the same topic.

9 If your book has an index (an alphabetical list printed at the back showing which page a subject, name, etc., is found on), this can be a quick way of finding out if the information you are interested in is covered in the book.

10 Flicking quickly through the book will give you an idea of whether you like the way it is presented. Do you want lots of examples and illustrations? Do you want activities and tasks? Do you want plain text?

Task 7.6
British couple hurt in earthquake

A British couple were seriously injured in an earthquake which struck Greece yesterday. Tom and Sylvia Steen were walking beside cliffs on the island of Lefkada when the earthquake struck, sending rocks raining down on them. The tremor, which measured 6.4 on the Richter scale, hit in the early hours. They were taken to hospital where Mr Steen received a blood transfusion after breaking his leg. His wife suffered head injuries.

1 In Greece.
2 Mr and Mrs Steen.
3 Walking on the cliffs.
4 6.4 on the Richter scale.
5 A blood transfusion.
6 Head injuries.

At least <u>22</u> other <u>people</u> were <u>hurt</u>, including <u>four</u> rock <u>climbers</u> who <u>fell</u> into the <u>sea</u> and <u>two</u> Italian <u>tourists</u> <u>hit</u> by falling <u>rocks</u>. A <u>bridge</u> linking the <u>island</u> with the <u>mainland</u> was <u>clogged</u> by <u>traffic</u> as <u>people</u> tried to <u>flee</u>.

Task 7.7
Did you notice how you read the text? You should not have read every word. Looking at headings, subheadings or pictures can give you a lot of information very quickly. Reading the very beginning and very end of a passage is useful as main ideas are often introduced at the start and summarized at the end. Reading the first line of each paragraph may indicate its main point. You might notice that some key words are repeated or recognize words that belong to the same *semantic field*. These words will help you to identify what the topic of the text is.

Semantic field: semantics is the study of meanings in a language. A semantic field is a group of words that can be grouped together by meaning. For example, 'bed', 'snore', 'dream', 'pyjamas' and 'tired' all belong to the semantic field of 'sleep'.

Task 7.9

A scientific report. Although a newspaper report will usually contain some facts, it can also be written from a specific viewpoint, either the journalist's point of view or in accordance with the political leanings of the newspaper. However, a scientific report would be based on proven data and would not necessarily include any opinion at all.

You would probably expect him or her to write *subjectively,* as he or she would have a vested interest – a strong personal interest in the topic because he or she could benefit from it.

Task 7.10

Depending on what dictionary you used, you should have found at least seven or eight different meanings for the word 'register'. The first meaning is similar to a list, and this can be used as a verb – to put something on to an official list – or as a noun – the book or record of a list of names. However, there are six further uses of the word, three nouns and three verbs, where you would have to understand the context in order to know which interpretation of the word to use.

For example, the verb 'to register' can also mean to show, record or express something, to be aware of something or to register a letter or parcel so that it is delivered using a special postal service.

'Register' the noun can mean the range of notes a musical instrument or a person's voice can produce, the style of language, grammar and words used for particular situations or a cash register – the American English word for 'till'.

Task 7.11

1 'Elevator' is American English. The British English word for this is 'lift'.
2 'Subway'-is British English. The American English for this is 'underpass'. In American English a 'subway' is an underground railway.
3 'Gas' is American English. The British English for this is 'petrol'. In British English 'gas' is 'a substance in air-like form that is used as a fuel for heating and cooking'.

Task 7.12

1 'Don't rock the boat': do not cause change, do not upset anything.
2 'More than meets the eye': part of the story has not been told.

Task 7.13

5 'What kind of problems does the world's growing population bring?' is the best answer.

8 Making notes

By studying and doing the activities in this chapter you should:

♦ be aware of the importance of note-making;
♦ learn how to make active notes;
♦ consider different note-making styles;
♦ develop strategies for making notes from reading and from lectures; and
♦ understand how to use notes for revising, thinking and planning.

GLOSSARY

These key words will be useful to you while reading this chapter:

Brainstorm: To suggest a lot of ideas for a future activity very quickly before considering some of them more carefully.
Concise: Short and clear, expressing what needs to be said without unnecessary words.
Dam: A wall built across a river which stops the river's flow and collects the water.
Dictaphone: A machine used to record spoken words and later repeat them aloud so that they can be written down.
Hierarchy: A system in which people or things are arranged according to their importance.
Illegible: Impossible to read because of being very unclear or untidy.
Legible: Describes writing or print that can be read easily.

Plagiarism: To use another person's idea or a part of his or her work and pretend that it is your own.

Rhyme: A word which has the same last sound as another word; a short poem.

Quotation: A phrase or short piece of writing taken from a longer work, or what someone else has said.

Synthesize: To combine different ideas, facts or experiences to form a single idea.

Trigger: To cause something to start.

Why do we make notes?

Note-making helps understanding and memory, so I have to be sure of what the important points are.

Japanese student

Task 8. 1

Think about notes you have made in the past, or are making now, and answer the following two questions:

1 When do you make notes?
2 Why do you make notes?

Compare your ideas with ours below.

WHEN DO YOU MAKE NOTES?

You will want to make notes from your lectures and seminars and from your reading, but you may also make notes when you are revising for exams or planning assignments.

WHY DO YOU MAKE NOTES?

To act as a memory aid

One of the main reasons we make notes is to help us remember what we have learnt. Although you may think at the time that you will remember the information, research has shown (Buzan, 1988) that we forget 98% of what we have read or heard after only three weeks!

To use
You will have to use what you have learnt for specific tasks, such as writing an essay or report, giving a presentation or sitting an exam.

To learn and understand
If you make notes in the right way, it means that you are thinking about what you have read or heard while you are making them. Engaging with the material in this way can help your understanding of it.

WHAT SHOULD I MAKE NOTES OF?

Example: making notes

Consider this example:

Two students have been researching information for an essay. After a few hours spent reading in the library, student A leaves with 10 pages of densely written notes. Student B, on the other hand, leaves with 3 sheets of paper, one for each of the articles she has read, with brief notes. Which student do you think is the more effective note-maker?

It is probably student B who will have made more effective notes. She is more likely to have selected the information she needs, written a few key words to remind her of the main ideas and left with notes that will be easy for her to use in the future. This is much more effective than writing down almost everything you read! There is no point in copying out information that you do not understand or that you do not need.

For your notes to be useful you need to make sure that you:

- ◆ know why you are making notes and what you will use them for; and
- ◆ only make notes of relevant and important points.

Remember, your notes should be shorter than the original source!

ACTIVE NOTE-MAKING

You may have noticed that in this chapter we use the phrase *making* notes rather than *taking* notes. What do you think is the difference between the two?

> *I have learned to make notes not to take notes. Before, when the teacher told me something I just wrote it down, but this was very passive and limited my understanding. Now I know I should make notes only of the important things. We don't need to remember every detail, but we need to reflect on the important ones.*
> **(Korean student)**

Taking notes
This implies a passive approach where you simply copy down what your lecturer says, or what you think are important passages from a text. You may not really be thinking about the ideas you are writing down and you might even write down information that you do not understand! Students who *take* notes tend to write too much and find their notes difficult to use.

Making notes
This implies a much more active approach. When you make notes you try to understand the ideas and decide which points will be useful for you to make a record of. You are selecting information and thinking actively about how you want to use it. Students who *make* notes tend to write down key words or phrases rather than sentences and also add their own ideas. Their notes are shorter but more relevant and therefore easier to use and remember.

Task 8.2

What kind of notes do you make? Look back at some notes you have made recently and answer the following questions:

Can you read and understand them easily?

+ Have you written anything down that you cannot understand?
+ Does reading them again help you to remember other information on the topic?
+ Is it easy to see which ideas are more important than others?

◆ Is there a structure to your notes?
◆ Are they brief and written in key words, or are they detailed and written in sentences?
◆ Have you written down where the information came from?

Imagine you had to use these notes to help you write an essay. Rate their usefulness on a scale of 1 to 10, where 1 is not very useful at all and 10 is extremely useful.

In the rest of the chapter we will look at strategies for making your notes as useful as possible.

Making notes from reading

Task 8.3

How do you make notes when you are reading? Look at the list below and tick any of the things you do:

◆ Print out pages from the Internet.
◆ Copy and paste useful information from electronic sources.
◆ Copy out important words, phrases and sentences.
◆ Copy out useful quotations.
◆ Write down key words for each paragraph.
◆ Underline or highlight important words, phrases and sentences on the page.
◆ Summarize the main ideas of each paragraph.
◆ Memorize and learn by heart important words, phrases or sentences.
◆ Make notes on a separate piece of paper.
◆ Write down where the information came from.

Key

For comments on this task, see 'Key to tasks' at the end of this chapter.

COPYING PARTS OF WHAT YOU READ

Many students print out or copy and paste information from electronic sources, as this is a fast way of recording useful information you have found. On paper texts it is common for students to highlight important ideas on the page, or to copy, word for word, parts they think will be useful.

The problem with these methods is that your notes will be very difficult for you to use effectively in the future. When you come to write your essay or give your presentation, you will be expected to synthesize the ideas that you have found from a variety of sources and discuss them in your own words. If, in your notes, you have copied directly from your sources, it will be very difficult for you to write the ideas in your own words in the assignment. This means you may be accused of plagiarism, which is a very serious offence in academic writing.

Plagiarism is not just when you use someone else's words but also when you use someone else's ideas without acknowledging them. If you do not write down where the information came from, you will not be able to acknowledge your sources in your assignment.

Signpost

See Chapter 9, 'Writing', for more information on writing references.

The only time it is acceptable to copy parts of what you read is if you read a phrase or a short sentence that you think you would like to use as a quotation. Then you must write this out in full. You need to make sure that you:

- use quotation marks (" " or ' ') to open and close the quotation;
- copy it exactly as it is written in the text; and
- write down who said it and on what page of the text it appears.

Quotations can be useful but you should not use too many of them and you should avoid using long quotations.

MAKING NOTES IN YOUR OWN WORDS

A problem is that before you make notes from a passage you must understand what the passage is about, but sometimes I can't understand it very well because my English reading skills are poor. I find it hard to decide which point is important and which is not. **(Chinese student)**

It is impossible to make useful notes unless you have understood what you have read. This will get easier as your knowledge of your subject and your English reading skills increase.

However, sometimes the problem is that students try to make notes too soon, before they have given themselves time really to think about the content or about what they are making notes for.

Signpost

You should read Chapter 7 for ideas about reading in English.

Know your purpose for making notes and make sure you understand the text
First, make sure you know why you are reading. What information are you looking for? What will you use it to do? It is a good idea to put your pen down when you read the passage for the first time so that you can concentrate on understanding the text. When you have finished reading, stop to think about what you have understood. If you have not understood the passage, go back and read it again. It is fine to underline and highlight points on the page (or on a photocopy) while you are reading, but you will have to make your own notes as well.

Make notes on a separate piece of paper
Put the text to one side and take a fresh piece of paper. Without looking back at the text, write down what you can remember. Do not write in sentences. Write down in a few words what you think the main idea is. Then write down key words that remind you of the points that are relevant to you. Making notes on a separate piece of paper will help you to:

- focus on what you have understood; and
- avoid copying chunks of text.

I found note-making difficult. I wanted to write the information down in a short and easy way. But I always write the whole sentence. I think this problem is because of my English.
(Japanese student)

It can be difficult to make notes of ideas that you have read in your own words if you have a limited range of English to use. Again, as your English vocabulary increases this will become easier. Meanwhile, do not try to memorize chunks of text. Concentrate on the ideas that you have understood, and only write down key words – the words that carry meaning. Do not write in full sentences.

When you come to use your notes, you will be constructing the sentences yourself from the key words:

Signpost

If you are not sure about how to identify key words, Task 7.6 in Chapter 7 will help you.

It was very difficult for me to write down big sentences in a few words but learning about note-making helped me to realize that I do not have to copy everything down and that it is easier for me to write just a word that gives the meaning.
(Cypriot student)

Task 8.4

Read the short passage below and try to understand it. Do not write anything until you think you have understood the main ideas. Then, without looking back at the passage, write down the key words on a separate piece of paper. Remember, you are interested in the main ideas, not the details:

In the mid-nineteenth century, an average worker clocked up around 75 hours a week at work. The Factory Act of 1844 legislated that women and children were not allowed to work longer than 12-hour days, which was seen as a major concession to the rights of workers. At the end of the century, a 54-hour week was still common, made up of six nine-hour days. By the early decades of the last century, manual workers were putting in 47-hour weeks. That had dropped to 44 hours by the Fifties.

In short, the number of hours worked in this country dropped steadily for 150 years. But then, in the Eighties, it started going up again; from 44.3 to 47 hours a week for men working full time, and from 40 to 43 for women. (approx. 130 words)
(From 'Work–life balance', in *Realtime*, supplement to the *Observer*, 2003)

Now write a summary from your key words. Do not look back at the article until you have finished writing.

Key

For suggested answers, see 'Key to tasks' at the end of this chapter.

Summarize
Writing brief summaries like this can be a useful way of making notes. It provides you with a concise overview of the main points. Always make sure that you understand first, then write the key words, and then construct your sentences. Look at the number of words used in the original text compared with the summary. Notice how much shorter than the original the summary is.

Task 8.5

Find the verbs 'dropped' and 'going up' in the text in Task 8.4. What verbs were used instead of these in the summary?

Key

For suggested answers, see 'Key to tasks' at the end of this chapter.

These are synonyms – words that have the same or similar meanings to other words. It can be useful to use synonyms in your notes to help you express ideas in your own words.

MAKING NOTES OF CONNECTIONS AND QUESTIONS

You should include any connections that you make when reading in your notes. For example, is there anything that is particularly relevant to your purpose – a quotation you could use? Does anything remind you of something you have read or heard before? Does anything you read make you think of another question you would like answered? What is your personal reaction to what you read? Include any thoughts you have on your notes.

It is also important that you make a note of anything you have not understood, so that you remember to go and find out about it later.

Example: Index cards

Study the example index card below:

Topic	1 *READING*
Author(s)	2 *Fairbairn, G. and Fairnbairn, S.*
Year of publication	3 *2001*
Title	4 *Reading at University – A Guide for Students*
Edition	5 *1st edition*
Publisher	6 *Buckingham and Philadelphia – Open University Press (OUP)*
Where to find a copy	7 *Learning Centre (London Metropolitan University). Shelf mark: StudyCol 37.17028?FAI*
Summary of contents	8 *Reading as a student, developing reading skills, active reading, deciding what to read, note-taking, writing where and when to read, collaborative reading, proofreading.*

KEEP A RECORD OF WHAT YOU HAVE READ

It is essential that you keep a record of where you found the information you are recording. When you come to use your notes, you will need this information to reference ideas taken from your reading. You may also want to go back to the text to check information at a later stage. It is much easier for you to do this if you keep a record of what you read as you go along. If you do not keep a record you can waste a lot of time trying to remember which text the information was in and where you found it. This can be very frustrating! A good method is to use index cards.

Task 8.6

Write an index card for a text you are studying. If you are not studying at the moment, write one for this book.

Making notes from lectures

I sometimes miss a lot of important things in lectures, because I am too busy taking notes.
(Japanese student)

I believe that I have improved my manner of studying because now I write notes when the teacher is speaking, whereas before I just listened in class.
(Filipino student)

If you try to write down everything your lecturer tells you about (taking notes) you will miss a lot of what he or she says. If you listen but do not write any notes at all, you may understand more of the lecture but you will probably not remember the information later on. Just like making notes from reading, the idea is to try to understand the main ideas and write down the key words that will help you to remember them. You should also make a note of any references the lecturer makes of experts or specific texts that you can consult afterwards for more information.

POINTS THAT CAN HELP

Try to understand the way the lecturer structures his or her lecture. Try to structure your notes in the same way. Notice signposting language.

This language often indicates the way the lecture is structured and when new or important points are being made.

Signpost

See Chapter 6, 'Giving oral presentations', pages 133–4, for more information about this.

Make use of any visual aids the lecturer uses. These may contain key points which you could use for your notes.

Remember that there is often a time at the end of the lecture for questions. This may give you the opportunity to clarify anything you are not sure about. Do not be shy about approaching the lecturer. Most are only too happy to spend a few minutes helping you (see below).

As your skill at understanding spoken English grows you will find it easier to understand your lectures.

If there is anything that you missed or did not understand, put a question mark ('?') on your notes so that you remember to check this information afterwards.

Signpost

See Chapter 3 for ideas about understanding spoken English.

REVIEW YOUR NOTES AFTER THE LECTURE

You have less time to make notes in a lecture than when you are making notes from reading. You cannot go back to listen again to anything you are unsure of. Therefore, it is very important that you review your notes immediately after the lecture has finished:

When I read my notes again, I need to understand what I have learned. I need to work on making my notes clear because otherwise I will not be able to read them again. Tip: take time after class. It is so easy to do, but if you don't it takes only 15 minutes before you forget the important points of the lecture.
(Japanese student)

Discuss the lecture with other students
It is always a good idea to discuss your notes with other students as soon as possible after the lecture. Your friends might be able to answer some of your questions, explain things that you have not understood or fill in the gaps that you have missed and you can do the same for them. Ensure that you make notes here too, so that you do not forget the important information you share.

Discussing the lecture afterwards will also help you engage with the information you have heard and reinforce your learning. You may find that the discussion helps you to understand how the lecture fits in with the rest of your studies, or is relevant to particular assignments. It is an opportunity for you to look at the way other students are making notes which can help you to become a more effective-note maker. This kind of group work, perhaps over a cup of coffee, can be a very enjoyable and motivating way to study.

Talk to your lecturer

> *I think the tutor already knows me as a student who always asks a lot of questions because after every class I speak to him about what I haven't understood and write notes of what he says to me.*
> **(Filipino student)**

You might be able to clarify points that you have not understood with your lecturer after the lecture. If this is not possible, because there are too many students or if the lecturer is busy, you could make notes of points to ask about in a tutorial or via email, if these methods of communication are available to you.

Are your notes legible?
Because you have to make notes so quickly during lectures, you may find that you have written something down but that, later on, you cannot read your own writing! You should check your notes immediately after the lecture has finished. If you do this you are likely to remember what the strange untidy writing on the page is supposed to mean but if you leave it any longer, you may never remember.

KEEP A RECORD

Make sure you include the name of your lecturer and the title and date of the lecture in your notes. It will make them much easier to find and use in the future.

Different note-making styles

LINEAR NOTES AND PATTERN NOTES

There is a variety of note-making styles. Some suit some people more than others:

> *Note-making is going to help me when I have to make notes from lectures and talks or from a text. I have to improve and choose a note-making style. I will improve by practice and practice.*
> **(Cypriot student)**

Task 8.7

Look at the examples of linear and pattern notes. They are both sets of notes on this chapter so far. Read them and decide which you prefer. The questions below might help you to decide:

- Do you think the notes would have been easy to make?
- Are they easy to read and understand?
- Would they be easy to use?
- Would they be easy to remember?

There is not one correct note-making style. You should choose a style that suits you. However, you cannot choose sensibly if you have not tried different options. Many students are familiar with the kind of linear notes illustrated here but have not tried pattern notes before. They are uncomfortable with pattern notes at first because they are not used to them but often find that, with practice, this more active and creative note-making style is the most useful:

> *We agreed that pattern note-making is difficult when making notes but easier to use and understand. Most of my notes now are pattern notes.*
> **(Ethiopian student)**

Some advantages of pattern notes over linear notes are as follows:

- The main idea is in the centre so it stands out more.
- It is easier to see the relative importance of each idea, as the more important ideas are nearer the centre.

NOTES (from Chp 8 'Making Notes')

Why? memory aid, use for essay etc., active learning

When? lectures, seminars, reading, revising, thinking & planning

What? main points <u>only</u>. Info. that is relevant & impt (key words)

How? making notes = being active:
1) understand
2) select info (what is it pr?)
3) write key words
keep it short → easy to remember → personal
– Linear notes v pattern notes?

<u>Notes from reading</u>
Don't copy (except quotes)
Use own words — key words on separate paper
Write connections and questions
Keep a record of the book /source

<u>Notes from listening</u>
As above: main ideas → key words
Review immediately ┬ with friends /ask lecturer
                    └ check I can read & understand
Keep a record: name of lecturer, title of lecture
& date (I always forget this!)

Linear notes

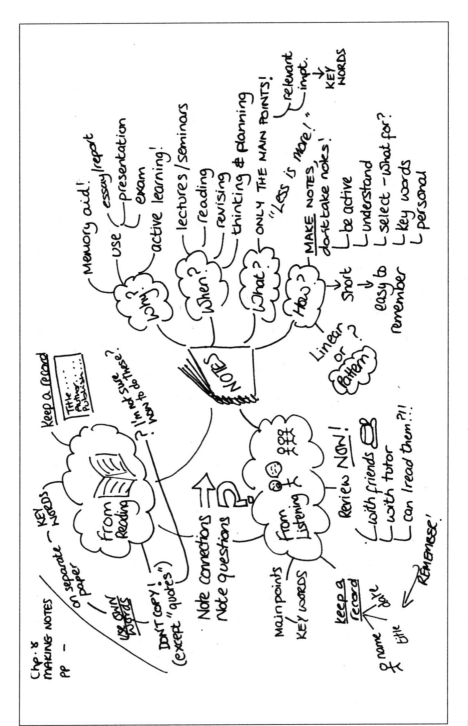

Pattern notes

- It is easy to indicate links and relationships between ideas.
- It is easy to add new information or ideas at a later date.
- It is a more creative and active way of note-making which promotes learning (Buzan, 1988).

We would strongly recommend that you practise different note-making styles until you are familiar with them. Then you can make a real decision about which ones work best for you. Use the questions in Task 8.7 to help you evaluate how you use the different styles.

WHAT KIND OF LEARNER ARE YOU?

Signpost

In Chapter 2, 'Being an effective learner', you started to think about what kind of learner you are: for example visual, auditory or physical. Thinking about your personal learning style may help you decide which note-making style might be the most suitable for you.

If you are a visual learner, someone who likes to see things, most of the styles we have mentioned may work for you. However, if you like to see pictures rather than words, you may find pattern notes easier to use and remember.

If you are an auditory learner, someone who likes to hear things, it may be that you could use a different style altogether:

I definitely remember things better when I hear them. I speak my notes into a dictaphone and then listen to them.
(Bangladeshi student)

If you are a physical learner, most note-making styles might suit you because by making notes you are *doing* something when you are listening and reading. Try putting your notes on cards that you can then order and rearrange.

MAKING YOUR NOTES PERSONAL AND MEMORABLE

Whichever style you decide to use, try to make your notes as personal and memorable as possible.

Memory triggers

Think about what kind of impact your notes make. Try to keep notes for one topic on one page if you can. You may find that when you try to remember the topic, you remember the page as a shape and you can recall specific points by remembering their position on the page.

Using colours, pictures or cartoons, and even rhymes, can make your notes more interesting, more personal and more fun. This all helps to make them easier to remember.

Organization

> *I could hardly understand the notes I had made myself, especially the disordered hierarchy of the notes.*
> **(Chinese student)**

It is essential that there is some sort of organization to your notes if you are going to understand and remember what your key words mean. How are the points related to each other? Which points are more important than other points? If this is not indicated then you are left with a disorderly mixture of unrelated ideas.

Using colour can be very effective. For example, if you are making notes on the advantages and disadvantages of a particular topic, you could write all the plus points in red and all the minus points in blue. One student who was studying German told me that she used colour when learning verb endings of tenses. In her notes the root of the verb was always written in black, but the endings were recorded in a different colour to highlight them.

You can use arrows → to link related ideas, or use a numbering system, 1 ..., 2 ..., 3 ...., to show the order or hierarchy of points.

There are other ways of highlighting important ideas:

underlining
using CAPITAL LETTERS

◆ using bullet points

putting ideas in boxes

or shapes

Look back at the illustrations and notice how the notes are organized.

Abbreviations, acronyms and symbols
These can all be useful in note-making. They can save time when making notes and save space on the page. They can make your notes more personal and help recall.

An abbreviation is a short form of a word. For example 'UK' is an abbreviation for 'United Kingdom'.

Task 8.8

Which of the following abbreviations do you know?

◆ Dr
◆ pg.
◆ impt
◆ info.
◆ 22nd

Key

For suggested answers, see 'Key to tasks' at the end of this chapter.

Some abbreviations are common – in other words, most people will recognize them and know what they stand for. Some may be specific to your subject. However, you can invent your own abbreviations for words that often come up in your notes – just make sure that you do not forget what your abbreviations mean!

An acronym is a word which is made up of the initial letters of the words in a phrase. For example, 'NATO' is an acronym of the 'North Atlantic Treaty Organization'.

Task 8.9

Which of the following acronyms do you know?

- ROM
- ASAP
- CD
- MA
- LASER

Key

For suggested answers, see 'Key to tasks' at the end of this chapter.

Again, you might want to invent your own acronyms.

You can also use symbols in your notes. For example, the symbol = is often used in notes to mean that something is the same as something else.

Task 8.10

What do you think the following symbols mean?

1 ∴
2 & or +
3 >
4 C20th
5 ☺

Key

For suggested answers, see 'Key to tasks' at the end of this chapter.

Using symbols and abbreviations is very useful for us when we are making notes. For example, if we are making notes in a lecture it is very difficult to write down the whole word 'information' because of not having enough time. Using 'info' is much shorter and quicker.
(Bangladeshi student)

MAKING NOTES FOR OTHERS

So far we have talked about notes that you make for yourself to use. It is important that they are neat and easy to understand because you may have to go back and use them months after you first made them. However, it is only necessary that *you* understand them, so you should make them as personal as possible to help you recall them easily.

There may be occasions where you are required to make notes for other people to read and use. For example:

- *Group work*: you may make notes for other members of your group to use.
- *Tutorials*: you may want to discuss notes you are making for an assignment with your tutor in a tutorial.
- *Assignments*: you might have to submit a set of notes of a lecture, notes of what you have read or an essay plan, for example, as part of a piece of assessed work.

If you are making notes for others to read it is important that the notes are as clear and easy to understand for them as they are for you. You will need to make sure that:

- your notes have a clear title;
- the source of the notes is clear;
- the organization and structure of your notes is obvious;
- any abbreviations or symbols used are commonly shared rather than personal to you; and
- the notes are legible and well presented.

CAN I USE MY FIRST LANGUAGE WHEN I AM MAKING NOTES?

It can be useful to use your first language in your notes. If what you read or hear reminds you of something you already know, one word in your own language may trigger memories and ideas quicker than a key word in English. Also, if a word in your first language is shorter than the word or expression in English, this can also be useful.

However, you should avoid making all your notes in your first language as, when you come to use your notes, you will have to translate them back into English and this can cause problems. Also, the more you practise making notes in English, the easier it will become. Writing notes in English helps you to understand, think and use the English language more effectively.

Signpost

See Chapter 7 for more information about reading in English.

Using your notes

Remember, we said that we forget 98% of what we have learnt in just three weeks. This means that even if your notes are active and creative you may still have forgotten what they mean in less than a month! Buzan (1988) suggests that students should constantly review what they have learnt. This helps you to move what you have learnt from your short-term memory into your long-term memory. In other words, it will help you to recall the information after a long time.

REVIEWING YOUR NOTES

You should review your notes after you have made them:

- Ten minutes after you have made your notes, rewrite them. This is where you can really think about using all the strategies suggested in the previous section to make your notes clear, memorable and easy to use.
- About 24 hours later, review your notes again. This time try to write down everything you can remember about the topic, before you look back at your notes. When you have finished, check what you have remembered with your notes. Fill in any gaps and correct any inaccuracies.
- Repeat this review one week later, and again one month later.

Although this may seem time-consuming, reviewing your notes in this way will help you to learn the information. You will remember it for a long time. It will become your knowledge rather than something you read or heard about and then forgot. This strategy will also save you a lot of time when you come to use your notes for an assignment or in an exam.

KNOW WHERE TO FIND YOUR NOTES

There is no point making beautiful notes if you cannot find them again when you need them! You should have some kind of filing system for each of your courses. For example, you might want to have a folder for each course. You could divide the folder according to weeks, classes, topics or assignments. You can also file the index cards you made to keep a record of your written sources. You could file these in alphabetical order by author or by topic. Do not put off filing your notes or you may lose them.

REVISING FROM NOTES

Signpost

See Chapter 11 for more advice about preparing for exams.

When you begin revising for exams you should make a revision plan. The notes you have made from your lectures and your reading are already a short version of what you learnt. They act as triggers to remind you of the details. However, at the end of a course you will probably have a large amount of notes – far too many to memorize for an exam! So, what is the best way to use your notes to revise?

Know what you need to know
You may not need to remember everything that you have learnt for the exam. Make sure you find out what you need to revise and find your notes on these topics.

Make notes of your notes
Read the notes you have selected and identify the most important points. Try to decide on one or two key words that will remind you of these points and write them down on an index card. Use colour or pictures if this helps. Remember, the idea is to condense your notes – to make them shorter – so that just a few words will act as triggers to remind you of the full set of notes.

Review your revision notes

Signpost

You can review your revision notes using a similar strategy to the one we mentioned on page 212.

After you have made them, look at the key words on your first index card and see how much you can remember. Check with your full set of notes and fill in any gaps and correct any mistakes. Continue with each of your index cards. Repeat this process until you are confident that the key words remind you of the information you will need. To test yourself you could ask a friend to read out each key word on your card and then tell him or her what this makes you remember.

Make notes of vocabulary
If there are words in English that you know will be useful in your exam but that you find difficult to remember, make index cards for these as well. Review them and test yourself in the same way.

Other reasons to make notes

So far we have looked at note-making as a way of recording ideas and information from what you have read or what you have listened to. There are also other important reasons why you might make notes at university.

BRAINSTORMING

When you brainstorm, you search your brain or your memory very quickly for everything and anything you know about a particular subject.

It is very useful to brainstorm a topic or an idea before you attend a lecture about it, before you read about it or before you prepare an assignment on it. Brainstorming will help you realize what you already know and what you might want to find out. This will make your reading and your listening more active and interesting and will help you to understand exactly what you need to do to prepare your assignments.

As Williams (1989) says, we have a lot of knowledge stored in our memories; the important skill is to be able to retrieve it! When you start to brainstorm a topic, you will be surprised by just how much you know. Remember, it is not just facts that you have learnt that are important. You can also include experiences you have had which have added to your knowledge and understanding. You will probably find that you have many experiences, examples and points of view that may be quite different from those of other students, especially if you are from different countries and cultures.

Activating this knowledge can enrich your study and help you to generate your own new and unique ideas.

However, if you are going to be able to use all the ideas you remember and generate, you will probably have to make notes of them. One of the most effective ways of doing this is by using pattern notes. Write your topic in the centre of a blank piece of paper. When you begin to brainstorm, make a note of all the ideas that come to you, as quickly as you can, on the blank space around the main idea. Do not stop to analyse the ideas, just get them down as quickly as you can. You will probably find that as you write down one idea it triggers another that you can add.

Example: brainstorming

Look at the example of notes made from brainstorming the topic 'The role of dams in water utilization' on page 216.

MAKING A PLAN

You should make a plan before you write an assignment.

You will use your plan when you are writing to help you remember what information you are going to write about at what stage. Using a plan will help to ensure that your written work is well structured, and that you do not forget any of the wonderful ideas you had when you were brainstorming and studying! Therefore your plan should be made up of key words, organized within a structure to remind you of what you want to say – a set of notes!

Signpost

See Chapter 9, 'Writing', for more information on planning written work.

Example: essay plan

Look at the example of part of an essay plan written by a Japanese student on a degree in women's studies on page 217.

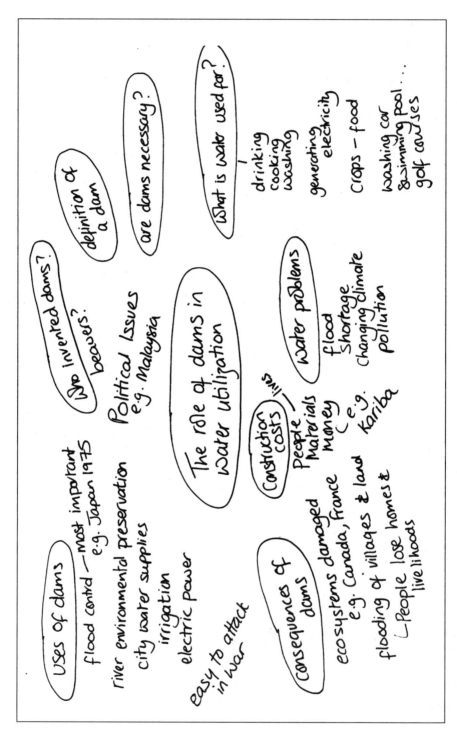

Brainstorming notes

Essay title: 'Does gender still matter in primary schools?' (1500 wds)

(Introduction – 250 wds)
'If boys and girls are different, they are not born but made that way. Gender is socially constructed' (B. Thorne, 1993).

Analysis of question
- *The reason why I chose this topic*
- *My experiences in Japan: in 70% of register, queuing for assembly & graduation etc – usually boys first, then girls follow*
- *Showing what I want to say in my essay: influences of teachers on children, problems of teaching material, possible way to deconstruct gender dichotomy in the classroom*

(Main body)

1 *'Hidden Curriculum' (L.A. Serbin, 1983)*
  Use her research conducted before Education reform Act (1998): how girls & boys behave differently, how teachers treat girls and boys and how this is constructed. (about 200 wds)
2 *Problem of teaching community in Japan & England: discrimination. Stereotyped gender roles, domination of male teacher and effect on children. (200 wds)*
3 *The ...*

It is important that your plan is detailed enough to be useful, but not as long as the final product. It is useful to indicate specific references you want to use, and also to think about how many words you will write in each section.

Sometimes, as in the example above, you will be asked to submit your plan as well as the finished product, as part of your assessed work.

Signpost

Look back to the section 'Making notes for others' earlier in this chapter.

Conclusion

Note-making will be useful for recording information, reviewing, remembering and using that information and for generating ideas and making plans.

The important thing is to make notes actively. Be selective: note down only the key words and do not copy! Your tutors will be interested in how you express your ideas about what you have learnt in your own English, and this will be much easier if you are working from personalized notes that you have made in your own words.

REFERENCES

Buzan, T. (1988) *Making the Most of your Mind*. London: Pan Books.

Buzan, T. (2003) *Use Your Head*. London: BBC Consumer Publishing.

Williams, K. (1989) *Study Skills*. Basingstoke: Macmillan.

USEFUL RESOURCES

http://www.deakin.edu.au/studentlife/academic_skills/online_workshops/note_making.php

This website has useful tips on making notes from lectures, in preparation for tutorials and in preparation for exams.

http://www.uefap.co.uk/reading/readfram.htm

This is part of the website for the University of Hertfordshire and it gives helpful advice for international students on making notes from reading in an academic context.

http://www.une.edu.au/tlc/aso/reading.htm

This site has a number of links to web pages with advice on effective strategies for making notes from reading.

http://www.unisanet.unisa.edu.au/learningconnection/learnres/learng/#Reading

This link takes you to a learning guide, 'Note making from reading', in the form of a Word document.

http://www.st-andrews.ac.uk/services/sss/selfhelptaking%20and%20making%20notes.htm

A concise guide to making notes from lectures and from reading.

http://www.yorku.ca/cdc/lsp/downloads/notes_brochure.PDF

This link takes you to a PDF file about making notes from lectures.

Burns, T. and Sinfield, S. (2003) *Essential Study Skills*. London: Sage.

> Chapter 6, 'How to learn creatively', includes advice on using pattern notes for note-making, brainstorming and planning.

Cottrell, S. (1999) *The Study Skills Handbook*. Basingstoke: Palgrave.

> Chapter 6, 'Research skills', includes ideas about making notes and Chapter 10, 'Memory', will help you to find out how you best remember information.

Fairbairn, G. and Fairbairn, S. (2001) *Reading at University*. Buckingham: Open University Press.

> Chapter 6, 'Reading and note taking'.

Seal, B. (1997) *Academic Encounters: Reading, Study Skills, and Writing*. Cambridge: Cambridge University Press.

> This book includes practical exercises for learners of English on reading texts and making notes.

Waters, A. and Waters, M. (1995) *Study Tasks in English*. Cambridge: Cambridge University Press.

> Unit 5, 'Taking and making good notes', is a useful task-based chapter aimed at international students studying in English.

KEY TO TASKS

Task 8.3

- *Print out pages from the Internet.*
- Copy and paste useful information from electronic sources.
- Copy out important words, phrases and sentences.
- **Copy out useful quotations.**
- **Write down key words for each paragraph.**
- *Underline or highlight important words, phrases and sentences on the page.*
- **Summarize the main ideas of each paragraph.**
- Memorize important words, phrases or sentences.
- **Make notes on a separate piece of paper.**
- **Write down where the information came from.**

If you do any of the things highlighted in **bold** then your notes are probably already quite effective!

As for those things highlighted in <u>italics</u>, you might like to print out pages from the Internet if you find it easier to work with paper sources. However, you should then make notes about this, not just file the piece of paper!

It is a good strategy when making notes from reading to underline or highlight important words, phrases and sentences on the page. However, you should *also* make your own notes on a separate piece of paper, especially if you find it difficult to write about other people's ideas in your own words.

The others are probably not good note-making strategies.

Task 8.4
Key word notes of the main ideas:

Working hours (Britain) dropped (1800s to 1980) (from 75 to 44 hours per week)
1980: going up

Summary:

The average working hours in Britain fell between the mid 19th century and 1980, from 75 to 44 hours per week. However, in 1980, they started to rise again. (29 words)

Of course, you may not have written the summary in exactly the same words, because you have written it in your own words, but the main ideas should be the same.

Task 8.5
'dropped' – 'fell'
'going up' – 'rising'

Task 8.8
Dr – doctor; pg. – page; impt – important; info. – information; 22nd – twenty-second.

Task 8.9
ROM – read-only memory; ASAP – as soon as possible; CD – compact disk; MA – Master of Arts (degree); LASER - light amplification (by) stimulated emission (of) radiation.

Task 8.10

1 Therefore.
2 And or in addition to.
3 Greater than.
4 The twentieth century.
5 This is a personal symbol. It could mean 'I like this idea' or 'I agree with this'.

9 Writing

By studying and doing the activities in this chapter you should:

- understand some of the different kinds of writing students do at university;
- consider cultural differences in writing styles;
- learn how arguments can be constructed in writing;
- understand plagiarism, what it is and how to avoid it;
- practise how to use information from your reading in your writing, through referencing and bibliography; and
- develop strategies for editing and proofreading your writing.

These key words will be useful to you while reading this chapter:

Abbreviation: A shortened word or phrase using only the first letters of each word.
Categorical: Without any doubt, certain.
Contraction: A shortened form of a word or combination of words.
Criteria: Standards by which you judge something.
Dissertation: A long piece of writing sometimes done in the last year of a degree.
Format: The structure and design of a written document.
Indenting: To make a space at the edge of something.
Plagiarism: Using another person's idea or a part of a person's work as if it is your own.
Priority: Something that is very important.
Reputable: Respected and able to be trusted.

Substantial: Large in size, value or importance.
Suspended: Temporarily not allowed to take part in an activity because you have done something wrong.

Different kinds of writing

At university you will have to write often and in various different formats, depending on the subjects you are studying. The most common form of writing is the essay, but you may also be asked to write reports, case studies, summaries, book reviews and, on some undergraduate programmes, there will be a dissertation in the final year. All pieces of writing will need to be structured in a particular way. Generally you will be given instructions by your tutors on how to structure your writing and what form to use. It is important to be clear about this so, if you are not sure what you should be doing, always ask the tutor. You will generally be expected to wordprocess your writing and you will be told how many words you should write, for example 2,000 to 3,000 words in your first year and sometimes 4,000 to 5,000 in the final year of a degree and about 10,000 words for an undergraduate dissertation. If you do not write enough words you may lose marks and, if you write too many, the tutor may not mark the extra words. All pieces of writing have an introduction and a conclusion with sections of information in between and all except summaries have references or a bibliography at the end.

Task 9. 1

What kind of writing are you familiar with already? Which do you enjoy?

Kinds of writing I can do	Kinds of writing I enjoy

ESSAYS

The purpose of an essay is to show the tutor that you have done some reading on the topic, have understood and thought about it and are able to explain what you have understood to the reader. Reading is a very important part of essay writing, but it is also essential to explain what you have read in your own words as much as possible to show that you have understood it and applied it to the title. An essay is a way of helping you develop your thoughts and knowledge on a topic. A good essay depends on the following points.

What you say

It is important that your essay:

- ◆ answers the question (or matches the title);
- ◆ gives information from different sources;
- ◆ gives more than one point of view; and
- ◆ includes some of your own thoughts.

We explain this in more detail below.

How you say it

It is important that your essay:

- ◆ is well organized;
- ◆ is easy to read;
- ◆ includes good grammar and spelling; and
- ◆ is in a suitable style.

Again, we explain this in more detail below.

What you say

The most important aim here is to show that you have understood the topic and have done what you were asked to do, including answering the question if there was one. The next most important thing is that you have demonstrated your understanding of the topic or question and that you show you have looked at it from different points of view. The third most important is that you show you have read about the topic and have used your reading in your answer.

How you say it

Here the most important aim is for the reader to be able to understand the information and your thoughts on it. This means writing in clear sentences and well organized paragraphs. It also means checking your English very carefully to make sure you have used the right words to say what you mean and your grammar and spelling are correct so as not to cause misunderstandings.

The structure of an essay

An essay is structured into an introduction, a series of paragraphs covering the main points of the essay and a conclusion.

The *introduction* (usually 7 or 8% of the whole essay) should:

- comment on the title of the essay;
- explain the meaning of any key terms in the title; and
- explain how you are going to approach the topic.

Each *paragraph* in an essay follows its own plan, including:

- a topic sentence which introduces the main idea;
- an explanation of the topic sentence;
- evidence to support what is said in the topic sentence;
- a comment on the evidence; and
- a conclusion which explains the implications of the evidence and links the paragraph to the next one.

Signpost

See also the section 'Argument' later in this chapter.

The *conclusion* (12–15% of the whole essay) should:

- give a short summary of the main ideas in the essay;
- refer back to the title and answer any question that was asked; and
- make some general concluding remarks (you might give your own views here or discuss how the topic relates to wider issues, but you should not introduce any new information).

In an essay the paragraphs are not numbered. Headings may be used but these are not underlined.

Example: essay titles

Here are some examples of essay titles:

- Compare and contrast the capital asset pricing model and the weighted average cost of capital as alternative ways of estimating the discount rate to be applied in investment appraisal (financial management).
- Give a brief account of the importance of the concept of equality and the difference in the thought of radical and liberal feminists (women's studies).
- Outline the similarities and differences between the organization of leisure and tourism policies of different states within Europe (leisure and tourism management).

REPORTS

Whereas an essay is something you only write at university or college, the report is a form of document which is used in many situations, particularly at work and in government. It is a practical document designed to achieve a task rather than a discussion to explore ideas, and it can be very short, just a few lines, or many volumes long. At university most reports will be between 1,500 and 5,000 words. A report is structured in short, numbered sections. This is so that if a report is being discussed in a meeting people can be directed easily to a particular section (for example, 'point 3.2, page 4'). A long report will start with a separate title page and contents page. A report may also include an appendix or appendices. This is information which is not written by you but which you think will be useful to the reader (for example, a table of statistics to back up your argument, a map or diagram or a section of a text written by another author). Appendices should always be referred to in the main body of the report. Below is an example pro forma for a report – that is, a model you can follow – but remember that different reports will have different layouts.

Example: report pro forma

TITLE

AUTHOR

DATE

1. INTRODUCTION

1.1   TERMS OF REFERENCE

This report is the result of an investigation into ....

1.2   PROCEDURE/METHODOLOGY

In order to investigate the ... the following procedures were adopted ...

1.2.1
1.2.2
1.2.3

2. FINDINGS

2.1
2.2
2.3

3. CONCLUSIONS

The principal conclusions drawn are as follows:

3.1
3.2
3.3

4. RECOMMENDATIONS

The following recommendations are proposed:

4.1
4.2
4.3

5. REFERENCES

6. APPENDICES

As you can see a report includes an introduction and a conclusion, like an essay, as well as references. However it also includes 'Terms of reference', which means the reason why the report is being written, and may include 'Recommendations' at the end, which means points for further action. The important skill with a report is to divide the information into short numbered sections in a logical way so that it is easy to understand. The headings of each section are numbered and in capital letters (as in the example) or underlined and, within each section, are subsections, also numbered, as can be seen in the pro forma.

Example: report title

Here is an example of a report title:

Read the case study 'An unmotivated building inspector' and, assuming you are the organization's human resource manager, write a report summarizing how motivation theories and practices could help to analyse, manage and improve the situation (business studies).

Task 9.2

What is the difference between a report and an essay? What do they look like? How are they structured? What kind of information do they contain? Fill in your answers below:

Essay	Report

Key

For suggested answers, see 'Key to tasks' at the end of this chapter.

LABORATORY (LAB) REPORTS

Science students and researchers have to write regular reports on their lab work. There is a format for these and they are written using the past tense and passive voice (e.g. 'The mixture was heated'). A lab report usually includes the following:

1   *A title.*
2   *An abstract,* summarizing the aim, method and result.
3   *An aim* – the reason for carrying out the experiment.
4   *An introduction* in which the theoretical background is explained.
5   *The method,* where you describe the equipment and materials used. This may include diagrams.
6   *The procedure,* where you describe the steps you followed in carrying out the experiment, usually written in the past passive.
7   *The results* – these are usually presented in the form of tables and graphs, clearly labelled.
8   *A discussion* – here is the place to comment on the results and identify any questions not resolved by the experiment.
9   *A conclusion,* which describes any conclusions you can draw from the results, being cautious by using phrases such as 'This evidence suggests that …' or 'One interpretation could be that …'
10 *References* – these will take the same form as references in any other written work.

SUMMARIES

A summary is an exercise where the student is required to read a text, such as an article or a chapter, and write down the information from the text in a much shorter form, picking out the main points. The following rules apply when writing a summary:

◆   It is written in the student's words, not words copied from the text, although you may include a few short quotations.
◆   It includes only the most important information from the text.
◆   No information which is not in the text can be added.

◆ It does not include the student's opinion on anything.
◆ It should be within the word limit asked for.

This is quite a hard piece of writing to do as it is necessary to understand the text very well in order to pick out the important parts and write them in your own words.

Signpost

For an example of a summary, see Chapter 8, Task 8.4.

BOOK REVIEWS

This activity may be used on humanities courses, particularly literature, but students may also be asked to review books or articles on other courses. In a review you are usually asked to comment on a range of aspects of the text you have been asked to read, including the following:

The *content*: what does it say? Is it interesting? Is it new information?
The *style*: is it easy to understand? Is the structure logical?
The *reader*: for whom is it intended?
You may be asked to give your opinion in a review.

Task 9.3

Write 'yes', 'no' or 'perhaps' in the boxes below, as appropriate:

	Essay	Report	Summary	Book review
You should give your opinion				
You should write an introduction				
You should include some quotation				
You should write a conclusion				
You should include references				

Key

For suggested answers, see 'Key to tasks' at the end of this chapter.

How to approach a piece of writing

With all pieces of writing it is a good idea to have a plan of action. One way to approach a task is as follows:

1 Analyse the title – you must be sure what you have to write about before you begin.
2 Brainstorm – this will help you to get ideas about the topic.
3 Make a plan – this will help you to find out what information you need.
4 Collect information.
5 Write a draft – you will always need to rewrite parts of your work at university.
6 Revise what you have written as many times as necessary.

The first priority is to be sure you understand the topic or question in the title, and the form in which it has to be presented (e.g. essay, report, case study, etc.) and the criteria for marking. Once you are sure of this try brainstorming ideas – that is, take a large sheet of paper, write your title in the middle, then write down all the ideas that come into your head, all over the sheet. This will help you to get some ideas and to work out how to respond to the topics.

Signpost

For an example of brainstorming, see Chapter 8 page 216 'Making notes'.

Task 9.4

Choose a title you have been given on one of your courses or use one from the examples above, and brainstorm ideas for it it. Write the title in the middle of a blank piece of paper and then write all your thoughts on it all over the paper.

The next stage is to use the notes you have made of your ideas to work out a plan – that is, the order in which you are going to write your ideas, what you are going to include and what you will leave out.

Example: plan

The following is an example of a plan:

Title: 'The differences between still and moving images'

Question: 'Do you need skill to understand an image?'

Introduction

Main body:
Introduce images (visual information)
Images as language (the medium for communication)
Why is the information in images important?
1 Recording information without a human point of view
2 Makes it easy to understand different experiences

Still images and moving images as typical information
What kind of information can you get from still and moving images?

Understanding the information
Comparing newspaper pictures and TV news
The difference between watching and seeing
How effective are they:
In conveying knowledge?
Quality and quantity?
Different types of expectation?
How to interpret information

Conclusion

Task 9.5

Make a plan for your piece of writing, using your ideas from Task 9.4.

After the plan, the next stage is to do the reading for your piece of writing. The plan will help you to know what you need to read and how much information you need. Only read what you need and make careful notes on your reading, making sure to write down the author, date, title, place of publication and publisher for your references, and page numbers as if you are planning to make a quotation.

Signpost

See Chapter 8 for more information on making notes.

When you have finished reading, write the first draft of your work. Then put it aside for at least 24 hours, longer if you can, to rest your brain so that when you reread it you can judge whether it meets the criteria and is relevant to the topic. Finally edit and proofread (see below) your work carefully before submitting it. It is often necessary to reread and edit a piece of work several times.

Writing styles

If you have not studied at university before, you will be learning the writing styles that are used at higher education level. Of course, styles vary from subject to subject, and if you have already studied at university in another country you may find that the English style is different from what you are used to in some general ways, too. There are certain ways of writing that all students writing at university are expected to use, and some basic features of these are as follows.

ACADEMIC STYLE

There are five points to note about style in academic writing:

1 Do not use contractions (use 'it is' instead of 'it's' and 'was not' instead of 'wasn't') or abbreviations (use 'for example' instead of 'e.g.' and 'that is' instead of 'i.e.').

2 Do not use colloquial expressions such as 'As I was saying', 'As a matter of fact', 'By the way' or 'Anyway'.

3 Use formal vocabulary.

4 Try to avoid using personal pronouns such as 'I', 'we', 'you'.

5 Be careful not to make categorical statements.

These points are explained in more detail below.

Contractions
This is a simple rule but one which many students have difficulty remembering. Always use the full form of a word, not a shortened form, in your academic writing.

Colloquial language
It will probably be difficult for you to know which expressions are colloquial and which are formal when you first start using formal English. This is something you will learn with practice, but it would be a good idea to ask a tutor, a language teacher or a friend who has experience of academic English if you are in doubt about an expression.

Formal language
The use of more formal vocabulary is something you will gradually get used to while you are at university. You can use a dictionary to help you learn more formal words and expressions, but you should also practise using terminology from your lectures and from your reading, first making sure you understand it.

Signpost

See Chapter 4, 'Building vocabulary', for ways to extend your vocabulary.

Personal pronouns
The general rule about using 'I', 'we' or 'you' does not always apply but you should always check with the tutor before using them. If you have been asked specifically to give your opinion, in a book review for example, it may be appropriate to use 'I'. Otherwise it can be avoided by using forms such as:

* 'It seems that … '
* 'There is evidence that … '
* 'It can be said that … '

Categorical statements

It is not considered appropriate to say without doubt that something is right or wrong, true or false, in academic writing. The convention is to phrase sentences using verbs such as 'may' or 'might' or adverbs such as 'perhaps' or 'possibly'. For example:

- Do not say: 'The Blair government is the best one since after the Second World War.' Say: 'The Blair government *may* be considered to be the most successful Labour government since Attlee's post-war administration.'
- Do not say: AIDS came from monkeys. Say: 'There is a view that AIDS *could possibly* have been transmitted to humans from apes.'

Task 9.6

Look at the following sentences and indicate by circling either the F or the I whether they are written in formal or informal style:

1 We didn't finish the experiment because we ran out of time   F   I
2 Such a proposal would need careful consideration before any funding could be awarded   F   I
3 Infection by pathogenic parasites may be a symptom of ill-health   F   I
4 If you think globalization is always a good thing then you're wrong   F   I
5 In the mid-nineteenth century the average worker clocked up 75 hours of work a week   F   I

Key

For suggested answers, see 'Key to tasks' at the end of this chapter.

CULTURAL DIFFERENCES IN WRITING

Different countries have different conventions. For example, Yamuna Kachru (1996) explains that in India it is appropriate to give much broader introductions to a topic and also to discuss more than one topic in a paragraph. The use of language can also be more ornate or flowery.

Cultural differences: example 1

Below is an example of an introduction to an essay on the 'Dowry system in India':

Growing up is a discarding of dreams and a realization of the various facts of life. A general awareness creeps in. It is a process of drinking deep the spring of knowledge and perceiving the different facets of life. Life is a panorama of events, moments of joys and sorrows. The world around us is manifested by both good and evil.

Dowry system is one of the prevalent evils of today. Like a diabolic adder it stings the life of many innocent people and is the burning topic of discussion. (Cited in Kachru, 1996)

In a British university the first paragraph would not be considered relevant to the topic, and the last sentence comparing the dowry system to an adder would be considered too poetic for an academic essay.

Another difference may be when a student adopts a very personal tone, which is almost never considered appropriate in academic writing in the UK.

Cultural differences: example 2

In the following example a Colombian student is writing a book review of *Jane Eyre*, a famous English novel:

This chapter almost overwhelmed me, but I liked it very much because, although it is fiction, during the time I spent reading it I was transported into another world. The image of Jane Eyre was vivid in my mind. I even nurtured a maternal love for her. Likewise, I created in my imagination the appearance of the other characters in the chapter, their facial expressions, gesticulations and so on.

Although it is sometimes acceptable to use 'I' in a book review, expressions such as 'overwhelmed', 'transported into another world' and 'nurtured a maternal love for her' would be considered much too dramatic and involved with personal feelings for this context. It is generally not good to try to look for very unusual words in your writing, but to use words that are often used in writing and discussion about the topic.

Hinds (1987) says that, whereas in English writing it is the responsibility of the writer to be clear, in Japan the reader has more responsibility for understanding and therefore writers may use more roundabout or circumlocutory ways of expressing their ideas.

Cultural differences: example 3

Here is an example of a Japanese student's writing:

It is sometimes said that art works, especially modern art, have several interpretations. If the only correct way of interpreting is the one done by the artist, this is going to be a reason for ordinary people to hesitate about appreciating art, because this idea gives ordinary people the threatening concept that they must study about art works in text books before they go to a gallery to see them. It is more delightful for us to find an interpretation by ourselves. Encountering two or more different works brings about new interpretations just like a chemical reaction.

This paragraph is clear but it takes more effort to understand than English people are used to having to make. We would probably use simpler, more straightforward sentences such as: 'It is possible to interpret a work of art in several ways.'

As one Japanese student said (cited in Fox, 1994: 8):

Japanese is more vague than English. It's supposed to be that way. You don't say what you mean right away. You don't criticize directly.

Kachru (1996) observes that, in many countries, including China and India, it may be considered polite to give a lot of background information which is not related to the topic, because this gives the reader more choices. In writing in Britain it is usual for the writer to argue their point of view rather than leaving the reader a choice.

It is considered important in Britain to be clear about what you are saying and to build up to your conclusion point by point, presenting your arguments (see below) and backing them up with evidence:

Style surely can be imitated but the more you imitate the more you lose your own style or your identity. At university I think our writing needs to be accurate, simplified and formal. Hence I should get used to writing this style of English.
(Chinese student)

Style is also important in other types of writing, such as letters, email messages and notes. Each type of writing has its own appropriate style. It is important to choose the right level of formality in order to communicate effectively and to make the right impression. Sometimes students are unsure of how formal they should be when communicating with their teachers.

Task 9.7

Look at this extract from an email sent by a student to his or her tutor. There are some problems with the style. Can you find them and think how you could change the language used?

Dear Michael,

Once again, I admit my gratitude to you for your valuable advice and co-operation. Your enthusiasm towards solving my problems and effort to helping me out to get this grant has really enthralled me and therefore I salute your endeavour.

So, I entreat you to write few lines from memory. I don't mind if you dash off a passage in the light of my undergraduate study. If you can, then please provide me with your postal address so that I can post the envelope with all documents within to you.

Key

For comments on this task, see 'Key to tasks' at the end of this chapter.

Argument

The way a writer convinces the reader of his or her view is through using argument. When we use this word informally it means to disagree. However, in writing at university it means to build up your ideas point by point, considering points which prove the opposite as well as those which support your views, in order to convince the reader to think like you. It may not be necessary to build an argument in all pieces of writing: a report may just be reporting findings or giving explanations; a summary will only be giving a shorter version of an original text. Can you distinguish between an argument and an explanation?

In an explanation the writer is giving some information and the reasons behind it but is not trying to convince the reader of anything. For example:

> Foreign direct investment means a company from one country invests in another. This brings finance into the country which is receiving the investment and expands the business of the investing company.

In an argument the writer wants the reader to believe his or her conclusion. This means giving reasons and often evidence. These are called premises. For example:

> Foreign direct investment creates jobs in the host country and also contributes expertise to the host economy. Therefore countries which are seeking economic growth should welcome it.

In the example above the first sentence contains two premises and the second one is a conclusion. This is what the writer wants the reader to believe. Conclusions often start with words or phrases such as 'therefore', 'so' or 'as a result', which indicate that the writer is about to say what he or she wants the reader to believe. They may also contain verbs such as 'must', 'should' or 'have to'.

Task 9.8

Can you think of two premises you could use to make someone believe the following conclusion?

As a result, in the future we will live in a more and more globalized world.

Key

For suggested answers, see 'Key to tasks' at the end of this chapter.

When putting forward an argument you will have more chance of convincing the reader of your point of view if you show you have thought about the opposite point of view and any arguments that might be put forward to support it. These are called counter-arguments. For example:

> Countries wishing to expand their economies will welcome foreign direct investment; however, investing companies may provide their own staff, limiting the number of jobs available to local people, and a large proportion of profits may be taken out of the host country. However the contribution of expertise by the investor and their investment in property and other local facilities will still make foreign direct investment advantageous for the host country.

The writer here shows that some points against foreign direct investment have been considered but also more points in favour are given so that the conclusion is still that it is a good thing.

It is important to give convincing reasons for the premises in an argument. You should ask yourself why your reader should believe you. If you are using someone else's ideas to support your argument, check that that person is reputable and what you have said is true and represents accurately what he or she has said.

Plagiarism

Plagiarism is a concept based on the Western idea that, when somebody writes something, it belongs to him or her and not to anyone else. So if you write an essay it is yours and, although other people can read it, they must not copy it. In the same way if you read a book, newspaper article, web page or any other text you cannot use the exact same words in your writing unless you say where you copied them from and use quotation marks. This is why we use references and bibliographies.

The rule in all UK universities is that students must use their own words in their writing. You may use short (maximum 8–10 lines) quotation from books, websites and other sources and you can use the ideas from these sources written in your own words but you must always give a reference in your text and list all details of the source at the end.

Signpost

How to do this is explained later in this chapter, in the section 'Referencing and bibliography'.

In other cultures plagiarism is not viewed in this way. For example:

Actually, the concept of plagiarism is not very familiar to us Chinese students due to the different teaching method and education attitude to an extent. We were encouraged in high school and in college to use more what famous people said before and what we learnt on the textbooks but we were not asked to note the name of the person and from which book we copied the words.
(Chinese student)

I never knew how strict the UK is about plagiarism until we spoke about this in class. This would be a major adjustment for me with writing essays, dissertations and projects for I have to keep in mind what I write. In the Philippines, rules on plagiarism are not that tough. I usually write long essays without giving references.
(Filipino student)

Task 9.9

In your country, how were you taught to use information from books and other sources? Did you learn to use quotations and references or did you do it differently? Write down what you did.

WHAT HAPPENS IF YOU PLAGIARIZE?

There are quite severe punishments for plagiarism. This means that if the lecturer marking your work thinks that substantial sections of it are copied from books, the web or other sources and you have not given references, you may be given a mark of zero and fail your course. If you do this more than once, you may be suspended from the university.

HOW CAN THE TUTOR KNOW IF A STUDENT HAS PLAGIARIZED?

Students from other countries usually use a different variety of English. In addition, if they are learning English, they often make mistakes of a particular kind, such as verb tenses and prepositions. Because of this, it is sometimes easy for the reader to tell that some parts of a piece of writing have been written by the student and some parts have been copied.

Example: plagiarism

Look at the example below, which shows two paragraphs in a student's essay:

Go shopping is one part of people's life; the majority of people *is still following* the traditional way *to go* to the department store. Nowadays the variety of technology *is* developed rapidly, there are so many ways *to shopping* and the most popular one is shopping online.

Online shopping offers consumers a vast array of goods and services from companies around the world. You may be able to get things that are not available locally and you may even pay less than you normally would in conventional shops.

The first part of the writing has some English mistakes (italicized) and, from the sentence structure, it seems that it has been written by a person who is learning English. In the second paragraph the English is perfect and the style is that of an English textbook. It looks as if the writer has copied the second paragraph from a textbook. As there is no reference given, this piece of work looks like an example of plagiarism.

When students download essays or parts of essays from the web, the tutor can easily find out by entering one or two sentences from the essay on a search engine like Google. Google will find the original text and the tutor will be able to see how much the student has copied.

If a student copies a piece of work or part of a piece of work belonging to another student and the tutor finds out, both students will be punished equally.

HOW TO AVOID PLAGIARISM

The best way to avoid plagiarism is to plan your writing, read the material you need to get the information from and make notes as you read. Then write your essay or report using your notes and without looking at the original texts you read. Of course, this is more difficult if you are learning English but it will help you develop your own ideas and arguments and your writing skills. Using books or other sources by copying bits of text and just changing a few words is not acceptable.

Example: avoiding plagiarism

Look at the text below, from a newspaper, and how two students used it. The first one has plagiarized because he or she used too many of the same phrases; the second has expressed the ideas in his or her own words:

Original text
The Royal Commission on Environmental Pollution told the Transport Secretary, Alistair Darling, that his expansion policy was 'deeply flawed'. A scathing report said ministers showed 'little sign of having recognised' the atmospheric damage caused by aircraft.

It recommended a freeze on airport expansion, together with a tax of between £40 and £100 on every ticket, which would double the price of many journeys. Sir Tom Blundell, the commission's chairman, said: 'We believe we should restrict airport development, rather than just expand in response to demand.' (*Guardian Unlimited*, Guardian Newspapers Ltd 2002, accessed December 2002)

Student 1
A scathing report believes ministers think *the atmospheric damage* is not *mostly caused by aircraft*, and *recommended* a slow down *on airport expansion* and *a tax of between £40 and £100 on every* single ticket.

Student 2
In the excerpts from the *Guardian* newspaper article (December 2002) there are different views on putting tax on flights. According to Sir Tom

> Blundell, the commission's chairman, we must stop responding to the
> airport authorities about their developing programs. At the same time
> the commission also announced 'a tax of between £40 and £100 on
> every ticket', which means passengers will have to pay double the amount
> of money for their flights.

If we compare the original text from the *Guardian* newspaper, we can see that student 1 has taken a lot of phrases from the original text (italicized) and used them without quotation marks. This is plagiarism. Student 2's summary, which uses his or her own words together with one quotation, signalled by quotation marks, is not plagiarism.

Task 9.10

Now read part of an article in a newspaper, journal or on the web, or a chapter in a book, make notes on it, put it away and then write a short paragraph on it without looking at the original. Make sure you use mainly your own words and put quotation marks round any phrases you use from the original text. If you can, ask a teacher to look at it.

Referencing and bibliography

This is a very important part of writing at university in the UK and it is difficult to get it right. Many English students find it hard to learn correct referencing. Referencing is important because it is the way you show that you have read enough material about your topic and have related your reading to the title of your work. Normally for an essay or report, you should have read four or five book chapters or articles in journals or on the web and all these should be referred to in your writing.

The method of referencing we are going to describe here is widely used and is called the Harvard system. Some lecturers like students to use different methods. When you are given instructions for an assignment you will normally be told what method of referencing to use, but it is always a good idea to clarify with the lecturer what is expected.

REFERENCING WITHIN YOUR TEXT

In the Harvard method there are four ways of referring to an author or text: The following examples use information taken from an article in the *Daily Telegraph* newspaper on 2 April 1989, written by April Robinson, a policewoman:

1 Describe the idea or point that you are using from the source, without mentioning the author in your sentence, then put the author's name and the date of publication in brackets at the end of the sentence: 'Nowadays nobody is surprised when police officers are attacked (Robinson, 1989).'

2. Use the author's name, followed by the date of publication in brackets in your sentence, when describing his or her ideas in your own words: 'Robinson (1989) believes that there is more and more violence in our society.' This can be done in a number of other ways, for example: 'As Robinson (1989) points out … ', 'According to Robinson (1989) … ', 'To quote from Robinson (1989) … ', 'Writing in the *Daily Telegraph*, Robinson (1989) explains that … ' or 'Writing in 1989, Robinson argues that … '

3. Use some of the author's own words in your sentence, putting these in quotation marks (also called inverted commas) ' … ' including the author's name and the date of publication in one of the two ways above: 'Robinson (1989) says that she really objects to " … people using the street as a rubbish bin".'

4. Use a long quotation from the source, but not more than 6–8 lines maximum, indenting this and using the author's name in one of the ways described in (1) and (2) above. When a quotation is indented it is not necessary to use quotation marks:

> Another thing that seems to have changed is people's attitudes to the things they own or want to own:
>
> > They seem to put more emphasis on material possessions than they do on human values. Material things have become too important. (Robinson, 1989)

If you are quoting from a source on the web, you should give the author's name and date as above if they are given on the site. If no author is given, you should give the title of the article and the date.

Task 9.11

Read a short article in a newspaper or on the web and then write sentences using information from the article in the four different ways shown above.

All the authors and websites mentioned in your writing have to be listed with full details in your references at the end of your work. We call this list 'references' when it only includes texts you have mentioned. If you make a list including other texts you have read in connection with the work but have not mentioned, the list is called 'bibliography'.

REFERENCES AND BIBLIOGRAPHY

The Harvard system for listing references and bibliography is as follows.

For a book
Author's surname, initial(s), date of publication in brackets, title in italics, place of publication, publisher. For example:

Fanon, F. (1986) *Black Skin, White Masks*. London: Pluto Press.

For a chapter in an edited book
Chapter author's surname, initial(s), date in brackets, title of the chapter in quotation marks ' ', book editor's initial(s) and surname, (ed.) or (eds), title of book in italics, place of publication, publisher. For example:

Castells, M. (2000) 'Information technology and global capitalism', in W. Hutton and A. Giddens, (eds) *On the Edge: Living with Global Capitalism*. London: Jonathan Cape.

For a paper in a journal
Paper author's surname, initial(s), date in brackets, title of the paper in quotation marks ' ', name of journal (in italics), volume and issue numbers, pages of paper. For example:

Fang, Y. (2001) 'Reporting the same events? A critical analysis of Chinese print news media texts,' *Discourse and Society*, Vol. 12, no. 5, pp. 585–613.

For a book, article or any other document on the web
The same rules as above apply but the web address and date the page was accessed are added. For example:

Gilligan, E. (1998) *Local Heroes* [online], Friends of the Earth, http:www.foe.co.uk/local/ rest.pdf (accessed 24 November 1998).

If there is no author given write the title of the article, date and web address. For example:

Media in Romania (1998) http://www.dds.nl/pressnow/dossier/romania.html

The full address of the page where the information was found should always be given. The list of references must be in alphabetical order by surname of the authors or title where there is no author.

Task 9.12

Using the books and articles you have collected to write an essay or report, write a list of references following the examples above, and making sure they are in alphabetical order. Try to include different kinds of references (for example, a book, a paper in a journal, an article from a website).

EDITING AND PROOFREADING

Editing and proofreading are the tasks you have to do when you have written your assignment and are ready to examine it again to make sure it is as good as possible before you hand it in. A good strategy is to write your essay, report or chapter, put it away for at least 24 hours, or a few days if possible, then read it again when you are rested and your brain is fresh. In this way you will be able to see if any changes are needed.

EDITING

Editing means checking your work to be sure that you have said what you wanted to say, including all the important information, and have done what you were asked to do. You can ask yourself the following questions:

- Is all the necessary information included?
- Is it all relevant to the title?
- Have I made my arguments clear?
- Have I given evidence by using examples and/or references to my sources?
- Do my paragraphs follow each other in a logical order?
- Have I explained what I am discussing in the introduction?
- Have I summed up and commented on the whole in the conclusion?
- Is my work too long or too short?

If you do not feel confident about your work you may be able to get help from tutors who specialize in writing at your university, but mainly your writing will improve with practice. However, even very experienced writers spend a lot of time editing and usually write several drafts of their work, so be prepared to rewrite your work as often as necessary.

Task 9.13

Reread a piece of writing you have done recently asking yourself the questions listed above.

PROOFREADING

When you have finished editing, you need to start proofreading. This is where you read each sentence carefully to check the details such as grammar, spelling, punctuation and vocabulary.

Spelling

You will probably be using a computer to write your assignments and will be using spell check. However, you must remember that the computer will only tell you if the word as you have spelt it does not exist. It will not tell you if you have used the wrong word for that sentence. For example 'to', 'too' and 'two' are all correct words but only one is right in this sentence:

It is possible to place *too* much importance on testing in primary schools (not '*to*' or '*two*').

Grammar
You will need to check whether you have used the right tense (past, present, future) and whether your verb and subject agree. If you have used a singular subject have you matched it with a singular verb? For example:

The drops of water were collected in a filter dish (not: The drops of water *was* collected … because the subject is '*the drops*' not '*water*').

You will also need to check that you have used articles ('the', 'a' and 'an') and prepositions ('of', 'to', 'from', etc.) correctly.

A word of warning: do not rely on the grammar check tool that comes as part of some popular wordprocessing packages. Frequently the advice it gives is totally wrong! It will tell you that a perfectly well formed sentence should be changed and offer an alternative which is incorrect English!

Punctuation
Are your sentences very long, or are they only half sentences? Have you used full stops, capital letters and commas where necessary? Have you put question marks after questions and quotation marks where you have used someone else's words?

Vocabulary
Have you used the right word for what you want to say? Does it have the right meaning in this context? Is the word formal enough or is it colloquial?

Signpost

See Chapter 4, 'Building vocabulary', for help with this.

Paragraphing
Paragraphs should be between about 10 lines and three quarters of a page and should have one main topic.

Proofreading can be difficult if you are not sure about some aspects of English. A good learner's dictionary of English can be a great help.

Signpost

See Chapter 4, 'Building vocabulary' for more information on using dictionaries.

Proofreading is more difficult, especially for we foreign students, because it is hard for us to proofread our writing in terms of the language of English. Correcting is achievable but perfection is unreachable.
(Chinese student).

A useful strategy is to be aware of your own particular weaknesses and to concentrate on them especially. For example, if you know you usually write very long sentences, check your sentences carefully and make them shorter if they are too long. If verb tenses are difficult for you, double check the verb forms you have used in your work. You could use a checklist like the one below to go through your work and to help you find out where you are making the most errors. Fill in a column for each piece of work you do, and add any extra categories of error in the empty spaces on the left:

CHECKLIST: proofreading

Type of error	Coursework 1	Coursework 2	Coursework 3	Coursework 4
Sentence length				
Commas				
Capital letters				
Verb tenses				
Agreement				
Articles				
Prepositions				
Spelling				
Paragraphs				

Task 9.14

Try proofreading this paragraph, written by a Business Studies undergraduate. You should find 20 mistakes:

The effect of tariffs on consumers

When a government of an importing nation imposes a tariff on imported goods, the consumer in the domestic market will reduce their consumption of that goods, as a result of the increases in the price of that goods (because tariff charges is passed into consumer), and in the case of the good been essential for the consumer, the consumption would not change very much, but the price will raise to include the tariff. In order to avoid demand collapsing altogether, suppliers have to absorb part of the tariff themselves, only if demand is totally inelastic will supplier be able to pass the entire Tariff on to the consumer.
Therefore the extend to which the Tariff is successful in reducing demand for The imported products depend largely on the elasticity of demand for that product. When Tariff imposed by a government on their imported product tariff tends to make the customer worse off.

Key

For suggested answers, see 'Key to tasks' at the end of this chapter.

Feedback

After all your hard work in preparing and writing a piece of work, once you hand it in, you may feel the work is finished. However, perhaps the most important learning can be done when you receive your work back and receive feedback from your teacher.

Always hand in your work on time, otherwise it may not be marked, and when it is returned to you, read the tutor's comments carefully. If you are lucky enough to have a tutor who gives you detailed feedback, you can learn a lot about your strengths and weaknesses in writing and about how far you manage to meet the requirements of your university. If your tutor has not given you enough information for you to understand why you got the mark you did, contact him or her and ask for more feedback. Remember, it is as important to understand what you did well as it is to understand anything you may have done less well. This is one of the most important ways for you to improve, because it has been shown that good quality feedback, which is then acted upon by the learner, leads to exceptional progress. Your tutors are a valuable source of information about the standards you need to reach and they are there to help you.

Conclusion

Writing is something we continue to develop throughout our lives, at university, at work and perhaps in our hobbies. It can be hard work writing in a language which is not your first language or the language you learnt at school, but the only answer is to read and write as much as possible and keep revising and improving. As one Taiwanese student said:

> I not only write daily but also make notes and remember what is important and what I have learned. Meanwhile I can improve my writing by reading. I have to think what kind of book will help me and be relevant to my subject. I have to do it and encourage myself immediately.

With practice and persistence, you will find you can make great progress and you will discover that what you learn by writing will help you in many other aspects of your studies.

REFERENCES

Fox, H. (1994) *Listening to the World: Cultural Issues in Academic Writing.* Urbana, IL: National Council of Teachers of English (NCTE).
Hinds, J. (1987) 'Reader versus writer responsibility: a new typology', in U. Connor and R. Kaplan (eds) *Writing Across Languages: Analysis of L2 Text.* Reading, MA: Addison-Wesley.

Kachru, Y. (1996) 'Culture in rhetorical styles: contrastive rhetoric and world Englishes,' in N. Mercer and J. Swan (eds) *Learning English: Development and Diversity*. London: Routledge.

USEFUL RESOURCES

http://www.uefap.com/writing/writfram.htm
   A good website on English for academic purposes.

http://www.macmillandictionary.com/MED.../08-language awareness-academic-UK.htm
   This site is a magazine, and numbers 08 and 09 look at aspects of academic writing.

http:www.ipl.org/div/aplus/linkswritingstyle.htm#logic
   This site covers writing style and techniques.

http://www.urich.edu/~writing/argument/html
   This site discusses how you can make effective arguments.

http://www.keele.ac.uk/depts/aa/handbook/section2/plagiarismanddishonesty.html
   A very clear site about plagiarism.

http://www.hamilton.edu/academics/resource/wc/AvoidingPlagiarism.html
   A site which tells you how to avoid plagiarism.

Crème, P. and Lea, M. (1997) *Writing at University: A Guide for students*. Buckingham: Open University Press.

Fairbairn, G. and Winch, C. (1996) *Reading, Writing and Reasoning*. Buckingham: SRHE and Open University Press.

Jordan, R.R. (1998) *Academic Writing Course*. Harlow: Longman.

McCarter, S. (1997) *A Book on Writing*. Ford, Midlothian: IntelliGene.

Rees, A. 'Guide to assignment writing for international students', available at www.bowbridgepublishing.com.

Swales, J.M. and Feak, C.B. (1994) *Academic Writing for Graduate Students: Essential Tasks and Skills*. Ann Arbor, MI: University of Michigan Press.

Williams, K. (1995) *Writing Essays*. Oxford: Oxford Centre for Staff Development.

Williams, K. (1995) *Writing Reports*. Oxford: Oxford Centre for Staff Development.

KEY TO TASKS

Task 9.2

Essay
- Discusses a topic.
- Gives different points of view.
- Puts forward arguments.
- Is divided into paragraphs but does not include headings, numbers, underlining or bold.

Report
- Gives an account of a situation.
- Makes recommendations.
- Seeks to inform rather than discuss.
- Is divided into numbered sections with headings, underlining, capitals and bold.

Task 9.3

	Essay	Report	Summary	Book review
You should give your opinion	Yes	Perhaps	No	Perhaps
You should write an introduction	Yes	Yes	Perhaps	Yes
You should include some quotations	Yes	Perhaps	Perhaps	Perhaps
You should write a conclusion	Yes	Yes	Perhaps	Yes
You should include references	Yes	Yes	Yes	Yes

Task 9.6

1 Informal – use of 'we didn't', 'we ran out of time'.
2 Formal – use of 'Such a proposal', 'would', 'funding', 'could be'.
3 Formal – vocabulary, use of 'may be'.
4 Informal – use of 'If you', 'then you're wrong'.
5 Formal but not entirely, the expression 'clocked up' is informal.

Task 9.7

Dear Michael,

Once again, *I admit my gratitude to you* for your valuable advice and co-operation. *Your enthusiasm towards solving my problems and effort to helping me out to get this grant has really enthralled me and therefore I salute your endeavour.* So, *I entreat you* to write few lines from memory. I don't mind if *you dash off a passage in the light of* my undergraduate study. If you can, then please *provide me* with your postal address so that I can post the envelope with all documents *within* to you.

The problem with this email is that, although the student intends to be friendly and quite informal, much of the language is rather formal and old fashioned and so the tone is odd. Only the phrase *dash off* is quite informal and in fact is not really suitable when talking about a reference, as it implies carelessness.

The phrases highlighted in italics do not work well. More suitable phrases are suggested below:

Dear Michael,

Once again, *thanks so much* for your valuable advice and co-operation. *I really appreciate your willingness to help me out.* So, *could you* write a few lines from memory? I don't mind if *you just write a short reference based on* my undergraduate study. If you can, then please *email me* your postal address so that I can post the envelope with all documents to you.

Task 9.8
Some possible premises:

- Communication over long distances is becoming easier all the time.
- Trade agreements are facilitating business between different countries.
- The spread of information is very rapid nowadays.
- More and more people around the world are speaking English.
- Multinationals dominate the market in many sectors.

Task 9.14
The effect of tariffs on consumers

When a government of an importing nation imposes a tariff on imported goods, the consumer in the domestic market will reduce their consumption of **that** goods, as a result of the increases in the price **of that goods** (because tariff charges **is** passed **into** consumer), and in the case of the **good been** essential for the consumer, the consumption would not change very much, but the price will **raise** to include the tariff. In order to avoid demand collapsing altogether, suppliers have to absorb part of the tariff themselves, only if demand is totally inelastic will ∧ supplier be able to pass the entire Tariff on to the consumer. Therefore the **extend** to which the **Tariff** is successful in reducing demand for The imported products **depend** largely on the elasticity of demand for that product. When ∧ tariff ∧ imposed by a government on their imported product ∧ tariff tends to make the consumer worse off.

The mistakes have been marked in **bold**. The insertion mark ∧ indicates where something is missing:

1 'those' not 'that' – goods is plural
2 full stop, new sentence
3 no 's' – singular
4 not necessary – delete
5 delete brackets and put commas instead
6 'are' not 'is' – plural
7 'on to' not 'into'
8 'the' needed
9 'goods'
10 'being' not 'been'
11 'rise' not 'raise'
12 full stop, new sentence
13 'the' needed
14 no capital letter
15 'extent' (noun) not 'extend' (verb)
16 no capital letters
17 'depends' singular subject
18 'a' needed
19 'is' needed
20 'the' needed

Below is a correct version of the text:

The effect of tariffs on consumers

When a government of an importing nation imposes a tariff on imported goods, the consumer in the domestic market will reduce their consumption of those goods. As a result of the increase in the price, because tariff charges are passed on to the consumer, and in the case of the goods being essential for the consumer, the consumption would not change very much, but the price will rise to include the tariff. In order to avoid demand collapsing altogether, suppliers have to absorb part of the tariff themselves. Only if demand is totally inelastic will the supplier be able to pass the entire tariff on to the consumer.

Therefore the extent to which the tariff is successful in reducing demand for the imported products depends largely on the elasticity of demand for that product. When a tariff is imposed by a government on their imported product, the tariff tends to make the consumer worse off.

10 Studying at postgraduate level

AIMS

By studying and doing the activities in this chapter you should:

- understand the difference between undergraduate and postgraduate study in the UK;
- learn how to carry out research and about the concept of methodology;
- become familiar with the kind of writing that is expected at postgraduate level;
- understand how to manage an extended piece of writing: MA or MSc dissertation, MPhil or PhD thesis; and
- gain some strategies for working with a supervisor.

GLOSSARY

These key words will be useful to you while reading this chapter:

Analytical: Examining things very carefully.
Component: A part which combines with other parts to form something bigger.
Confidentiality: Keeping something secret, in a formal situation.
Deceit: Keeping the truth hidden, especially to get an advantage.
Dissertation: A long piece of writing on a particular subject, done for a Master's degree and sometimes in the last year of undergraduate study.
Ethical: Related to a system of accepted beliefs which control behaviour, especially such a system based on morals.

Fieldwork: Study which consists of practical activities that are done away from university.

Hypotheses: Ideas or explanations that are based on known facts but have not yet been proved.

Investigate: To examine a problem carefully.

Methodology: A system of ways of studying something.

Phenomena: Things that exist and can be seen.

Statistics: Information based on a study of the number of times something happens or is present, or other numerical facts.

Supervisor: A person whose job is to communicate with another person to make certain that everything is done correctly.

Theoretical: Based on the ideas that relate to a subject, not the practical uses of that subject.

Thesis: A long piece of writing done for a PhD.

Viva: A spoken examination.

You, the postgraduate student

As a new postgraduate student in the UK, who are you? Did you study for your undergraduate qualification in your own or another language and are you now starting to study in English for the first time? Have you gained an undergraduate degree in an English medium institution but in another country? Have you been accepted on a postgraduate course because of your work experience or other qualifications and not studied at university before?

In any of these cases you may feel nervous about starting to study at postgraduate level and you may be wondering what the difference will be between this and your previous experience. You may also be wondering what your tutors' expectations of you will be and how you can meet those expectations.

Task 10.1

Take a sheet of paper and draw up a short list of the abilities and strengths you expect to develop in your postgraduate studies.

The difference between undergraduate and postgraduate study

One of the main differences between undergraduate and postgraduate study is the way you are expected to approach your studies and, in particular, your thinking. If you have been an undergraduate at a UK university you will have been encouraged towards the end of your degree to think more independently and to put more of your own ideas into your work. In other cultures this may not have been encouraged:

> *Independence is one of the virtues an international student should develop. Given that, the student should show enthusiasm to finish the course.*
> **(Filipino MA student)**

> *One of the key things I learned when I started was how important it is for students at postgraduate level to initiate and participate in their own learning.*
> **(Indian MSc student)**

> *In the UK there is more emphasis on questioning and critical analysis.*
> **(Kyrgyzstani MA student)**

Most Master's courses and some MPhil and PhD courses include a taught component, which will be similar to undergraduate study but at a higher level. However, there will also be an important research component and, on an MPhil or PhD, there may be no taught component at all. At postgraduate level you will be expected to build up your ability not only to understand and discuss other people's work but also to undertake new work yourself which will add to the existing academic knowledge in your field. You will be starting to become an expert and, if you produce a good masters dissertation, this may be kept in your university library for other students to read and consult, or published as a paper in a journal. As an undergraduate your main task was to learn about your field, although you were expected to contribute your own perspective as well. As a postgraduate you will, of course, still be learning about your field, but your task is to add to the knowledge in the field and contribute to its development. At Master's level you are on your way to becoming an academic. At MPhil and PhD level you are an academic, and you may be expected to teach undergraduate seminars and to publish papers on your research:

> *During my first year I taught computing and I have also taught food science. If available teaching is a good break from research and you get paid for it.*
> **(Indian PhD student)**

This means being even more of an independent learner than as an undergraduate. You will be learning more about how to undertake research and will develop the ability to:

- understand different analytical approaches and apply them;
- find information from a range of sources and critically evaluate it;
- develop theories and apply them to data;
- come up with ideas of your own, refine and focus them;
- develop arguments to support your ideas and predict counter-arguments;
- be aware of ethical issues in research; and
- evaluate your own work and develop it accordingly.

The Master's degree

A Master's degree (MA, MSc or MBA) will usually consist of taught courses or modules followed by a dissertation. The modules will help you to develop your knowledge in the field and your analytical skills. You will become familiar with theoretical approaches to your subject and how to apply them to data. You will also probably have to take a course in research methods. This will teach you how to plan research, how to carry it out and how to describe what you have done. It will give you the knowledge and skills you need to work on your dissertation. You will be taught how to make a wise choice of topic, taking into account such factors as:

- the subject or field in which you are studying;
- what you are interested in;
- the expectations of the tutors;
- the time you have been given to carry out the work;
- the resources that are available; and
- your own particular skills or abilities.

Example: Master's dissertations titles

Here are some examples of titles of Master's dissertations:

- Vision Japan: market entry strategies and the economic, social and cultural influences – an examination of possible links in the context of the Japanese market (management studies).

♦ Transport and tourism development in Botswana (MA in transport policy and management).

♦ An investigation into the quality of services in retail banking: a case study of the Cyprus Popular Bank (MA in management studies).

Task 10.2

Make a list of topics which you think you would be interested in researching.

Now make a list of the skills and abilities you have to help you in any research you do.

Most students will take a Master's degree before starting an MPhil or a PhD.

The MPhil and PhD

The MPhil (masters in philosophy) and the PhD (doctor of philosophy) are research degrees which can involve research carried out in any field, not just philosophy. They are awarded on completion of a thesis based on original research completed under the supervision of a lecturer at a university. You may not have to attend any classes, although often you can choose to take some courses which will help you with your research. However, you must have regular meetings with a supervisor. A PhD usually takes longer than an Mphil, although there is no fixed length, and the research for a PhD will be more substantial. When you have finished your thesis you will have to present it in an oral interview called a viva.

THE VIVA

This is generally the only oral examination you will have in the UK. After you have submitted your doctoral thesis and it has been marked by the examiners, you will be asked to meet them to discuss your work. This is so they can be sure that you did the work yourself, that you are able to discuss it with others and that you have genuinely contributed new knowledge to your field. The examiners will ask questions about the thesis, the ideas behind it, your research methods and your evaluation of your findings. Your research supervisor should help you with preparation for the viva. It will be a good idea to have a few practice sessions with the supervisor or with fellow students or friends. You will need to practise talking about your research and try to think of any questions the examiners may want to ask you about it.

Signpost

If you think you may be nervous, look at the section 'Exam nerves' in Chapter 11. There are also some videos of vivas listed in the 'Useful resources' section at the end of this chapter.

Carrying out research

The first stage of carrying out any research is to have an idea of what you want to find out. Whereas in most of your undergraduate studies you were told what topics to discuss, it is now up to you to decide what you want to investigate. This does not mean that you can choose anything you like. You will always have to decide in consultation with a tutor or supervisor and if you cannot think of any ideas, the tutor or supervisor will be able to make some suggestions. In choosing a topic for a dissertation or thesis it is important to be sure that nobody has done exactly what you are planning to do before. Your idea need not be completely new but you must be aiming to find out something new about the topic, either by looking at it from a different perspective or by taking it further than previous researchers have done. It is a good idea to look at previous students' dissertations and theses to see what topics they have covered and how they have approached them. Universities keep copies of all their students' PhD theses, and will probably have copies of good Master's dissertations as well in the library.

As a student from another country, you probably have specialist knowledge of areas which many UK students would not be familiar with. Many students choose research topics which relate in some way to their background or previous experience. This makes sense, especially if you are able to obtain information from sources in your home country or have access to experts there.

Example: specialist knowledge

Here are some examples of topics which reflect and draw on international students' specialist knowledge:

- The restructuring of integrated public transport in Latvia and Lithuania (transport and logistics).
- Maternal nutrition and infant development (visual maturation and mental development) in Thailand and Vietnam (brain chemistry and human nutrition).
- A novel idea for measuring displacement using low-cost optoelectronic and/or fibre optic components (electronics and communications engineering: optoelectronics).

Task 10.3

Make a list of any specialist areas of knowledge you have which would help you in any research you do.

Ideas do not often come to you fully formed, they develop over a period of time. When you choose a topic for research it will not be fixed but can be changed as you find out more about it and think things through. You also need to be sure you can find the information you need to develop your topic. If it is impossible to get information you may have to change to a different one.

For example, if you decide to carry out research on 'The impact of the call centre industry on the economy of the Philippines and its workforce' but you cannot find any data about the Filipino workforce, this will be a difficult topic for you to investigate. Also if you plan to collect data through telephone interviews but do not feel confident about speaking English on the phone, it might be better to change your plan.

So at postgraduate level you will be doing a lot of thinking about your subject, yourself and the relationship between the two.

FINDING INFORMATION

The topic you choose will influence what kind of information you will be looking for, but also the information available may influence the topic you choose. You will need to decide whether your research is going to take place in libraries, in laboratories or outside the university, in 'the field'.

Deskwork is research which is concerned with the study of documents. Fieldwork is concerned with collecting primary data outside the university for analysis.

DESKWORK

As a postgraduate student, you will probably have access to more libraries and resources than undergraduates. In some cases there are agreements whereby postgraduates can use the libraries of a number of universities and have access to specialist websites. You will need to find out about these in your university library. If your topic requires specialist materials you will be able to ask your library to obtain them through interlibrary loans. The specialist librarians will also be able to help you find the most useful websites for your research. When you are researching a topic, make an appointment with a librarian as this will save you time and ensure that you find out where to look for the information you need.

Of course, all information you use must be properly referenced and included in your bibliography, including web-based materials, information from radio or television or from newspapers articles as well as books and journals.

Signpost

See Chapter 9, 'Writing', for information on how to write references and bibliographies.

This is even more important at postgraduate level than for undergraduates. All writing at postgraduate level must demonstrate that before taking your research further you have read widely on the topic you are investigating and are aware of what others have written about it. This is why you must include references to other texts in the field, and it is most important that these should be accurate and give enough information for your reader to be able to find them easily. You may want to include information that you have read in your own language or other languages you know. If you use information in another language you must translate any quotations you use and also translate the details for the reference. For example:

- Amin, S. (1979) *L'Accumulation à l'echelle mondiale* (Accumulation on a global scale) Paris: Anthropos.
- Cheng, Jieyuan and Zhang, Yianhai (2000) *MBA Courses, Case-management Control and Management Economics Cases*. Yili: Yili People's Press.
- Maximov, S.V. (1871) *Sibir i Katorga* (Siberia and forced labour). St Petersburg.

FIELDWORK

This may involve collecting samples and data in many different kinds of situations. It may also involve contact with people through interviews or observations of people involved in certain activities such as meetings, teaching or other types of work-based activity. If you are researching activities in which you are involved yourself as a participant, this is called 'action research'. For example, if you have been working in the marketing department of a multinational in your country and you want to carry out research into why their methods of marketing have not been very successful with the local population, you might be examining both your own work and that of others to find your answers. You may also decide to use questionnaires if you want to find out information from a large number of people.

If you are researching in a scientific field, you may be carrying out research in a laboratory and with a team of researchers. In this case you may need to clarify with the rest of the team exactly what you are doing and how it will contribute to the research of the department as a whole.

METHODOLOGY

A research report, a dissertation or a thesis will all have a section on methodology. This will explain:

- where information was collected from (e.g. Internet sites, books, journals, TV, radio, interviews, questionnaires, observations);
- why these sources were chosen;

- how you found them and how you used them;
- what difficulties you had (if any);
- how you analysed the information; and
- any ethical issues.

ANALYSIS

Analysis is usually classified as qualitative or quantitative although, in many cases, these two types of analysis are combined. The distinctive features of the two types are as follows:

Qualitative analysis	Quantitative analysis
Explains phenomena	Tests hypotheses
Waits to see what will come up	Is deductive
Is inductive	Data are structured
Data are unstructured	Uses statistics
Looks for ideas	Looks for the 'truth'
Includes more detail	Deals with large amounts of data

An example of quantitative analysis would be distributing a questionnaire to a large sample of people and putting the results into a computer for analysis, or carrying out a series of experiments and analysing the data by electronic means. An example of qualitative analysis would be to use a case study or a series of observations or interviews to find out what is happening in a particular situation.

Most postgraduate courses will include the option of taking a module on using statistics. This will teach students how to use the statistical software packages necessary for quantitative analysis. There are also software packages available for qualitative analysis but these are less commonly used and it is not necessary to be familiar with them to carry out qualitative research.

When you have collected your information and started to analyse it, you will start to have some ideas about what you have found. Now you will begin to:

- clarify and elaborate the questions you are asking;
- examine how the evidence you have collected answers those questions;

 ◆ decide what you can conclude from the evidence; and
 ◆ draw up arguments for your conclusions.

Keeping a diary while you are carrying out the research will help you to formulate and clarify your ideas.

THE RESEARCH DIARY

It is helpful when you are researching a topic to keep a diary or log in which you can write down all the details of your sources as well as make notes about what you have read and what your thoughts are on your reading. You can also include notes on your meetings with your supervisor and any other discussions you have. You can write about any difficulties you experience, whether with finding information, understanding it or thinking through the questions you are addressing in your research. If you need practice with your writing in English, this is a good way to do it. In your diary you can experiment with ways of discussing the ideas you are working with and get into the habit of writing about them in English. This will help you when you come to describe the methods you used in your research.

A diary or log may include details of the following:

 ◆ What work you have done.
 ◆ Where, how and why you did it and perhaps how much time you spent on it.
 ◆ What you read.
 ◆ What data you have collected and what you plan to do with them.
 ◆ Any surprises.
 ◆ Any problems or difficulties you come up against and your ideas for overcoming them.
 ◆ Your thoughts and feelings about your work.

The last point, your thoughts and feelings, is a very important one. When you write a report on research you have done or a dissertation you will have to describe the process you went through in searching for and analysing information. The diary should help you to do this.

Example: students' diaries

Here are some extracts from students' diaries:

4 March 2003

I went to the library to read the books and write the proposal. For the whole afternoon I read only one book named <u>Megamergers in a Global Economy</u>, and made some notes which I might use for the further project writing. It is nearly impossible for me to read the whole book thoroughly because it would take a considerable long time, which is deficient, and should be organized very efficiently. Therefore I must force myself to read books quickly, and meanwhile catch the useful information and materials. Eventually I finished the proposal after the whole night writing. Next week I need to do some revising before the submission on Thursday.

(Chinese student)

12 February 2003

I went to the Tate Modern museum today. I have been there three times. There is an exhibition of Eva Hesse, who was born in Hamburg, Germany. Shortly before her death, Eva Hesse described her subject as 'the total absurdity of life'. 'If something is meaningful maybe it is more meaningful said ten times … if something is absurd, it is much more exaggerated, more absurd if it is repeated' said Hesse. Personally it seems to me a majority of artists have an incredible life. I am jealous of them but more I admire them. They make a fantastic life by themselves, which is better than none. 'Life doesn't last, art doesn't last, it doesn't matter,' said Hesse.

(Taiwanese student)

ETHICAL ISSUES

One aspect of study which becomes much more important at postgraduate level is the ethical aspect. Ethics are about being honest and telling the truth about what information you find and how you find it. Obviously in discovering and creating new knowledge it is very important to be honest. Some aspects of ethics are as follows.

Plagiarism

Plagiarism is one very important ethical issue. When a student or researcher finds information from a written or spoken source it is always important he or she says where that information comes from. At this level, where you may be writing material for publication, you can be in trouble with the law as well as with the university authorities if you use other people's materials without acknowledging it, so your references and bibliographies will be of very great importance.

Signpost

For more information on plagiarism, see Chapter 9, 'Writing'.

Confidentiality

Another ethical issue concerns how you obtain and use information. If you interview people or ask them to fill in a questionnaire you must tell them exactly how you are going to use the information you are asking them to give you. If you promise people you will not use their names then you must make sure these are kept secret and that people are not identifiable through other details (e.g. if you say 'I interviewed one Vietnamese female student and one Indian male in the group' and there is only one Vietnamese female student and one Indian male you will not be keeping those people's identities secret).

Deceit

It is not ethical to obtain information by pretending to be someone that you are not, or by pretending that you are going to use the information for a different purpose from your real intention. A researcher should not use information he or she was asked not to use, or for example, tape record a conversation either on the phone or face to face without telling the person or people being taped that you are doing so. If you were carrying out experiments or analysing statistics it would also be unethical to give false results.

In other words, ethics is about always being perfectly honest about what you are doing and how you are doing it. This is important in research because, otherwise, false knowledge will be created.

Task 10.4

Look at the following examples and say whether you think they are ethical or not:

1 Your friend works in a big company and has said she can get you some information about staff turnover in the company as long as her boss doesn't find out. Do you accept her offer?

2 You have found an interesting article about the topic you are researching, but there is no information to tell you who wrote it or where the information came from. Do you use the information and pretend you wrote it yourself?

3 You have collected quite a large amount of statistical data on your computer and are ready to analyse them, but a small but important section of it disappears. You don't want to collect it again so you imply that it has been included in your results even though it hasn't.

4 You are researching people's behaviour in meetings and have been observing different meetings. You happen to be in a meeting where you haven't told anyone about your research, but you make some notes anyway on the participants' behaviour and use them in your analysis.

Key

For suggested answers see the 'Key to Tasks' at the end of this chapter

Writing at postgraduate level

We have already mentioned the fact that what you write at postgraduate level may be published in journals or books, so it is obvious that it must be written in good English, that it should be properly referenced and with a full bibliography. You will be expected to refer to your reading on the topic in a 'literature review' which explains what other people before you have said about the topic and what you think about what they have said.

Example: literature review

Here is an example of a short paragraph taken from a literature review. The student has examined a number of views on reward systems and is summing up:

Many of the books focus on incentive features. These are an important aspect of reward systems because they are the inner

> power of operating reward systems. Woodley (1990) considered
> that incentives stimulate a higher level of satisfactory
> output than pay arrangements lacking that feature. Many
> people who have benefited from it, like R.M. Currie, who
> adopted incentive bonus schemes and Wilfrid Brown who
> recommended that piecework be abandoned, recognized this.
> (Luptin and Bowey, 1975, p. 79). (Chinese student)

You will also be expected to explain at the beginning what you were attempting to do in your research, what questions you were seeking answers to and how you tried to find answers to those questions (see the section on methodology above).

Example: desk research

Here a student is explaining how he carried out some of the desk research for a project:

Several texts on the topic of globalization and related
subjects were read. These included books, Caribbean
magazines, Caribbean newspapers, policy documents on the
issue of globalization and trade liberalization from the
Organization of Eastern Caribbean States (OECS) Government
offices and secretariat. It was also useful to take a
historical perspective and visit a few texts on world trade
policy, including the Adam Smith theory and the industrial
revolution. This afforded me a view of the historical
perspective on trade and world economics as well as helping
me to make a distinction between the economic movements in
the past and present. (Student from St Kitts-Nevis)

You will then need to explain what you have found and what you think about this. This is where you will be saying something new about whatever topic you are addressing. You will need to think about how you present your findings so that they are easy to understand and convincing. Here you will need to put forward arguments and predict any counter-arguments that your readers might think of.

Finally, you will end with a conclusion which summarizes what has gone before and perhaps says what else should be looked for or what other questions need to be answered.

The principles which apply in writing at undergraduate level will also apply at postgraduate level. However, your tutors will have higher expectations of you in terms of style, vocabulary and accuracy, so it will be necessary to work hard at writing. Whether you are writing a short paper or a thesis the structure will be fairly similar but on a different scale. Many people feel nervous or discouraged by the thought of having to write a very long piece. The answer is to build it up gradually. This is where your diary can help you. If you are in the habit of writing a little every day, you can slowly develop a long piece of writing. If you are writing a dissertation, you will have two or three months in which to write it. If it is a thesis, you will have two or three years. Also you will be editing, proofreading and rewriting your work several times. Your supervisor will be helping you to improve as you go along and your knowledge, as well as your writing skills, will be developing. Many universities will also have workshops where you can get help with writing skills on a one-to-one or a group basis:

> *I used the university's Writing and Communication Workshop because my English writing skills were not good enough for the level of the MA course.*
> **(Pakistani MA student)**

> *I was surprised how quickly English came to me and after a couple of months I was used to the class and the modules.*
> **(Turkish MA student)**

Here are some suggestions for developing your writing:

1 Make notes on whatever you read and on any conversations relevant to your research.
2 Always keep a notebook with you to write down any ideas you have.
3 Give yourself deadlines (e.g. 'by the end of the week I will have written 500 words' or 'by 1 May I will have written Chapter 3').
4 Show what you have written to a friend or fellow researcher and discuss it.
5 Make lists of points that you want to cover.
6 Plan each chapter and gradually add more detail to each plan.
7 Write regularly and give yourself a reward when you have written something (e.g. 'if I have written 1000 words by Friday, I will go out for dinner with friends').
8 Reread what you wrote before and add to it and improve it.

Task 10.5

Make a list of your strengths and weaknesses as a writer, and choose which of the suggestions above might help you.

Working with a supervisor

When you are preparing a dissertation or thesis you will work with a supervisor who will guide your work and give you advice throughout the process. The supervisor is the person who can help you most with your research, so it is important to develop a good relationship with him or her. When you are starting out the supervisor will help you choose your topic and advise you on where to look for data. He or she will then set up a series of meetings with you and will expect you to produce some fresh work to be discussed at each meeting.

The supervisor's role is to:

- ◆ make sure the student is on the right track;
- ◆ advise the student on finding useful information;
- ◆ read the student's work;
- ◆ give constructive criticism; and
- ◆ help the student if he or she gets into difficulties with the research.

The student must:

- ◆ work independently;
- ◆ produce written work for the supervisor to read;
- ◆ attend meetings with the supervisor; and
- ◆ follow the advice he or she is given.

A supervisor is usually a very busy person so it is important to make the most of your time with him or her. When you have an appointment with your supervisor, be sure to send him or her some of your work to read in advance and to prepare any questions you want to ask your supervisor. When the supervisor comments on your work, make

Task 10.6

What would you do in the following situations?

1 You have a meeting with your supervisor tomorrow but you haven't completed the work you agreed to do at your last meeting. Do you:

   a phone up and ask to postpone the meeting
   b stay up all night trying to write something
   c go to the meeting with nothing and say you are sorry

2 Your supervisor cancelled the last meeting with you and now she has phoned to say that she needs to postpone your next meeting because she is very busy. But you feel you cannot continue your work at this stage unless you get some advice. Do you:

   a write or email her with a list of your questions asking if she can reply in writing
   b go to complain to the head of department
   c ask another lecturer to help you

3 Your supervisor talks quite fast and seems to assume that you know more than you feel you do. Sometimes you don't understand what he is explaining. Do you

   a pretend you understand so as not to look stupid
   b take as many notes as you can and ask someone else about it afterwards
   c explain your difficulties to the supervisor and ask him to cover the material more slowly

Key

For suggested answers, see 'Key to tasks' at the end of this chapter.

sure you understand what he or she is saying and ask him or her to explain if you do not understand. Your supervisor can help you best if you can tell him or her what you need and what your difficulties are if you have any.

Conclusion

The most important thing to remember as a postgraduate student is that you are part of an academic community; you are not alone. You need to learn how to make the most of the resources that are available to you: the material resources, libraries, laboratories and other sources of information, and the people who share them with you, your supervisor, your lecturers and fellow students and the other sources of advice in the university such as student advisers. Always ask for help if you need it.

USEFUL RESOURCES

Bell, J. (1999) *Doing your Research Project*. Buckingham: Open University Press.

Blaxter, L., Hughes, C. and Tight, M. (2001) *How to Research*. Buckingham: Open University Press.

Brause, R.S. (2000) *Writing your Doctoral Dissertation: Invisible Rules for Success*. London: Falmer.

Brown, S., McDowell, L. and Race, P. (1995) *500 Tips for Research*. London: Kogan Page.

Cryer, P. (1996) *The Research Student's Guide to Success*. Buckingham: Open University Press.

Fitzpatrick, J., Secrist, J. and Wright, D.J. (1998) *Secrets for a Successful Dissertation*. London: Sage.

Green, D.H. (1998) *The Postgraduate Viva: A Closer Look* (video). Leeds: Leeds Metropolitan University.

Murray, R. (1995) *Thesis Writing* (video and notes). Glasgow: University of Strathclyde.

Murray, R. (1998) *The Viva* (video and notes). Glasgow: University of Strathclyde.

Murray, R. (2002) *How to Write a Thesis*. Buckingham: Open University Press.

Phillips, E.M. and Pugh, D.S. (2000) *How to get a PhD: A Handbook for Students and their Supervisors*. Buckingham: Open University Press.

Rees, A. 'Guide to dissertation writing for international students', available at www.bowbridgepublishing.com

Swales, J.M. and Feak, C.B. (1994) *Academic Writing for Graduate Students: Essential Tasks and Skills*. Ann Arbor, MI: University of Michigan Press.

KEY TO TASKS

Task 10.4

1 Unethical. You should always get permission from those in charge for any information to be used.
2 Unethical. If you can't explain where information comes from, you can't use it as it will not be verifiable.
3 Unethical. All statistical data should be scrupulously accurate.
4 Unethical. You must always ask people's permission if you are going to use them in any way in your research.

Task 10.6

1 (a) would probably be best, as there is no point in having a meeting if you have no work to discuss.
2 (a) would be best. It would not be a good idea to go to the head of department unless the problem is really serious, and another lecturer would probably not be well informed about your work.
3 (c) definitely. It is really important to communicate frankly with the supervisor otherwise it will be difficult for him or her to help you appropriately.

11 Preparing for exams

AIMS

By studying and doing the activities in this chapter you should:

- be able to understand approaches and attitudes to exams in the UK;
- learn about some of the different types of exams you may take at university;
- discover some useful ideas to help you prepare for exams; and
- know how to do your best in an exam.

GLOSSARY

These key words will be useful to you while reading this chapter:

Anonymously: Without knowing the person's name.
Compulsory: Something that you must do.
Crucial: Extremely important or necessary.
Expelled: Officially forced to leave.
Impersonating: Attempting to deceive someone by pretending that you are another person.
Invigilator: Someone who watches people taking an exam in order to check that they do not cheat.
Legibly: In a way that can be read easily.
Stressful: Difficult and worrying.
Terminology: Special words or expressions used in relation to a particular subject or activity.

Exams and you

Do you like exams or do you find them difficult? Why is this? Some people find the exam situation stressful. This could be because the time in which to write your answers is limited or because it is hard to concentrate in a room with lots of other students. Other people like exams because it gives them a chance to show what they know and they enjoy answering questions. Probably if you have done well in exams in the past, you will do well in the UK, although there may be some differences and you may not be used to writing exams in English. Some courses may not even have exams at the end but will be assessed through coursework only, or a combination of coursework and a presentation. Other courses may include a combination of exam and coursework or may be assessed only by an exam.

Signpost

See Chapter 9, 'Writing', for more information on coursework and Chapter 6 for more information on giving oral presentations.

In my country final exams are very important as if you don't pass then you will have to do all subjects all over again. Here exams are important as well but in a different way. For example we don't have exams in all subjects and I was really happy and relieved when I heard that.
(Cypriot student)

Task 11.1

Think about the exams you have taken in the past and write below why you thought you did well, and what you think you could do to improve your performance, if necessary:

I do well in exams because ...	I think I could do better in exams if I ...

Exams in the UK

Exams in the UK, as in most countries, are very formal and strictly controlled; they are also nearly always written, except for special cases like the viva for the PhD thesis. They are supervised by invigilators, one of whom will usually be your lecturer. You must arrive before the time the exam is due to start, show your identity (ID) card to be admitted, sit where you are told to sit (usually you are given a seat number) and leave all your belongings except your pens and pencils outside or in a special area of the room. For most exams you will not be allowed to take any books or papers in with you. You will have to switch off your mobile (cell phone) and leave it with your other belongings. You will not be allowed to speak or get up out of your seat after the exam has begun and will have to put your hand up if you need anything. If you need to go to the toilet, an invigilator will go with you. Once the exam has started, you will not be allowed to ask the invigilators any questions about the exam paper, even if you do not understand it. If you do ask them, they will tell you they cannot answer you. During the exam the invigilators will walk up and down watching the students. At the end of the exam you will be told to stop writing and you must do so immediately. Then you must wait in your seat until the invigilators have collected your paper.

If a student cheats in any way during an exam, by looking at another student's answers, talking to another student, taking in notes on paper or on his or her skin or anywhere else, or impersonating another student, the punishment will be very serious. It could be having to take the whole course again, being suspended temporarily or being expelled from the university.

One difference you may find in the UK is that you have to write your answers in a special booklet, on the front of which you will be asked to write your ID number and the details of the exam. You are not normally asked to write your name as exams are generally marked anonymously. This is so that markers will not be influenced in the case of students they know well. During an exam you are usually only allowed to write in the exam booklet, so rough work has to be written there and then crossed out when you have completed the final version of your answer:

> *Another important issue about examinations is the examination answer book, which is a book of about ten blank pages for answers. When I studied in college we just used our own common blank papers of blank notebook as the answer sheet and then wrote the title of the subject and name and student ID on the first page. It was quite simple and easier.*
> **(Chinese student)**

Task 11.2

Are exams in the UK the same as exams where you have previously studied? Write down any differences on a sheet of paper.

The thought of taking exams in a new country may seem quite frightening. They are often stressful for students, wherever they take them, but understanding of the process and good preparation can reduce your worries and enable you to feel confident. Below we will give some ideas on how to prepare for your exams, but first a description of some different kinds of exams.

Different kinds of exams

There are quite a few different kinds of exams in the UK. They may last between one and three hours, ask just one question or many, and the questions may all be equally important or some may be more important than others:

> *I was introduced to what are the examination rules in Britain and I found many different examination styles between different countries, but the most important thing is that I was taught how to revise effectively.*
> **(Chinese student)**

SOME TYPES OF EXAMS

Closed
This means you must not take anything into the exam room except pens, pencils and rubbers and, if allowed, a calculator or drawing instruments. The lecturer will always tell you in advance if you can take a calculator or instruments but if you are not sure, it is best to ask. Electronic dictionaries will not be allowed.

Restricted
This means that you may be allowed to take certain texts into the exam (for example, a case study or other text that you have been asked to prepare). You will not be able to

take anything except this text so, again, it is important to find out exactly what is allowed beforehand.

Open

Some exams allow students to bring in any material they want to, including books, articles and their own notes. Do not think that because you are taking an open examination you do not need to revise. However much material you take with you, you will not have time to read it all and answer the questions, so you will still need to revise carefully in advance.

Prepared

In this case you are given a text to prepare before the exam and can bring it in with any notes you have written on it. However, you will not know in advance what the questions will be.

Seen

This means that you will be given the questions in advance of the exam so that you can prepare answers. However, you will not be able to take any notes or papers into the exam room so you will have to remember the information you have prepared.

DIFFERENT TYPES OF QUESTIONS

Different exams also include different types of questions. Some of these are described below.

Multiple choice

This means there will be a large number of questions and, for each one, you will be given four possible answers from which to choose. All you will have to do is mark the correct answer. This means that you do not have to do any writing in the exam, but you will have to read very quickly and understand all the terminology. These exams are common in science subjects such as chemistry and biology or information technology.

Example: multiple-choice question

Here is an example of a multiple-choice question:

1. Data redundancy _____

    a could lead to data integrity problems
    b should always be eliminated
    c is of concern only for database systems
    d is an essential feature of file and database control

Here all you need to do to answer the question is write the letter (a), (b), (c) or (d) beside the correct answer in the space provided above.

Short answer
This means you will have to write a short answer to each question. Again there will be a large number of questions but your answers will only be one or two sentences long or may only require you to write 'yes' or 'no.

Example: short answer question

The following is an example of a short answer question:
Answer each question with a Y or N in the space provided.

13 A data flow symbol must never connect to two processes ___

14 Each data flow must always be connected to at least one data store symbol___

Essay-type answers
This is the most common form of exam. Students usually have to answer three or four questions in three hours. This means you have to write short essays for each question.

There is usually a choice of questions although one may be compulsory.

Example: essays

Here is an example of two questions from a paper for a BA in leisure and tourism management. Candidates are asked to choose three questions to answer in three hours:

1 The main aim of public policy in leisure and tourism is a desire to meet people's needs. Discuss.

2 Public policy in leisure and tourism can only be understood as a product of political ideology. Demonstrate how two political ideologies have shaped leisure and tourism policy development.

How to prepare for exams

REVISION

Revision is the work of preparing for an examination by reviewing what you have studied previously and making sure you understand and remember it. As you will probably have several exams within a short period, it will be very important to plan your revision well in advance. It is a good idea to make a timetable for yourself, including all the activities you will be doing during the weeks before the exams such as attending lectures, meeting friends, spending time with your family, sleeping, eating, sports and watching TV. Make sure you have marked more than enough time on your timetable to revise the subjects you have exams for, as you never know when something unexpected may happen and take up some of your time, such as visitors from home or catching a cold or flu.

Many people like to revise alone, but it can be helpful to work with a friend or in a small group. This way you can check any points you don't understand and discuss topics with others to develop your ideas. However, you should be careful not to waste time just chatting.

Here are a few points to remember when revising:

- ◆ Start early (a few weeks before the exams start).
- ◆ Make a timetable.
- ◆ Stick to the timetable as much as possible.
- ◆ Start with the subjects you find hardest.
- ◆ Go through the syllabus for each subject.
- ◆ Get old exam papers and practise answering questions.

GOING THROUGH THE SYLLABUS

If you have taken notes carefully during your lectures and from reading you have done, you will have a good record of information on the different areas of your syllabus. These notes will help you know what is important to revise and will also inform you of what extra reading you could do on the subject. You will probably also have a course handbook with an outline of the syllabus and reading lists.

Signpost

See Chapter 8 for more information on making notes.

As you read for your revision, make notes or underline or highlight sections. Then condense these into a shorter form, keeping information on small cards or divided into sections on paper. Use coloured pens to highlight parts of your notes. Remember what type of learner you are and apply this knowledge to your revision. If you learn better by listening, you can record information on tape. If you like to learn through physical movement, you can walk up and down while going over your notes. If you have all the important information on cards or in short notes, you can put them away while you revise another subject, then get them out and go over them a day or two before the exam.

Signpost

See Chapter 2, 'Being an effective learner', to find out what type of learner you are.

MEMORIZING

There may be some information that you need to learn by heart, such as formulae in maths, the abbreviations for elements in chemistry or the names and dates of cases in law. Some hints for memorizing are as follows:

- Never try to memorize what you don't understand.
- Go over material regularly every few days.
- Start each session by revising what you did in the previous one.
- Keep your information in a logical sequence (e.g. alphabetical or chronological for dates).
- Learn short pieces at a time.
- Use rhythm when reciting (for example, use the tune of a song you like).

Tony Buzan's books, *Use your Head* and *Make the Most of your Mind*, will give you some good ideas for remembering.

Signpost

See the 'Useful resources' section at the end of this chapter for details).

PRACTICE

Time is crucial in exams, so it is important to practise answering quickly. One of the best ways to prepare, especially if you are worried about your English, is to get hold of some questions from previous exams and practise answering them. Usually your lecturer will give you some examples or you will be able to get them from the university library. Prepare to answer a question by reading on the subject and memorizing the information you need to answer the question. However, do not memorize word for word and write down what you have memorized from a book or article in the exam. Like an essay, the exam answer must be written in your own words. When you feel ready to answer, give yourself one hour or 45 minutes to write the answer and then do it without looking at your books or notes. When you have finished, check your writing to be sure it makes sense and answers the question. Count the number of words you have written. If you are revising with other students you can ask one of them to read your answer and comment on it. This will tell you whether your handwriting is legible and how much you can write in the time. You should aim to write at least 500 words for an essay-type question. The more practice answers you write, the better you will know your subject, the faster you will be and the more you will be used to writing in English, using the vocabulary of your subject. As one Chinese student said:

I found I was weak in writing. I thought I ought to do more reading and writing work for improvement purposes and I will have to pay attention to time control when I attend an examination, because all examinations are time limited.

If you are going to have a multiple-choice exam or short answers you should also practise doing past papers. Again, prepare carefully, learn as much as you can and then try to answer in the time limit given.

How to do your best in exams

The most common reasons why students fail exams are as follows:

- Lack of revision and preparation.
- Not writing enough.
- Not answering the question.
- Running out of time.
- Illegible handwriting.

Task 11.3

Have you ever done less well than you hoped for any of the above reasons? If so describe what happened on a sheet of paper.

We have discussed revision strategies above and explained how practice can help you to write quickly enough and improve your handwriting. However the most important thing to remember in an exam, just as it is with an essay, is to answer the question that is asked.

FOLLOWING INSTRUCTIONS

In your exams you will have to be prepared to read carefully and quickly as well as to write legibly and fast. It is most important that you read the instructions on the exam paper very carefully so that you know how many questions to answer and which, if any, are compulsory. You also need to know how the marks will be distributed between the questions.

Example: instructions

Here are some examples of instructions:

Example 1

INSTRUCTIONS TO CANDIDATE, PLEASE READ CAREFULLY

You are required to answer three questions.

All questions carry equal marks.

Example 2

You must answer Part 1, question 1 and <u>two</u> questions from Part 2. Question 1 carries 50% of the marks for the exam, and the other questions 25% each.

Example 3

EXAM CASE STUDY

Read the attached case study CAREFULLY. It is issued to you prior to the examination to enable you to identify potential issues and research those areas. You will be required to answer THREE COMPULSORY QUESTIONS in the examination based on the case study and ONE question relating to the topic you researched for your coursework.

In the Example 1, you should divide your time evenly between the three questions. In Example 2 you should spend twice as much time on question 1 Part 1 than you do on each of the questions from Part 2.

Next you must read all the questions carefully and make a choice if you are instructed to do so. When you have chosen your questions, make sure you understand exactly what each question is asking:

> *I have to read the instructions very carefully and then continue with answering the questions.*
> **(Greek student)**

Task 11.4

Read this exam question carefully then decide which one of the answers summarized below (numbered 1–6) would most accurately respond to the question:

Question

The Internet has had a major impact on the world of business in a number of ways. Using the example of *one* of the following:

banking, the retail trade, insurance

describe how *two* of the facilities below have impacted in the field of your chosen example:

a   websites
b   email
c   conferencing
d   spam

Summarized answers:

1 The use of websites for customer communication in banking.
2 Email and online conferencing in banking and insurance.

3 Spam as a means of advertising in the retail trade.

4 How the retail trade has responded to developments online: websites, email, online conferencing and spam.

5 The changes that have been brought about in banking by the introduction of websites and email.

6 New developments in the insurance business: how have websites, email and spam transformed the business?

Key

For suggested answers, see 'Key to tasks' at the end of this chapter.

CHOOSING YOUR QUESTIONS

Once you have read all the questions and understood exactly what each one is asking, it is important to choose carefully which ones you are going to answer. Do not choose two questions where you may find you are repeating the same information in both answers, as you will lose marks for this. Choose questions when you feel confident about knowing the information needed to answer and when you can answer the question in the way it is asked. For example, in the Task above you could answer the question well even if you know nothing about banking and insurance, because you can choose the retail trade as an example. You will also be able to answer if you know about websites and email but not conferencing and spam. However, you will not be able to answer well if you only know about email. Of course, if you find you do not know enough about the subject to answer the number of questions required, you should still try to answer the right number as best you can.

ANSWERING THE QUESTION

If you are answering essay-type questions, make some notes and a short plan for each question at the beginning and plan your answers. If you run out of time later, you may get some marks for your notes and plans. Write your answers like a short essay, with an introduction, paragraphs for each main point and a conclusion. In the introduction explain how you are going to answer the question. Refer back to the question in your conclusion.

Signpost

See Chapter 9, 'Writing', for more information on writing essays.

Example: answering the question

Here is an example of a question for an exam in business policy, and the conclusion of one student's answer:

Question
Explain Porter's Five Forces Model. Use examples from the Ice Cream Industry to illustrate strategies which may be used to create barriers to entry.

The conclusion to the student's answer
It is interesting to point out that barriers can be put up using the generic strategies from which all these barriers stem, whether it is low cost leadership or differentiation or focus. Companies use these strategies in one way or another to keep entrants out, but this also gives entrants the ability to see why barriers are there and by using a focus strategy they may be able to break into a small area of the market. Thus Porter's five forces model offers a useful tool for examining the competitive environment in which businesses operate.

Notice that the student uses some of the words from the question to show how he or she has answered it. The student summarizes the main points and adds a concluding sentence.

TIMING

If you are doing a multiple-choice or short question exam, go through the questions as quickly as possible. If you find you can't answer one, do not waste too much time before moving on to the next question. When you have finished, go back to the beginning, checking your answers and trying again with any questions you didn't manage to answer the first time. With multiple-choice questions, if you definitely don't know the answer, make a guess and mark one answer. Never mark more than one because you will get no marks if you do. If there are four possible answers and you decide to guess, there is a one in four chance that you will be right and will get a mark. In an exam with essay-type questions, it is important to divide your time up evenly between the questions. For example, if you have to answer three questions in three hours, make sure you spend no more than one hour on each. It is essential, too, to leave some time at the end to read through and check your answers.

WRITING IN EXAMS

Write as clearly as possible in your exam. If you know that your handwriting is hard to read, make sure you get plenty of practice at writing answers quickly. Edit and proofread your answers very carefully checking especially for any mistakes you know you tend to make.

Signpost

See the section 'Editing and proofreading' in Chapter 9, 'Writing'.

Always leave space between paragraphs and answers so that you can add more information when you reread at the end. You may cross out but always be sure to write neatly and legibly when you add information. No one will expect your English to be perfect but make sure you have used the terminology of your subject correctly and structured your sentences clearly. Remember to include examples and refer to theories and books if you can. It may be possible for you to use a bilingual dictionary in exams. You should find out about this from the assessment unit in the university at least a few weeks before the exams start:

Writing is the weak part of my exam. I make some mistakes such as grammar mistakes and spelling mistakes. I have to use my memory to try to remember the words which I usually get wrong. I will remember it firmly and try to do better next time.
(Chinese student)

EXAMS AND DISABLED STUDENTS

If you have any disability, for example dyslexia, claustrophobia (fear of confined spaces), agoraphobia (fear of crowds), blindness or partial blindness or any other condition which affects your study, it will be possible for you to take your exams in special conditions, in a room alone with the invigilator, and in some cases to have extra time to write your answers. If you have already been in contact with the disabilities officer of the university, he or she will have helped you to make arrangements for your exam. If your disability only affects you in exam conditions, you must inform the disabilities officer and the assessment unit at the university about two months before the exams so that he or she can make the arrangements. This can also be done if you are a person who panics seriously so that you become ill in exams.

Signpost

For more information on where to go for advice, see Chapter 12, 'Coping with life as an international student'.

EXAM NERVES

I really hate exams. I don't know why but usually I get really nervous even when I hear the word exams. It is not something new to me although I feel I will never get used to it. Everyone agrees with me as we all believe that exams are the most unpleasant part of study.
(Chinese student)

Many students feel nervous about exams. Of course, the best way of building your confidence is to prepare really well for each exam. If you feel that you have revised your subject thoroughly and have also practised writing answers to questions within the time you know you will be allowed in the exam, you have no reason to feel nervous. However, nerves are physical, and there are some things you can do to make sure you are physically well prepared, too:

- Don't stay up all night doing last-minute revision before an exam. Finish your revision early and do something relaxing like going for a walk, or going swimming before going to bed.
- Get up early and give yourself plenty of time to get ready if your exam is in the morning.
- Don't drink too much coffee or other stimulating drinks as they will make you more nervous.
- When you arrive at the exam room, don't chat with other students. Stay quiet and breathe slowly, concentrating on your breathing. You can also do this during the exam if you find you are having difficulty concentrating.

On the day of your exam

The following are some points to help you do your best on examination day.

ARRIVE EARLY

Always find out a day or two before where your exam is going to be held, and make sure you know how to find the room and how much time you need to get there from home. Also check the time of the exam and arrive 10–15 minutes before it is due to begin. If you are late you may not be allowed into the exam.

READ EVERYTHING VERY CAREFULLY

Once you are settled in your seat and you are given the question paper, read all instructions and questions before starting to write anything. You can underline words and mark the questions you have chosen on the paper.

PLAN YOUR TIME

Divide up the time you have left according to the number of marks for each question, remembering to leave 5–10 minutes at the end for checking and proofreading what you have written.

PLAN YOUR ANSWERS

Write a short plan for each of the answers you have chosen, listing the main points you will cover and any sources you may refer to.

WRITE YOUR ANSWERS LEGIBLY

Make sure that your handwriting is legible and leave a space between each line and a space at the end of each question. This is so that you can add information later when you reread, without making your page look too messy.

CHECK YOUR ANSWERS

Reread all your answers carefully, checking the information, the sentence structure and the spelling and grammar.

After the exams

You will usually have a long wait after the exams to get your results. You will be told the date of publication of the results before you take the exam. Results are usually pinned up on noticeboards according to subject. Your name will not be listed, only your ID number, so that only you will know your results.

When you get your results, remember that in the UK it is very unusual for students to get marks above 80% except in subjects like maths or chemistry. Generally an excellent mark is one which is over 70%, which is grade A or distinction. This means that a mark of between 60 and 69% is very good and one between 50 and 59 is good. The pass mark is generally 40%.

If you do well, you can relax and look forward to the next course. If you are disappointed in your result, you will need to think through carefully what you did and plan your strategy to do better next time. If you fail an exam, you will have an opportunity to take it again. In this case you may be able to find out from your tutor what was wrong with your exam. There may also be revision sessions organized to help you prepare for your resit. Many students have to take the same exam more than once, and many of them pass the second time, so don't despair or worry too much. Make sure that you understand where you went wrong and that you revise more thoroughly and prepare yourself better the next time:

> I should read the question paper carefully and try to know the right answer method. For that I did badly in section three. I need to practise more.
> **(Bangladeshi student)**

Conclusion

The best way to succeed in exams is to attend lectures and seminars throughout the semester, do all coursework and assignments, and read as many of the recommended texts as possible. In this way you will not have to do all the work at the last minute. Remember that the same rule applies for exams as for any other issue at university: if you don't understand or you are worried about something, always ask for help. There will be someone to help you whatever the problem is. Your lecturers want you to succeed just as much as you do.

USEFUL RESOURCES

Acres, D. (1994) *How to Pass Exams without Anxiety: Every Candidate's Guide to Success.* Oxford: How to Books.

Burns, R. (1997) *The Student's Guide to Passing Exams.* London: Kogan Page.

Buzan, T. (1988) *Make the Most of your Mind.* London: Pan Books.

Buzan, T. (2000) *Use your Memory.* London: BBC Publications.

Buzan, T. (2000) *Use your Head.* London: BBC Publications (also sound recording and video recording).

Duncalf, B. (1999) *How to Pass any Exam.* London: Kyle Cathie.

Henderson, P. (1995) *How to Succeed in Exams and Assessments.* London: Collins Educational.

Madders, J. (1988) *Stress and Relaxation: Self-help Techniques for Everyone.* London: Macdonald Optima.

Tracy, E. (2002) *The Student's Guide to Exam Success.* Buckingham: Open University Press.

KEY TO TASK

Task 11.4

The answer is (5). This is because the question asks you to choose one area from the three listed and write about two of the facilities, from the four listed. Summarized answer (5) covers the area of banking and the facilities of websites and email.

12 Coping with life as an international student

AIMS

By studying and doing the activities in this chapter you should:
- gain some understanding of social life at university in the UK;
- find out information on the kinds of sporting and leisure activities available;
- get an idea of what facilities are provided for students to assist them practically;
- start thinking about financial aspects of being a student, including part-time work; and
- discover some hints on how to make the most of your time, and enjoy yourself too!

GLOSSARY

These key words will be useful to you while reading this chapter:

Affiliated: Part of or in a close relationship with another, usually larger, group or organization.

Bursary: A sum of money given to a person by an organization, such as a university, to pay for him or her to study.

Culture shock: A feeling of confusion felt by someone visiting a country or place he or she does not know.

Excluded: To be kept out of something.

Extra-curricular: Activities which are not part of the usual school or college course.

Lobby: To try to persuade a politician, the government or an official group that a particular thing should or should not happen, or that a law should be changed.

Socialize: To spend the time when you are not working, with friends or with other people in order to enjoy yourself.

Voluntary: Done willingly, without being forced or paid to do it.

Social life at university in the UK

Many UK students, especially those who go to university straight after leaving school, see their time there as a time to enjoy themselves, meet new people and try out activities they have not done before, as well as a time for study. Universities in the UK have a number of different facilities which cater for students' social life, such as places to eat, sports facilities, leisure facilities and clubs.

SOCIALIZING

There are cafes and bars where students meet to eat and drink and there are often events organized with live music or discos. There is usually a lot of drinking of alcohol, but there are always people who do not drink alcohol and there are plenty of other drinks available, so if you do not drink alcohol you will not feel out of place. However, if you come from a society where it is not customary to drink alcohol, you may not be used to seeing people drinking all around you.

One thing which you may find surprising is that teachers sometimes organize parties for students, especially at the beginning or end of the year or at Christmas. They may also go out with groups of students for a meal or for a drink in a pub. As we have explained in Chapter 5, students and teachers relate to each other more informally in the UK than in some other countries. They usually call each other by their first names, for example, and some students from overseas find it strange or embarrassing at first when they find they are expected to socialize with teachers:

> At first, I did not love party-life. I thought it would not be good for me to be in a party. I can remember, in the international student party arranged by the university, I could not participate in the funny game where my teachers were dancing, poking fun, enjoying. However, after participating in two or three parties I realized I was wrong ... it is a challenge to adapt to different social customs. Party-life gives me a chance to meet many new people and to be sociable.
> **(Bangladeshi student)**

> After the lecture, since it was the last class, the lecturer invited us all to go to a pub for a drink with another group of students on MA courses. About 20 people, we occupied two tables and all the boys drank beer. We chatted, laughed, made fun of one another including the teacher. He was very kind and smart and good at dealing with our curiosity and nosiness. It was a really nice party and we all enjoyed it very much.
> **(Chinese student)**

If you do not feel like socializing there is no obligation to join in this type of activity and nobody will mind if you choose not to. However, by participating, you can get to know people and improve your knowledge of the language and culture.

CLUBS AND SOCIETIES

As well as eating, drinking and music there will also be many different clubs and societies for students to join. At the beginning of the academic year in September there will be a 'freshers' fair'. This is an event organized for students who have recently started studying at a college or university. It is held before classes start and events are organized by the students' union for new students to inform them about all the activities available. Every student is automatically a member of the students' union and it is free of charge. Student unions in all the different universities are affiliated to the National Union of Students (NUS), which is a powerful lobby for student rights across the country. Many student unions produce a regular newspaper which gives information about issues and activities. The students' union will give you an NUS membership card which will entitle you to discounts in museums, art galleries, cinemas, theatres, travel agents and some shops.

Here are some examples of clubs and societies. Different universities will have different ones:

- The Christian Union.
- The Creative Writing Society.
- The Drama Performing Society.
- The Fine Art Club.
- The Hindu Society.
- The International Students' Society.
- The Lesbian, Gay, Bisexual and Transgender Society.
- The Muslim Women's Society.
- The Computing Society.
- The Rock Society.
- The Utopia Society (Politics and Modern History).
- The Pan African Society.

As you can see from the list above, they cater for a very wide range of interests, so there should be something for everyone.

There may also be societies for students from particular countries, for example a Chinese Students' Society, or a Greek Students' Society. Joining one of these, if there is one for students from your country, will obviously be enjoyable and reassuring for you, as you will meet other students who speak your language and who may share your ideas and interests. However, it will also be a good idea to join other clubs or societies which interest you because in this way you will meet students from the UK and other countries, discover new activities or develop your existing hobbies, and learn a lot of English. Even if you are already a fluent speaker you will learn the local ways of speaking, specialist language and colloquial expressions which will be new to you if you are new to the country or the region.

Sport and leisure activities

Universities will have sports facilities either on campus or further away if the university is located in the middle of a big city like London or Birmingham. It is quite common for Wednesday afternoons to be left free of lectures so that students can participate in team sports. If the playing fields are not on campus, buses will be arranged to take students to play football, rugby, cricket, hockey, netball and so on, and there will be matches against teams from other universities which may involve travelling around the country. Playing a team sport is a very good way to meet people and keep yourself fit and healthy. If you have played in a team at home, the university will be very happy to have you as a player and if you are a beginner, you will be able to get training. There will probably be some sports facilities on the campus wherever it is (for example, a gym, squash or badminton courts or perhaps a swimming pool if you are lucky). You can find out about sports at the freshers' fair or through the students' union, which will have an office somewhere on the campus where you will find friendly fellow students who will give you any information you need.

There may also be activities which involve short trips away from the university such as rock climbing or caving, bird watching or environmental projects. These will be a great way for you to get to know more of the country.

Here are some examples of sport and leisure activities:

- *Team sports*: basketball, cricket, football, hockey, netball, rugby, volleyball.
- *Individual sports*: badminton, squash, tennis, athletics.
- *Outdoor activities*: canoeing, climbing, horse riding, rowing, parachuting, ski-ing.

Task 12.1

If you are already in the UK, find out what activities are available in your university and make a list of those you would like to join.

If you have not yet arrived but have access to the Internet, look at the website of the university you are planning to attend and find out what is available. If you do not have access to the Internet, write to the university and ask them to send you information about extracurricular activities.

Adjusting to your new surroundings

Studying and living in a new country is an exciting and rewarding experience. Nevertheless, there may be times that you feel anxious or homesick because there are many things around you that are unfamiliar. Do not worry – it is quite usual to experience some sort of 'culture shock'. Make sure you keep in touch with friends and family at home, but also find out about and join in the social life at your new university. There will be many people around you who will be able to offer you explanations, friendship and support.

Student services

You will find that all universities have a range of services to deal with any problems or difficulties students might have during their time there. These will include specialists in the following:

ACCOMMODATION

They will help you get a place in a university hall of residence or find a 'homestay' with an English family. They may also be able to give you lists of other accommodation if you want to live independently.

FINANCE

They will help you open a bank account and sort out your fees and accommodation expenses and give you any other financial advice you need.

CAREERS

They may be able to help you to find part-time work while you study and will advise you about future career opportunities and work placements.

DISABILITIES

They will help you if you have any special needs while you study because of any disability or medical condition. There is now legislation in the UK that says that universities must provide for the needs of disabled students. If you are blind or partially sighted, deaf, use a wheelchair, have a hidden disability such as epilepsy or diabetes or suffer from any form of mental illness, contact the disability adviser in your university and he or she will help you get any assistance you need for your study. It is best to tell your adviser what you need well in advance of your arrival so that he or she can have arrangements in place for when your course starts, but he or she will help you at any time.

COUNSELLING

Universities have counsellors to help students who become unhappy or upset for any reason. These counsellors will talk to you about your problem in confidence and give you support and advice.

Most universities will also have a special adviser for international students who will help you with applications for visa renewals, advice if your family want to visit you or if you want to visit other European countries.

Task 12.2

Look at the website or the prospectus of your university or any university where you think you may be studying and find out which of the services listed above they offer.

Finance

EXPENSES

Often the biggest problem students from other countries face in the UK is finance. Of course, everybody knows how high the fees are for international students, but on top of that the cost of living is also very high. Everything is expensive: food, clothes, transport, books. If you are studying Architecture, design subjects or Fine Art you will need to spend a lot of money on materials. You will also have to pay for printing work that you do on the computers at the university, for any photocopying you do and for fines if you keep your library books out too long. One thing that is free, though, at university is unlimited access to the Internet. You will find that prices in London are higher than in the rest of the country, especially for accommodation and transport. On the other hand, you can find markets in London where you can buy everything you need cheaply, but you need to know where to find them.

GRANTS AND SCHOLARSHIPS

Find out before you start at university whether any scholarships, grants or discounts are available for you. Some universities offer special discounts for students who have had a member of their family study at the university. Some have scholarships for people from specific countries. There are also lots of grants and bursaries offered by other organizations for specific groups of people, sometimes based on religion, gender, age, country of origin or subject of study. These are usually small sums of money up to a few hundred pounds but everything helps. You can find out about these either from the financial adviser or the international adviser of your university, or from UCKOSA.

Signpost

See the 'Useful resources' section at the end of this chapter.

PART-TIME WORK

Many students in the UK have part-time jobs. As an international student you will have the right to work for 20 hours per week maximum. Students often work in supermarkets, fast-food outlets, restaurants, hotels or bars because they can fit the hours in with their studies by working in the evenings and at weekends. Bigger chains are more flexible in their hours than smaller restaurants with fewer staff. It is harder to work in a shop or an office because these are usually daytime jobs. However, you may find that your timetable gives you one or two free days a week on which you can work in a job. Remember, though, that it is important to attend your lectures and seminars and to do all your coursework and preparation. As a student this must be your first priority because your success depends on it, and so does your visa.

The careers adviser in your university may be able to help you find part-time work. You can also go along the nearest high street and ask in the different shops and restaurants if they need any help, or look in the local newspaper for advertisements. If you have relatives or friends they will also be able to help you. There may be some part-time work in the university, putting books back on the shelves in the library or helping to welcome new students or show visitors round. However, there is usually a lot of competition for these jobs and you will be more likely to get one in your second or third year, when you know the university better. It is a good idea to get involved in voluntary work, either at the university or for charitable organizations, because this gives you work experience in the UK and helps improve your knowledge and confidence. It could also help you find paid employment.

Task 12.3

Work out a budget for one year at university. Include all the expenses you will have to pay: fees, accommodation, transport, food, books and materials, clothes, entertainment, mobile phone.

Now work out where the money is going to come from.

Plan carefully. If you fall behind with payment of your fees or payment for university accommodation you may be excluded from the university. This could seriously affect your studies and also your right to stay in the UK.

Health care

If you are planning to study for more than six months you will be entitled to free health care from the National Health Service (NHS). The first thing to do when you have found your accommodation is to register with a doctor (called a general practitioner or GP). You must do this straightaway, not when you get sick, because often they are full or have waiting lists and you do not want to be searching for a doctor if you are feeling unwell. Also it will be important to get a medical certificate from your doctor if you miss any coursework deadlines or exams because you are ill. If you are living in a university hall of residence, they will inform you of where to find a doctor. If you are living with a family, you will be entitled to register with their doctor. If you are living independently, you can go to the nearest public library and they will give you a list of doctors (GPs) in your area. Then you should go there and register with the doctor, taking evidence that you are a student with you. You will not pay to see the doctor but you will have to pay a charge at the chemist for any medicine the doctor prescribes. If you have an accident or fall ill when the doctor is not available, you can go to the nearest hospital which has an accident and emergency department.

Transport

As a full-time student you may be entitled to a discount on travel. Some students in London can get a 30% reduction in fares. In order to get this you need to apply to your university for a special card.

All students up to the age of 25 can get a card for cheap travel on the railways all over the UK. This is called a 'young person's railcard' and costs £18 for a year. With this card you will get a third off rail fares. You can get the card at your local station or at www.youngpersonsrailcard.co.uk

All students up to the age of 25 can also get a discount 'Coach card' for travel on coaches all over the UK. This costs £10 and also gives you a 30% reduction in fares. You can find out about it at www.GoByCoach.com

Safety

Always be careful of yourself and your belongings. If you go out at night, go where there are plenty of other people and use public transport or official cabs. Don't get into a car unless you know the driver or it is marked as a cab, with a light on top and a registration number. Do not carry large sums of money and do not walk about talking on your mobile phone, as someone may try to take it. If anyone does grab your bag or phone, let them have it. Do not get into a fight. If you do have a bad experience, go to see the counsellors at your university. They will help you and give you advice.

Making the most of your time

It is very exciting to go abroad to study in a new country, and there is a lot to discover both in your studies and in life outside the university. There will be many aspects of life which are different from home, some of them we have mentioned in previous chapters. Expect things to be different. Expect to be surprised and to have to get used to a different kind of life. Then you will not be disappointed. It is not easy to be far from home for the first time and you may find it difficult to get used to the climate, especially in winter, the food and, most importantly, the people and customs. You may find these very strange but be sure that, if you do, they probably find you a bit strange, too. Be tolerant of people's differences and they will be tolerant of yours.

If you are unhappy for any reason, be it practical, because you don't understand something or can't find a solution for something, or emotional because you are homesick or lonely or confused, talk to someone about it. You can go to any of the advisers in student services, you can go to one of your tutors or you can talk to a relative, a friend or a fellow student, but make sure you talk to someone and get the help you need. There will always be someone to help you if you can find that person.

Conclusion

We hope you have found this book useful and that if it has not given you all the information you need, at least it has informed you of how you can get that information. Please contact us if you have any suggestions for improving the book, any useful ideas or any problems you have come across which we have not mentioned. Make the most of your time as a student, enjoy your studies and enjoy your time in the UK.

USEFUL RESOURCES

The British Council publishes a free information sheet for international students on 'Tuition fees and the cost of living'. Phone 020 7389 4383 or email educationenquiries@britishcouncil.org.

www.nusonline.co.uk
  The National Union of Students (NUS) is a very useful source of advice and information.
www.skill.org.uk
  Skill – the National Bureau of Students with Disabilities has an information sheet for international students.
www.uckosa.org.uk
  UCKOSA – the Council for International Education gives advice on immigration and welfare matters and other useful information. Phone 020 7107 9922 or visit their website.

How to contact us
Write to us with any comments or suggestions at:

The Learning Centre
London Metropolitan University
236–50 Holloway Road
London N7 6PP

Index

accommodation, 302
aims,
    personal, 7
    of presentations, 123–4
audio-visual aids, 144–8

bias, *see* reading
bibliographies, 246–7, 265–6
brainstorm, 191, 214–15, 216
bursary, 297, 304

clubs and societies, 299–300
comprehension, *see* listening
counselling, 303
courses, choosing, 18–19
cultural differences, 2, 306
    in approaches to studying, 4–5
    in behaviour, 3–4
    in speaking, 100
    in writing, 235–8
    in reading, 180–1
cultural knowledge in listening, 55–6
culture shock, 297, 301–2, 306–7

dictionaries, 85–6, 109–11, 187
    choosing 72–5
    subject specific, 84, 183, 187
    using, 75–6, 77

disabilities, 302, 307
dissertation, 258, 261–2, 273

English, *see also* language, 3
    learning, 35–7
    presentations in, 138–43
    studying through, 20–22
exams, 278–96,
    and disabled students, 292–3
    instructions, 288–90
    nerves, 293
    practice, 286–7,
    questions, 282–3
    regulations, 280
    revision, 284–6
    results, 295
    types, 281–2
    writing in, 292
extra-curricular activities, 298–301

feedback, 251–2
finance, 302, 303–5, 306

grants, 304

health, 305

internet, 168

jobs, *see* work

language,
  specialist language, 51, 83–4
  formal and informal, 71–2, 91–5,
    139–4
learning, 14–39
  conditions for, 31–2
  cultural differences in, 25–7
  English, 35–7
  independent, 15–17
  learning styles, 32–4, 207, 285
  motivation, 17–20
  observing your learning, 29–30
  planning, 34–5
  previous, 22–4
  quotes on, 38–9
  responsibility for, 15–17
  theories of, 28–32
lectures, 59–61, 162, 201–3
leisure, *see* sports
library, 166–9
listening, *see also* understanding spoken
  English, 40–65
  assess your level, 41–2
  being a good listener, 57–9
  and cultural knowledge, 55–6
  effective listening, 46–9
  extensive, 48–9
  improving, 62–4
  intensive, 48
  to lectures, 59–61
  and pronunciation, 53–5
  and vocabulary, 51

medical care, *see* health

National Union of Students, 299, 307

notes, 191–221
  index cards, 200–1
  from lectures, 201–3
  linear and pattern, 204–7
  from reading, 195–201
  in presentations, 136–7
  reasons for making, 192–3
  revising, 213–14
  selecting information, 193–5
  techniques, 208–10
  using, 212–17

plagiarism, 140, 196, 240–4, 269
postgraduate study, 258–77
  deskwork, 265–6
  differences from undergraduate
    study, 260–1
  ethics, 269–71
  fieldwork, 258, 266
  Master's degree, 261–2
  methodology, 266–7
  MPhil and PhD, 262–3
  research, 263–71
  supervisor, 259, 274–6
  viva, 262–3
  writing, 271–4
presentations, 120–59
  audio-visual aids, 144–8
  body language, 143–4
  communication with audience,
    124–7, 134–8
  delivery, 134–44
  formality, 139–40
  group presentations, 154–5
  nerves, 149–53
  notes, 130, 136–7
  planning and preparing, 122–34
  questions, 53

structuring, 128–34
timing, 127–8
voice, 142–3
pronunciation, 53–5, 107–13, 141, 142

questions,
in presentations, 131, 153
in seminars, 98–9, 103–6, 116–18

research, 261, 262, 263–71
reading, 160–90
articles, 168
cultural differences, 180–1
improving, 176
making notes, 195–201
recognising bias, 160, 173–5
reflective, 163, 170–5
selecting, 164–6
SQ3R, 170–5
strategies, 182–5
surveying books, 165–6
and translating, 177–9
referencing, 244–6

scholarships, 304
seminars, 96–106
preparing, 97–9
social life, 298–300
societies, *see* clubs
speaking 88–119
confidence, 99–101
formal & informal style, 91–5
in groups, 106–7
in presentations, 138–44
pronunciation, 108
in seminars, 96–106

to tutors, 95
sports, 300–1
students' union, *see* National Union of
Students

thesis, 262

understanding spoken English, 40–65 *see
also* listening
factors in understanding, 49–57
strategies for coping, 43–5

vocabulary, 66–87
dictionaries, *see* dictionaries
of English, 67–8
knowing a word, 69–72
learning, 76–83
selecting, 69, 80–1, 83–4

work, 302, 304–5
writing, 222–57
argument, 239–40
book reviews, 230
bibliographies *see* bibliographies
cultural differences, 235–8
dissertations, 223, 273
editing, 247–8
essays, 224–6
plagiarism, *see* plagiarism
planning, 231–3
postgraduate, *see* postgraduate study
Proofreading, 248–51
reports, 226–9
references, *see* references
style, 233–8
summaries, 229–30